I0889925

Reading for the Planet

READING FOR THE PLANET
Toward a Geomethodology

Christian Moraru

UNIVERSITY OF MICHIGAN PRESS • ANN ARBOR

Copyright © Christian Moraru 2015
All rights reserved

This book may not be reproduced, in whole or in part, including illustrations, in any form (beyond that copying permitted by Sections 107 and 108 of the U.S. Copyright Law and except by reviewers for the public press), without written permission from the publisher.

Published in the United States of America by the
University of Michigan Press
Manufactured in the United States of America
♾ Printed on acid-free paper

2018 2017 2016 2015 4 3 2 1

A CIP catalog record for this book is available from the British Library.

ISBN 978-0-472-07279-8 (cloth : alk. paper)
ISBN 978-0-472-05279-0 (paper)
ISBN 978-0-472-12132-8 (ebook)

To see a World in a Grain of Sand . . .

—WILLIAM BLAKE, "Auguries of Innocence"

Imagination alone enables us to see things in their proper perspective, to be strong enough to put that which is too close at a certain distance so that we can see and understand it without bias and prejudice, to be generous enough to bridge abysses of remoteness until we can see and understand everything that is too far away from us as though it were our own affair. This distancing of some things and bridging the abysses to others is part of the dialogue of understanding, for whose purposes direct experience establishes too close a contact and mere knowledge erects artificial barriers.

Without this kind of imagination, which actually is understanding, we would never be able to take our bearings in the world. It is the only inner compass we have. We are contemporaries only so far as our understanding reaches.

—HANNAH ARENDT, *Essays in Understanding, 1930–1954: Formation, Exile, and Totalitarianism*

Planetarity is not a threat[. I]t is an opportunity. It means leaving the comfort zone for the contact zone.

—SUSAN STANFORD FRIEDMAN, "Planetarity: Musing Modernist Studies"

CONTENTS

PROLOGUE 🌐 A WELL-TEMPERED MANIFESTO

[T[he world has moved back to [the] centre of political consciousness, not in the traditional sense of the "earth as garden," but as new technologically worlded and neo-stoic cosmopolitical percept of the "earth-as-planet."

—NEIL TURNBULL, "The Ontological Consequences of Copernicus"

Both theoretically and historically-culturally, literature furnishes the display or screen affording the dominant systems of ideology, might, social administration, and technology, what might be termed the Prevailing Operating System of their place and moment, their most vivid and unfettered registration or tracing. Literatures, then, are not merely the basis for a broad range of institutions configured around cultural and aesthetic contracts, those concerning, for instance, sciences, technologies, historical phenomena, and art forms and their notable practitioners. They open the very arena, platform, or space for the critical registration, recapitulation, analysis, and reimagination or supplementation of the prevailing systems of actuality.

—HENRY SUSSMAN, *Around the Book: Systems and Literacy*

§1. A Book with an Edge

Hailed as the first "to perfectly capture the bizarre collection of emotional modes we juggled . . . after the [initial] shocks of September 11,"[1] Frédéric Beigbeder's 2003 novel *Windows on the World* has Frédéric, one of the two narrators and pseudo-alter ego of the author, and his friend Troy chat in New York City's Life Café. The place is "aptly named" not only because it is "full of highbrow claptrap that makes you want to change the world" but also because Troy does want to change the world.[2] Revolving around his world governance project, the conversation goes like this:

> "Tell me, Troy, what are you going to call this idea of yours? You know you've got to have an 'ism,' otherwise no one will take your utopia seriously. I suggest 'alt-globalism' to contrast with globalization, or maybe

> 'Internationalism.' Except that sounds too commie. . . . 'Multilateralism'? 'Cosmopolitanism'? 'Globalism'? No, sounds too capitalist."
>
> "Well, I hadn't really thought about it, but it seems to me it's pretty incidental . . ."
>
> "Oh, no! Not at all. It's very important to have a name that makes people want to get involved. 'Universalism'? No, sounds too much like Vivendi. I've got it: 'Planetarism.' There you go. We're all planetarists."[3]

Indubitably, we are not. And I am not sure we should all become *des planétaristes* right away either. More modestly, *Reading for the Planet* proposes instead that we give some thought to a planetary model of cultural production and interpretation. Neither Troy nor Frédéric has this model in mind. One is too "utopian"; the other, too cynical. Besides, the "planetarism" I am offering for consideration has nothing to do with Troy's "World Parliament"[4] or with Frédéric's *planétarisme* for that matter. But the French author's stance on things planetary should not be confused with his hero's.[5] Beigbeder's light, acidly humorous, and self-deprecating tone can be, and has been, misleading. Running underneath it is a serious, genuine dedication to the world and its humanity, as well as an uncommon sense of urgency.

I share them both, which is why my book has a bit of an edge to it. A "bleeding edge," possibly. This is more than a wink to the Thomas Pynchon aficionados out there. It is also a formal statement to the effect that *Reading for the Planet* participates in several genre protocols. Argument remains, of course, decisive in these pages. Making a case, step by step, is what they fundamentally do. At the end of the day, there is no substitute for rigorous marshaling of evidence, in British and North American essay tradition, as well as in others. But, at the same time, the argumentative, along with its expositorily sanguine, primarily denotative register, bleeds occasionally into more poetic tonalities and, with greater frequency toward the end, into a slightly more "activist" tone. Consequently, there is something of a manifesto element to my intervention, in which, on this account, "nowness" and "newness" intersect rhetorically, as genre expert Mary Ann Caws might say.[6]

I would like to think, along these lines, of *Reading for the Planet* as a somewhat impassioned essay pertaining chiefly to literary-cultural theory and criticism, calling first and foremost on fellow theorists and critics, but taking up issues broader than literature and addressing a larger public.[7] Otherwise, whoever my audiences are—literati in general, dedicated "planiterati,"[8] or non-specialists—I trust they will find the platform laid out here also historicized, theorized, and implemented in a book that takes its time with the discussion proper but only to submit that we are running out of time. The prevalent, nationalist-territorialist (nation-state-bounded) methodologies do seem to be, throughout the humanities, out of time, out of sync with our supra- and transnational times. Retooling or, as I put it, "planetarizing" this methodology so as to bring it in line with our times, that is, with the post-1989 world, cannot wait. This world is both highly webbed and decentered, prone to volatility and entropy and fraught with considerable dangers. Following the deep freeze of the Cold War, we have entered an era where reaching others, into their lives, homes, and cultures, is easier than ever but also an ambiguous gesture that can result in mutually enriching exchanges, genocide, and anything in between. Equivocal, working alongside—and sometimes furthering—the weakening of nation-states and other decentralizing processes, interconnectivity and the policies and technologies making it possible have fostered contacts on an unprecedented scale but have also triggered or compounded a flurry of geopolitical crises worldwide since the 1990s: wild expansions and contractions of corporations, financial markets, and economic activity overall inside, across, and even against nations; the regional rekindling of religious sectarianism, ethnic separatism, and similar conflicts on most continents; explosive, often quasi-instantaneous global spread of viruses, diseases, and epidemics, but also of ideas, images, lifestyles, and culture overall, of pathogenic and nonpathogenic agents and phenomena up until now either "endemic," corralled inside their places of origin, or contaminating literally or metaphorically other places and people at a slower pace; at-distance, cross-statal, cultural and political censorship, which is de facto what North Korean hackers apparently managed to inflict, at least initially, on Sony Pictures, its comedy *The Interview*, and moviegoers alike in late November 2014; brash land grabs and other attempts by transnationally networked terrorism and empires such as Russia and China to redraw state borders in the Middle East, Eastern Europe, and the South China Sea; and, indeed, one border incident after another, whether on the southern frontier of the United States, in Gaza, Anatolia, West Africa, or Ukraine. Picked out at random from a much longer litany, such disasters, emergencies, and aggressions speak to a certain worldview, to a way of settling thorny issues of location, limit, and spatiality, and their articulations—territorializations—of identity, belonging, sovereignty, community, and culture. More to the point, these incidents betray a worrisome grasp of the dialectic of place and "situated" humanity ("here," "me," "us," "ours," "our tradition"), on one side, and the larger world of places and collectivities, on the other.

However, this skewed view of the world and of being in it is, fortunately, not the only one, as contemporary art, literature, and philosophy prove. Alongside more encouraging sociopolitical and economic responses to the turbulence of our times, the world images many literary works paint are critical, implicitly and explicitly, of the world mappings and politics behind the catastrophic and bellicose occurrences listed above. If, as David Harvey concludes in his epilogue to *Cosmopolitanism and the Geographies of Freedom*, "our geography has been made and remade again and again by human endeavor, then it can be remade yet again to accord more fully with our political ambitions."[9] Harvey's own "relational" reconstruction of place and community, as well as of the world and of its cartographic representation, is instrumental to this remaking, and so are a plethora of landmarks in late twentieth and early twenty-first-century literature.[10]

To be sure, this is heartening. But do these artistic interventions, these planetary "counter-images," show up on our critical radars? Further, if they do, are we up to the epistemological challenges they pose? What do they look like to us: meaningless blips or meaningful structures? These questions are pressing, and the stakes of the answers could not be bigger. This is why, analytic for the most part, the considerations that follow become sometimes mildly exhortative. They set forth a personal understanding or critical awareness that presupposes taking up a stance—a *prise de conscience*, as the French call it, and a *prise de position*, all rolled into one. That said, *Reading for the Planet* will probably strike many as a rather lame, perhaps stylistically toothless manifesto if compared to the genre's early twentieth-century incendiary masterpieces. That would be a correct assessment because, all in all, the book aspires to be at once tightly reasoned and thought-provoking, compelling as a demonstration *and* ethical option. It does not purport to stir up and appeal through fiery language, rash extrapolations, and grandiose claims, but by virtue of its specific, painstakingly theorized and contextualized contentions and of the critical prose couching them.

For this reason, too, this monograph is shorter than my previous one. Nevertheless, its relative conciseness does not rule out, at the other end of the formal spectrum, arborescent syntax, punnily self-indulging language, and strategic reiterations, all designed to drive home, consolidate, and qualify my central points. Rhetorical gambits aside, *Reading for the Planet* does not shy away from a more condensed and precise mode of enunciation; more accurately, it seeks to occupy a middle ground between the nuanced and the axiomatic. This is because it behooves a project like this to cultivate the sort of biting brevitas that cuts to the chase without oversimplifying things, but also because extensive historical and theoretical expatiations, if sound, usually lend themselves to compacting into pronouncements intellectually and, here and there, typographically "italicized": trenchant, clear, and ambitiously systematic, as they both attend to the incrementally world-systemic literary-cultural phenomenology and organize themselves into a theoretical system. And yet, I believe, they are never gratuitously apodictic.

The reader familiar with my work will also discover that they come on the heels of my recent research. In fact, beginning with "Authors in Debt: Credit Lines in the Global Economy of Representation," the conclusion to my 2005 *Memorious Discourse,* my main publications have variously paved the road to the present book's argument for a planetary epistemology necessarily underwritten by an apposite ethics.[11] Setting out to think through the problem of how to read *with* and *for* the planet whatever we happen to be reading (viewing, listening to, and so forth), of how to look at or turn to the planet and "face it," in every sense of the word, as the planet itself is turning to us, this volume extends particularly the line of inquiry of my 2011 *Cosmodernism: American Narrative, Late Globalization, and the New Cultural Imaginary* and of the 2015 essay collection, *The Planetary Turn: Relationality and Geoaesthetics in the Twenty-First Century.*[12] Co-edited with Amy J. Elias, *The Planetary Turn* features, as acknowledged below, a piece of mine that draws out some methodological implications of *Cosmodernism*'s core concept for the planetary paradigm. Centered on post–September 11, 2001 American and world literature, philosophy, and cultural theory, *Reading for the Planet* expands that article with an eye to theorizing a geocultural model of interpretation—a *geomethodology*—in a fashion that, to reemphasize, both elaborates a full-dress critical rationale and issues a call to action inside and outside literary-cultural criticism.

§2. Cosmodernism and the Planet

Neither the sole "new thing" to supersede postmodernism nor a distinct movement or school so far, cosmodernism is, as I introduce it in my 2011 book, (a) a more and more recognizable imaginary pattern, to wit, a modality of mapping out today's world as a cultural geography of relationality; (b) by the same token, an also better, and better-marked, scenario of discourse and subjectivity formation; (c) an ethical imperative pointing to the present as much as to the future; and (d) a critical technique for interpreting and assembling a range of post-1989 narrative and theoretical U.S. imaginings into a coherent and ahead-looking model.

Building on these meanings, *Reading for the Planet* adds a fifth: as an inchoate, still "soft" trend, cosmodernism is for American and other Euroatlantic cultures a transition to, harbinger of, and sometimes a blueprint for that which planetarism is becoming for the entire world on the threshold of the twenty-first century. That is to say, the North American "cosmodernization" (cosmodern-becoming) of the postmodern—a subject tackled more insistently in *Cosmodernism*'s epilogue and in a couple of other places after that[13]—is a world-fractal phenomenon, namely, an isomorphic *subset* of a highly complex, fairly discontinuous, and at times contradictory shift of larger proportions and longer-lasting consequences; cosmodernity and cosmodernization are to the United States and the West generally what planetarity and planetarization are becoming to the world, its present, and its foreseeable future.

Therefore—and most notably—while the cosmodern can be described as a planetary synecdoche, cosmodernism is *not* the Ur-paradigm the rest of the world replicates. Planetarism is scarcely cultural imperialism redivivus even though writers' intimations of planetarity are not wholly immune to imperial lapses and neoimperialist, totalist-globalist temptations. It is the other way around, rather: socioaesthetic mutations in North America, Europe, and elsewhere cannot circumvent the broader, ecumenical transformations affecting how artists, thinkers, and laypeople worldwide see themselves, their places, and the world. Thus, *Reading for the Planet* restages the cosmodern "algorithm" of interpretation discriminately, rehearses some of its tenets (e.g., the role of relationality), and revamps, repurposes, or casts aside others to work out a mechanism for reading planetarism—for teasing out the inscriptions of planetarity, the world's reemergence *qua* planet, in early twenty-first-century literary, cultural, and theoretical practices.

The structure of this presence rests, as we shall notice repeatedly, on a characteristic *geocultural logic*: the heterotopic co-presence deployed by the greater elsewhere's ever more aggressive bid for redefining the cultural "here"—nearness, locality, the "regionally specific," and the putative, and usually problematic, autochthonous—topologically as well as typologically (anthropologically). This logic has been behind one of the most salient world developments since the collapse of the Berlin Wall: the overhaul of the traditional dynamic of place and culture. Some critics have indeed underscored the weakening of the "umbilical cord" between determinate locations, on one side, and, on the other, cultural formations such as discourse, identity, and community, which have been customarily deemed as "stemming" or "coming from" a particular, well-contoured, and largely stable territory whose political, economic, and epistemological sovereignty has been enforced by the nation-state and its administrative-corporatist and educational institutions. Others have hypothesized that this link has been severed altogether culturally, politically, and in many other ways—witness the 2014 Romanian presidential elections, whose outcome was reportedly decided by voters residing outside Romania. Still others have maintained that such ties have been supplanted by a less bounded model of cultural origination. According to this model, indigenous roots become rerouted first cross-regionally, trans- and inter-continentally, and then globally, while inherited filiation yields to voluntary affiliation and "vertical" derivation to horizontal *dérive* ("drift") and its sometimes cosmopolitan fantasies of playful self-fashioning. In any case, there is little doubt that the path, makeup, functioning, and understanding of the locus-culture nexus have been shifting, faster and faster, across countries, cultures, as well as disciplines, where, consequently, we are running into problems testing the effectiveness of our approaches, the boundaries of our discourses and of the "scholarly" more generally, the limitations of our epistemologies, and the germane limits of our academic setups and units.

Both concomitant and homologous to the geopolitical shifts and troubles enumerated earlier, these problems too bear witness to the staggering upswing in interconnectedness and mobility around the world, in the quasi-universal instability and vulnerability of borders, in the fluidity of territorial-institutional jurisdiction, in the growing "fuzziness" of location, and in the cultural-discursive and socioeconomic unmooring of formerly dependable, "steadfast" categories such as place, origin, tradition, and the like. They include the risks taken by the reader of Yoko Tawada's "Metamorphosen des Heidenrösleins," whose "language games," as Marjorie Perloff has shown with great display of erudition, put one on a "cultural collision" course with Johann Wolfgang von Goethe as much as with Japan's history, literature, and national idiom;[14] the revelation of the Faulknerian scholar forced to travel these days, methodologically if not physically also, to Haiti and even farther away, to western Africa to uncover the sources of the southern anxieties buried deep in *Absalom, Absalom!*; the bemusement of the critic who, alongside the characters of *White Noise* and other, later Don DeLillo novels, might wonder if the American heartland's glorious sunsets are no more than "fallout from a war in China";[15] or the conundrum one faces in Joseph O'Neill's masterpiece *Netherland*, where, as we will learn later in the epilogue (§32), the bigger world becomes legible in the unlikely yet refreshing "civility" spectacle put up for our benefit on a Long Island cricket field.[16]

§3. Planetarism: History, the Cultural Imaginary, and the Problem of Interpretation

Neither such critical provocations nor the world realities mounting them are entirely new. Their European origins, for instance, can be traced to the voyages of the fourteenth-century Venetian and Portuguese explorers if not farther back. Nevertheless, as I stress throughout, both the omnipresence of these realities and the intensity with which they level such challenges day in and day out at the dawn of the third millennium are historically unmatched and demand solutions without delay. In that, they tell or highlight one way of telling both the world's time and our cultural-intellectual time in the world. They attest to the world's "condition" or modality of being: planetarity. Embodying this ontology is the planet, which my book defines as *the geocultural matrix increasingly fashioning human expressivity and comprehension worldwide, the emerging "single unit" of cultural discourse and analysis, of world-writing and world-reading.*[17]

Reading for the Planet, then, is not an ecocritical inquiry. Here, the planet is not an environmental concept even though, as I will clarify later on, one of its main parameters is spatiality and, further, it would not be possible without the concept nor without the recent work done around it by critics such as Lawrence Buell, Ursula K. Heise, and Karen L. Kilcup. The kind of ecology that concerns my foray into the planetary, as it does critics such as Henry Sussman, Hubert Zapf, Michael Wutz, and Joseph Tabbi, is *cultural*, more exactly, *geocultural*. Conversely, I am interested in a *planetarily framed practice of culture*, in culture defined as a world "ecosystem" to whose welfare the socio-discursive, ethno-racial, and gender-, class-, and faith-inflected here-there and self-other relations, and relationality more broadly, are crucial. Obviously, the ecosystem is more than a metaphor for cultural give-and-take within the human sphere. Nor can human relationality be fully conceptualized without factoring into it our dealings with non-human others such as the animal, the biosphere largely, the inanimate, the divine, and so on. But, again, my discussion focuses, here as elsewhere in my work, on intra-anthropological relatedness, deliberately narrowing down alterity to the cultural, more exactly, the *geocultural other*.[18]

With this important proviso, one can look, I think, at the tellings, narrations, representations, and measurements mentioned above, and also at the critical struggles to make sense of them, as the characteristic "species" of the human ecosystem, all of them subsisting—expressing something, producing meaning, or trying to figure this meaning out—according to a certain figuring or imagining protocol: planetarism. The cultural imaginary of planetarity, planetarism constitutes *both a reality and a metareality, a historical phenomenon and an aesthetic-conceptual construal thereof.* Further, as constructions, the stories and figurations of planetarism are simultaneously *descriptive and normative, contemporary and future*, a reality, "under construction" as it may be, and a reality to be or set of directives for present reality's change. Ontologically, as already existing reality, the planet is partially already in place ("in the world") and can be described as such; most significantly, this partial presence is being augmented aesthetically and critically, as subject to a prescriptive planetary imagination. As cultural form, imaginary configuration, and *Weltanschauung*, planetarism is then both aligned and at odds with the historical and political circumstances of its birth. The post-1990s, ever-accelerating de-linking and unorthodox recoupling of locale and material-discursive production in manufacturing, trade, finance, communications, sciences, and the arts are the backdrop against which new, planetary ways of experiencing and viewing the world have risen and with them the possibility of a new cultural paradigm inside and outside the United States. Thus, at the core of what may well amount to a sea change "out there," in the "real world," planetarism is, more and more markedly every day, the twenty-first-century imaginary's "Prevailing Operating System," to borrow Sussman's term.[19] Neither entirely unprecedented nor everywhere the same nor subtending the entire earth, the planetary is *the pivotal dimension in which the world's cultures are fostered.* In this sense, rather than in the more holistic-integrative one, of which critics like Gayatri Chakravorty Spivak remain understandably leery, this dimension is unique in terms of the force with which it leaves its imprint on how people are now picturing themselves and their environments.[20] A highly complex, material-aesthetic operator, the planet is becoming a dominant, shaping, as well as illuminating context, an arena, a modulating drive, and a mode of cultural production. No question about it.

The question is how to tackle this output. More precisely, the question is—aesthetically, ethically, and politically—how to handle the imagination system so as to enlist its own *episteme* in a "reimagination" of the world's "prevailing systems of actuality."[21] One might ask, therefore, how are we to respond to planetarism critically? How are we to sort out a planetary cultural symptomatology ranging from free-floating, disembodied fantasies of fluidity, hyperconnectivity, and "contagious" *mode* and modality of affect and aesthetic self-definition to the nitty-gritty of migrant lives and quasi-generalized diaspora of a world that seems to be, as we shall see in part 1 under §13, in search of the postcolonial's "beyond"; from extreme forms of "time-space compression" (Harvey) to the global "spectacle society" and the world panopticon of touristic voyeurism, military surveillance, intervention, annexation, and aggressive data gathering by government agencies; from the shrinking-cum-dilation and the conflict-ridden intermingling of private and public spheres to the ebb and flow of identities—from the deterritorialization of subjectivities to the reterritorialization of allegiances as supra-national consumer options, fashion statements, and professional memberships? How are we to make sense of cultures' pathos of being in the bigger world—how do we understand them *in their patent or disguised worldliness*—while distinguishing between this legitimate aspiration and the homogenization and "banalization of the world" that Baudrillardian "telemorphosis" and other categories of overmediatization threaten as with?[22] How do we interpret novel X from culture Y geoculturally? Once again, how do we read "with" the planet, and what would be the intellectual mechanics as well as the ethical ramifications of such a planetary form of interpretation?

§4. Steps toward a Geomethodology: Brief Outline

> A drop of blood is like a novel, it contains the world.
> —BHARATI MUKHERJEE, *The Tree Bride*

In answering these questions, the book builds toward a reading model for the projections of planetarity encrypted in cultural practices or artifacts. Putting together the planetary interpretive grid takes a two-step process. The steps are *Reading for the Planet*'s main parts, which in turn are split into two sub-parts or chapters. Part 1 lays the groundwork for the geomethodology developed in part 2. Part 1's opening chapter (§5–§9) comprises the critique of globalist theory and terminology, thus setting the stage for part 1, II, in which I articulate—again, based on the previous section's theoretical-conceptual "housecleaning"—the planetary paradigm. This paradigm is completed in part 2, I, where I lay out its key feature: the planetary reading model. I show how this works in part 2, II, while the epilogue details the ethical ramifications of the model's applications—how reading with the planet can become reading *for* the planet or "critical stewardship."

Specifically, the book's prolegomena (§5–§14) consists of a series of historical and conceptual dissociations helping contextualize the rise of planetarism and define its core critical lexicon over and against post–Cold War globalization, global studies, and the latter's "global" family vocabulary. By no means synonymous although routinely conflated, *world* (the broadest term), *globe*, and *planet* make up this part's fundamental notional triad, with the last two understood as intertwined processings ("worldings") of the first: the world has to undergo a process to become globe, planet, or something else. While, similarly to "planetarism," "planet," and the like, "globalism," "global," and their brethren do correspond to either fully shaped or emerging *empirical realities*, to how things are or are about to be in the world, *Reading for the Planet* remains keen on such worldly signifiers as discourse formations, ways of talking about what is happening to the world. For it is on this world-performative terrain, where the contemporary world is construed, discursively formed, and, in an important yet often neglected sense, also *produced*, that *alternate* formations and reformations are first envisioned.[23]

The end result of these deconstructive/reconstructive procedures can be described as a critical equivalent to linguistic back-formation. Needless to say, "globe" and "planet" did not come into being, nor were they defined ontologically, in what they are and do, as globalism and planetarism had their multiple suffixes clipped (by whom?); it was the other way around, actually. But, if globalism, globalization, and globality, on one side, and planetarism, planetarization, and planetarity, on the other side, entail worldly maneuverings, certain ways of fashioning the world, then planetarism may be well poised to refashion, reimagine, or reworld the world into a shape, structure, or meaning distinct from, if not outright critical of, the shape, structure, or meaning "world" acquired (or lost) as it "worlded" as "globe" (as it "globalized"), *and* as it was "worded" as such by global studies. This is why "globe" and "planet" are so insistently treated here as *competing constructions of the worlding world, of the world that is coming together, or, in brief, the world-as-world. They are alike insofar as they share the relational modus operandi, and they diverge in their different management of relationality.* My book both queries and dwells on this contrast to take a stand by putting forth its own planetary alternative. This makes *Reading for the Planet* a critical-theoretical counteroffer twice: while not restricted to issues of discourse, textuality, and perusal, literary or otherwise, its greater objective is another—planetary—reading. The critical review of global studies in part 1's first half, especially the revisiting of this scholarship's rhetorical production of globalization, is a stepping-stone toward this reading.

"Idiosyncratic" on occasion, and so not unlike all new (or "newish") terminology, the planetarity repertoire is introduced and defined in part 1's final segments (§10-§14) and then put to work accordingly. As far as I know, neither the definitions—at least these definitions—nor their uses have been attempted more systematically elsewhere although Spivak's "globe"-"planet" dyad, Eric Hayot's work on "world" semantics, and Emily Apter's exquisite inquiry into "Untranslatables" (Barbara Cassin's *intraduisibles*) like "*Welt, Mundus, World, Terre, Cosmos, Chôra, Globe*[,] *Planetarity,* [and] *irdisch*" move all in this direction.[24] I realize that getting into the wooly business of such terminologically contrastive elucidations as I am ups the ante once more in a book that, as I have said, insists on walking the fine line between high-stakes claims and theoretical sobriety. Nonetheless, these differentiations must be undertaken. They are key to my discussion overall, in particular to its critical retrofitting of the more established, perhaps already ossified dictionary that also comes into play alongside and in tension with the planetary nomenclature: "culture," "cultural practice," "originality," "tradition," "patrimony," "sovereignty," "community," "identity," "subjectivity," "contemporary"/"present," "space"/"territory," and so on. As with "globe" and "globalization," the overabundance of scare quotes signals an awareness of the *conventions*—assumptions, expectations, and agendas, in sum, rhetoricity—these words body forth. Thus, in conjunction with the distinctions introduced under §10-§14, this older and broader category of notions is inevitably "planetarized" throughout: reassessed, complicated, and otherwise fine-tuned for a historical moment (planetary) and for an endeavor (planetary reading) that were lying well beyond the horizon of the 1970s and early 1980s, when critical theory originally forged this class of terms. Obviously, some theoretical and terminological heavy lifting is to be expected here too, as is the relative density of reasoning and style. But I think the patient reader will agree that they all pay off in what comes next. He or she will also appreciate, I hope, not only the hoops my argument is going through but also the moves it declines to make. Either way, the goal remains setting up, as clearly and effectively as possible, the planetary reading model.

In concert with the historical and conceptual revisionism of part 1, the following step taken by *Reading for the Planet* arises from the conviction that a planetarily minded reading should work out a flexibly comparatist interpretive modality able to approach ethically, with an epistemologically auspicious humility, a culture's planetary "fine print" and thus unscramble or decompress the encodings of planetarity—turn to the planet's face, distinguish and make it visible for others also—in the putatively or "genuinely" local, regional, cloistered, and culturally-anthropologically peerless. I flesh out this interpretive apparatus or geomethodology in the first half of part 2

(§15–§20). Still theoretical in its ambitions, the second half (§21–§31) canvases mainly early twenty-first-century fiction alongside some criticism and philosophy. In particular, I attend to writers of various backgrounds to formulate, back up, and illustrate planetary reading's main contentions, components, and operations. I am drawn, admittedly, to a certain type of fictional prose. However, despite the important specifications under §14, there is no planetary genre per se at this stage in world literary history, and so I cannot claim I am focusing on a particular form. What I examine—appositely, "planetarily"—is novels that (a) belong to what I call in part 1 (§13) "the planetary age," most of them having come out after 9/11; (b) are, characteristically, as exemplars of our time's world network culture, intertextually and interculturally supersaturated; (c) project, oftentimes critically, a planetary vision on recent, post–World War II and especially post-1980s events in the form of certain narrativizations of world space ("geoaesthetics") suspicious of the rationales behind ongoing geopolitics, geoeconomics, and their official or implied cartographies; and, therefore, (d) as upshots of such intellectual-affective mappings of the world,[25] present themselves, overtly in writers like Bharati Mukherjee, less so in others, as ethical "world containers" subtended not only by a geoaesthetics but also by a *geoethics*. Like a speck of somebody's blood or a raindrop in a haiku, these narratives piece together the world's broken body and cradle multitudes; they are "hemo-synecdoche[s] of the world," as Mukherjee has a character reflect in her 2004 novel *The Tree Bride*.[26] I also contend that they "want" to be read this way. Obligingly, my planetary reading model measures this synecdochic dimension, the fervor and ability of such world-containing, world-heavy, or, more simply, "worlded" works to take in the world while their immediate concerns may or may not be, at first blush at least, the wide world as such.

Of late, the number of this kind of works has skyrocketed. As far as I can tell, the trend foregrounds national literatures' deepening worldliness rather than their imperialist propensities. In this regard, U.S. literature is no exception. Nor should it receive special treatment. True, I tend to look primarily at American works, but I am an Americanist first and a comparatist next—and *because* I am an Americanist. The model's applications in part 2, II, show that, and in a good way too, I would like to think. What I seek to build, though, as an American literature specialist in conversation with *histoire croisée* advocates, comparatists, world literature proponents, global studies scholars, "neocosmopolitans" and their critique of epistemological nationalism, ecocritics, and translation theorists, is a methodological basis for "planetary criticism," viz., for coming to terms with the literature and culture *of the planet*.

I wish to clarify the ambiguous genitive right away, for it is less presumptuous than it sounds. What I have in mind is not all "worlded" literature and culture on the planet, in the sweeping-quantitative sense that has all-too-often discounted, or has just been unable to see, the qualitatively unique, the singular. My ambition is not another critical grand narrative. It is not this kind of literary production from "all over the world" that I bring under the epistemological purview of my geomethodology. Actually, this is not "world literature" either. Or, if it is, it is insofar the world's literature, no matter where in the world it hails from, is more and more becoming worlded literature or a literature of worldedness in a planetarily discursive, thematic, and at times even formal sense: novels, plays, poetry, and other evocations of cultural-historical incidents and sites in which, however small, unassuming, and geographically and politically circumscribed these gestures, occasions, and places may be, the world "worlds" itself nevertheless, gathers itself together, and, in displaying the animate and inanimate texture of this throbbing, ever-changing, and kaleidoscopic worldly togetherness, shows its face *as* world.

In closing, I underline the ethical import of the geomethodological. To this end, the epilogue trades on Emmanuel Levinas's response to the Heideggerian critique of "planetarized" technology to propose a linguistic-deontological retooling of "reading-*with*" as "reading-*for*" the planet and of literary-cultural criticism as planetary stewardship. Does this put on the book a spin that is ultimately ethical rather than political? The question is not unwarranted. There is no shortage of political agendas and proposals these days, though. In fact, there is an abundance of them even if we check only within the liberal quarters where *Reading for the Planet* too stakes out its territory. What the majority of these *different* initiatives are lacking, it seems to me, is an ethically shared ground in whose absence they hardly stand a chance of changing much in today's worlded world. This foundation is not a depoliticizing *commonality*, a politically disabling "consensus" that, as Jacques Rancière claims, "transform[s] . . . [t]he political community . . . into an *ethical* community" and allegedly cancels the political out.[27] This is, instead, a loose *communality* of thought and attitude; this is, digitally, geoculturally, and otherwise, a worldly mise ensemble that opens up a meeting space and thereby "instigates" a coming together—if not a wholly new "social contract," then surely new forms, possibilities, and arenas of sociality;[28] thus, this is a togetherness that, before being and in order to *be* some day strategically coalitional by buying into a single, clearly identified, and vastly accommodating political option, *must be* ethical. In other words, it must be by *being-with* first, in an ethical *with-world*, one whose topoethical structure of "conviviality," we shall note in part 1, great minds like Goethe had already foreseen.[29] Before remapping the world, we have to think about the cartographic ethic of such a political gesture.

It is by carrying on and refining this trajectory of thought that I also maintain—programmatically against recent rejections of the ethical by Rancière and his ilk—that what we, cultural critics and theorists of planetarity, need to accomplish first, but for *political reasons* also, is ground ourselves in an ethic. Oriented by Levinas in its "consideration" of and for the planet's luminously elusive yet exigent face and the geophenomenological relationality embedded in it, this ethic is here principally one of critical-theoretical practice. Its ethos obtains as a corollary of the literary and culturally "decompressive" analysis of the "telescoping" scenes surveyed in part 2. But, in keeping with this book's inter- and supra-disciplinary designs, the conclusion offers up this ethos as a plausible rallying hypothesis for all humanists, inside, across, and outside the humanities.

On the other hand, affirming this ethos implies an unapologetic reaffirmation, albeit rather unfashionable these days, of culture as a vigorously transformative force in the world, of culture's worldedness in a geoontological and political sense. Planetarism, a counter-imagination, can be, and often is, oppositional. As suggested in §1 and amply illustrated in part 2, planetary spatial poetics often upsets the spatial politics "on the ground." In turn, planetary reading, the rigorous reading of planetarism's counter-imaginings, cannot miss the seeds of such oppositions, affirmations, and transformations, the eventfulness potential in all those small and unassuming places and scenes. In theorizing and reading planetarity, this book's main efforts, then, deliberately bring culture back to the center of a world-system usually dismissive, in its classical—and classically economistic articulations—of culture's systemic value and, hence, of its political relevance. Are these endeavors "culturalist"? They may well be, but that hardly makes them systemically or, I should say, planetarily irrelevant. At any rate, the answer to the question is less important than what they ultimately accomplish as they throw light on literary-aesthetic representation's centrality to both what the world is and to what planetarism shows that the world can be.

I could not have brought this project to fruition without the generous help of many people and institutions. My first thanks go to Amy J. Elias, distinguished Americanist, widely recognized authority in postmodern and digital studies, and good friend. In 2011, as I was still reeling from having just wrapped up *Cosmodernism*, she approached me with an idea that led to *The Planetary Turn*. For that collection, I wrote an essay, which I then reworked into this book's part 2, and I also composed an earlier form of the introduction. Eventually, only some of that version went into the opening piece of *The Planetary Turn*. I have revised and augmented that initial draft quite a bit, and the outcome—virtually a new text—has become *Reading for the Planet*'s part 1. These revisions, expansions, and the like do not document only a personal preoccupation traceable, as I have noted, to my earlier work. They are also a testimony to three years of working with Amy, to hundreds of e-mails, phone calls, editorial dilemmas, and, on the more substantial side, to theoretical problems and even to language that *Reading for the Planet* and its companion, *The Planetary Turn*, unavoidably share. In this sense, our collaboration goes on within this individually authored book, one for whose shortcomings I remain otherwise exclusively responsible.

I also want to recognize the following institutions, programs, and persons who have provided much-needed funding, guidance, and venues of critical exchange: the Fulbright Foreign Scholarship Board, the Bureau of Education and Cultural Affairs of the United States Department of State, and the Council for International Exchange of Scholars for a 2014 Fulbright Specialist Grant in U.S. Studies at Radboud University in Nijmegen, the Netherlands; the German Alexander von Humboldt Foundation, for a 2012 research stipend locally, and most generously, sponsored in Munich by Raoul Eshelman; the University of North Carolina, Greensboro, for a 2012 Summer Excellence Fellowship and a fall 2014 research assignment leave; also at UNCG, the College of Arts and Sciences, specifically for the assistance generously extended by the College's Dean, Timothy Johnston, over the past few years; UNCG's English Department, its past and present heads, Professor Anne Wallace and Professor Scott Romine, and its superbly collegial faculty; UNCG's dynamic Atlantic World Research Network and its Director, Professor Christopher Hodgkins, whose support, encouragement, and genuine interest in the thorny issues broached in *Reading for the Planet* have been invaluable; UNCG's Office of Research and Economic Development and its Vice Chancellor, Dr. Terri L. Shelton, for vital help throughout; UNCG's International Programs Center, for a 2012 Kohler Research Award and other grants enabling travel and work leading to this book, and the University's Walter Clinton Jackson Interlibrary Loan Department staff; colleagues and graceful hosts at Ludwig Maximilian University of Munich, the University of Konstanz, and the University of Freiburg (Germany), the University of Limoges (France), the University of Maryland, Ohio State University, the University of Bucharest, the University of Cluj-Napoca (Romania), and Radboud University and the University of Amsterdam (the Netherlands). John McGowan, John Protevi, and Jeffrey J. Williams have given useful feedback on an earlier draft of *Reading for the Planet*'s closing pages (§31–§33). In the summer of 2014, I enjoyed the opportunity to discuss my geomethodology at Petru Maior University, Târgu-Mureş, Transylvania University, Braşov, and Lucian Blaga University, Sibiu (Romania), in particular with members of the new Romanian "school" of global studies such as Andrei Terian, Alex Goldiş, and Oana Strugaru.

Gratefully acknowledged is also the support of Liedeke Plate and Timotheus Vermeulen, my gracious Radboud hosts. Marjorie Perloff, David Cowart, Paul Allen Miller, Brian McHale, Ursula Heise, Paul Maltby, Bertrand Westphal, Emily Apter, Brian Richardson, Jerome Klinkowitz, John Frow, Vincent B. Leitch, Zahi Zalloua, Nicole Simek, Keith Cushman, Karen Kilcup, Stephen Yarbrough, Hephzibah Roskelly, Monika Fludernik, Jan Alber, Robin van der Akker, Yra van Dijk, Basarab Nicolescu, Jean-Michel Rabaté, Rodica Mihăilă, Mircea Martin, Ştefan Borbely, Corin Braga, Andrei Bodiu, Caius Dobrescu, Alexandru Muşina, Adrian Lăcătuş, Iulian Boldea, and Alexandra Mitrea have offered advice, assistance, and fellowship. I am thankful too to Radu Ţurcanu, leading psychoanalyst and old friend, for extending his hospitality, humor, and wisdom when I needed them. Jeffrey R. Di Leo, distinguished cultural theorist and Executive Director of the Society for Critical Exchange, has been my generous host at University of Houston–Victoria's Winter Theory Institute, where, over the last couple of years, I have presented portions and versions of *Reading for the Planet*'s argument. Kir Kuiken deserves credit for mentioning to me Rodolphe Gasché's latest book. And Henry Sussman's inspiring scholarship and kindness remain the luminous and firm guide that, directly and indirectly, has saved this book innumerable hesitations and about-faces.

Some of the insights set forth here have been tested out in my classes. I am thankful, therefore, to my UNCG undergraduate and graduate students in post-2010 courses such as English 208: "Topics in Global Literature," English 740: "Studies in Contemporary and Postmodern American Literature," and English 704: "Studies in Contemporary Literary and Cultural Theory." Finally, I appreciate the unwavering support and interest in my work shown at the University of Michigan Press by Editorial Director Aaron McCollough. I am also indebted to Christopher Dreyer, Tom Dwyer, the copyediting and marketing staff, and the Press's three anonymous external readers for their constructive comments.

Finally, a few sections of *Reading for the Planet* have originally appeared, in different form, as follows: "'A foreign tongue to unite us': Book Traveling with Dai Sijie," in *Canadian Review of Comparative Literature* 36, no. 2 (June 2009): 120–136; "Melancholy Nation," in *American Book Review* 35, no. 1 (November–December 2013): 19–20; part 2's §21–§23 fragments have been adapted from my essay "Decompressing Culture: Three Steps toward a Geo-methodology," text included in *The Planetary Turn: Relationality and Geo-aesthetics in the Twenty-First Century*, edited by Amy J. Elias and Christian Moraru. Copyright © 2015 by Northwestern University Press. Published 2015. All rights reserved; "The Forster Connection or, Cosmopolitanism Redux: Zadie Smith's *On Beauty, Howards End*, and the Schlegels." Adapted from the *Comparatist*, 35 (May 2011): 133–147. Copyright © 2011 by the Southern Comparative Literature Association. Used by permission of the University of North Carolina Press. I am grateful to these publications, their editors, and publishers for permission to reprint modified segments of these articles, as I am to Elke Claus (www.elkeworks.com) and Chicago's Morpho Gallery (www.morphogallery.com) for allowing me to use a visual reproduction of Claus's mixed media on paper "To You Alone" on this book's front cover. Also, all translations from German, French, Romanian, and other languages are mine unless otherwise indicated.

PART 1 WORLD, GLOBE, PLANET

planaō (Gk.): "lead astray," "wander," "wander in mind," "be at a loss"
—*Pocket Oxford Classical Greek Dictionary*

The globe is not the world.
—PHENG CHEAH, "What Is a World? On World Literature as World-Making Activity"

I

§5. Wording the World, Worlding the Word

> Can we now identify an emergent planetary optic that can be grounded anywhere and that creates historical possibilities not available before?
> —MARY LOUISE PRATT, "Planetary Longings: Sitting in the Light of the Great Solar TV"

In his 1964 article on Wallace Stevens, "The Planetary Poet," John Crowe Ransom made a point to cut the commentary short and close with the "epilogue" Stevens himself had "deliver[ed] . . . in a roundabout manner" two years before he died.[1] A resplendent coda to the poet's career, the four stanzas of "The Planet on the Table" feature one of his alter egos, Ariel. In doing Prospero's bidding, Ariel steps into the role of a master of natural ceremonies, an illusion maker and thereby an imitator or, in Ancient Greek, *mimetés*. In brief, Stevens's Ariel is a poet. But the spirit is a special type of poet: his "self and the sun were one." His poems, Stevens further discloses, "although makings" of Ariel's own "self," "[w]ere no less makings of the sun." As Stevens glosses,

> It was not important that they survive.
> What mattered was that they should bear
> Some lineament of character,

Some affluence, if only half-perceived,
In the poverty of their words,
Of the planet of which they were part.[2]

Both friend and handler of the sun and the elements, elementary ("aery") himself, Ariel is in the planet-writing business. Arguably, so is Stevens. Conjuring up the planet, the 1953 poem performs an act as magical as it is aesthetic.

Central to this aesthetic performance is a *geoscopic* protocol. At once an invocation of the planet and a textual convocation, "The Planet on the Table" is a twofold calling forth that actualizes the planet by looking at it, more exactly, by gazing into the planet's face and treating it as a legible object—one that lends itself to reading. *Poiēsis* here entails and can ultimately be defined as "facing." Largely speaking, it boils down to an art of looking. In particular, it designates an aesthetic retraining of the ordinary gaze on the planet. More specifically still, it institutes an *ethoscopy*, a contemplation of the planet *as* planet, a multiple, creative-interpretive consideration of the planet's planetary "aspect" or *adspectum*, namely, of that which, on earth, makes for a worldly "expressive" face or *figura*. The latter is a material and cultural configuration at once planetarily pertinent (while fluctuating across the planet, its relevance overall seizes hold on a planetary scale), optically "remarkable" (it is visible, stands out "scopically"), semiotically meaningful (it signifies something), and, last but not least, ethically compelling. Thus, poetic writing, and any variety of artistic mimesis for that matter, whatever its subject, is not only planet-oriented (a commonplace, after all), but it also regards ("looks at") and portrays planetarity. It examines, in other words, the earth's face to draw its planetary portrait, to map out the planet poetically so that, on and between the poem's lines, the perspicacious reader might make out the planet's own, coherent and coherence-inducing, "lineaments." These are not—or not just—*ethnoscopies*. They do not trace coordinates, borders, boundaries, natural and political wrinkles and divides, scars and fault lines, itineraries, and historical tracks of change, suffering, and élan that mark off locations, positions, or venues of *discrete* ethnolinguistic groups (organized into national entities or not). They are, again, ethoscopies. For they bring out in high relief planetary "characters" or letters "re-lettering" all such locales, histories, and geopolitical units, "worlding" them into the geoscript of the planetary supra-unit. This geoscript, this poetic cartography, indexes a planetary consciousness.

In keeping with the neo-Romantic aesthetics Stevens carries so memorably to a modernist extreme, the rhetorical longitudes and latitudes of this sublime world-mapping remain oftentimes hesitant, blurry, and thus "half-perceived," for these "ma(r)kings" are quasi-mystical, obscurely allusive, highly metaphorical. The poem's words do embody the planet's appearance in some measure, but, more than anything else, they make up an introvert exercise in *self*-embodiment. Exquisite as they may be, their self-reflexivity lessens extrovert reflectiveness and its wealth of detail, which a more capacious, world-inclusive wording of the 1950s planet requires. Therefore, while they do testify to the greater world outside and the mimetic self behind them, the poems are planetary synecdoches ("part[s] . . . of the planet") rather allegorically. All its splendor notwithstanding, their metaphorics betrays, and at times deliberately cultivates, a paradoxical poverty—sketchiness, imprecision, abstruseness—of planetary representation. Self-acknowledged, as one might expect, this poetic paucity yields an apposite world picture, one in which an analogous scarcity, a certain studied reticence of planetary mimesis, is brought to bear on the planet's image.

At issue here is not just how Stevens's poetry is wording the world—for it is—but, conversely, also how and to what extent Stevens's world itself affords it, in what form and to what degree a sufficiently and adequately "worlded" post–World War II modernism—a "planetarized" modernism receptive to the world-as-world—is effectively and fully possible during the author's lifetime. The question, then, is not only style and, more broadly, aesthetics, but also history and the insights the particular historical moment enables in modernists like Stevens. Intriguingly enough, the poet sets about to put the planet on the table the way an ordinary worker might with the family's daily bread. And yet, partaking in the "solar" life of the world-as-world and sharing in the planet's planetarity to the point of rendering it a domestic item are affective and imaginary exploits neither the "makings" (poetics) of Stevens's late modernism nor the Cold War's adversarial-disjunctive, either-or geopolitics wholeheartedly sponsored.

At the height of the Cold War confrontation, Philip Roth also speaks directly to the era's geopolitical bearings on the private, the emotional, and their expression. One might say—in anticipation of the introduction of the "netosphere" concept in §9—that he is, as great artists often are, onto something here, to wit, onto a certain Cold War world configuration of what Lauren Berlant describes as "affectsphere."[3] A character of Roth's 1961 novel *Letting Go* complains, in fact, that nobody can love anybody anymore because "we are all of us living in the shadow of the Bomb" and its consequences: "emotional anarchy, separation, a withdrawal of people from people. A kind of moral isolationism."[4] This feeling of "feelinglessness" flies in the face of New Age "free love" and the like. More notably, and way ahead of the "affective turn" in the humanities and, subsequently, of the recent inquiries into the "geopolitics of emotions" and the interplay of the ideological and the emotional during and after the Cold War, the feeling underscores that individual affect and its representation are colored by the world-as-world, or, differently put, that people's emotional "withdrawal" from other people is articulated with, if not utterly touched off, by the forced, "politicized" separation of *peoples from peoples*: the love affair with the Bomb has profoundly alienating if not *geo*alienating upshots insofar as it tends to map private affairs onto world affairs—or something like that.[5] Of course, Roth is not alone in his insight. Pynchon, John Updike, Robert Coover, and Don DeLillo "feel" the same throughout their work. Likewise, Ian McEwan has a character of his 2012 Cold War novel *Sweet Tooth* dismiss as "monstrous solipsism" the temptation to "broo[d] about a stranger who caressed [her] palm with his thumb" while "civilization [is being] threatened by nuclear war."[6]

To be clear: even though, as Fredric Jameson and others have argued, "[l]ate modernism is a product of the Cold War,"[7] the period from the 1950s through the 1980s did witness, in works by Stevens and other visionaries of the era, wordings of a worlding world courageously and farsightedly overflowing the schismatic territorialities, bounded ideologies, and hemmed-in loyalties into which the actual post–World War II world was split. But such wordings were, to a notable extent, fleeting amphibologies, "intimations," "anticipations," and "premonitions" of planetarity. By and large peripheral in the economy of the modernist aesthetic system, these worldly tropisms were also geopolitically "impaired," as it were, understandably imprecise in their planetary "vision." When they did have the world-as-world in their sights, they typically provided figurative approximations of it, not in the least because a worlded world was not there yet to intrigue and guide them.

Following Martin Heidegger, thinkers and critics across disciplines tackle "worlding" as the world's rush toward worldedness, an innate tendency to juxtapose its pieces and thus morph into a worlded ontosyntax. This need not be a macro-entity monolithically "one," as even ethically minded "one-world" descriptions seem to suggest, but, as Jacques Derrida would say, a "haptical" world in which most if not all of its parts touch one another, interact and modify each other, derive their meanings from other parts within the whole as well as from this whole itself, and otherwise hang together so much so that the negotiation of their being-together is an axial routine of the everyday.[8] Compared to this worlded setup, Stevens's world—both the world in which he lived and that limned by his poetry, his Eastern influences notwithstanding—was at an earlier stage of worlding.[9] The decades coming immediately after the war were—again, comparatively speaking—poorly worlded. In some situations, the Cold War standoff made writers, especially on the other side of the Iron Curtain, world-hungry, but it overall put a check on the relational makeup of the world, and it could not but dampen—directly in the notorious case of socialist realism, obliquely in others—the relationality of the world's literary wordings. This poverty, this limitedness, this censorship even, did not quite stimulate artists' endeavors to "make out" the world-as-world, as it often inhibited the mar(k)ings, the poems' and stories' line(ament)s and wordings rather overtly.

By contrast, a world in which worlding ("togethering") has picked up speed, and still more so a *worlded world*, where worlding has entered an advanced phase, is a structurally *relational* world. This world is characterized by *relationality* at two levels. One is systemic. Here, the relational structure ensures that the majority if not all of this world's ingredients, places, and forms of life and expression thereof are, can be, or are likely to become one day interconnected and interdependent. The other is sub-systemic. At this level, everything or almost everything in this world is, can be, or is likely to become connected to and dependent on the broader world-system in terms of function and meaning. We will see below that the relational can also lead to *differently worlded worlds* depending on what type of worlding, global or planetary, is in play, which is in turn determined by the relational practice involved, by how relationality is understood, and by how it is carried out. Suffice it to say for now that, for aesthetic, political-economic, and technological reasons, relational wordings of the world—world pictures keen on the world's worldedness, on the world-as-world—did not supply, regardless of their orientation and despite the inevitable exceptions, the "cultural dominant" of Stevens's time. Neither would they become mainstream with late modernism's successor, postmodernism, which, of late, more and more scholars have been approaching as a Cold War phenomenon.[10]

It is only with the end of the Cold War that, in the United States and elsewhere, the panoply of world-relational imaginings starts taking center stage and their expressive dearth begins to give way to a less ambiguous plenitude: to more abundant, better-made and -marked makings and markings aspiring to paradigm-defining and even canonical status, to bolder lineaments and more distinct mappings, in sum, to a cornucopia of planetary representations and ultimately to a need to theorize them and deal with them systematically within a critical "field" of their own. In their most ethoscopically consistent manifestations, these figurations will bring about a whole rhetorical-thematic class in which "The Planet on the Table" would fit only with some approximation along other poems both anticipatory of, and geopolitically, culturally, and otherwise contemporary with, the late twentieth century: W. H. Auden's "Prologue at Sixty," Derek Walcott's "The Fortunate Traveller," Seamus Heaney's "Alphabets," and, to add just one example from outside the English-speaking world, Jorge Carrera Andrade's "geophysical," post-Whitmanesque lyrical monologue "Hombre Planetario" (Planetary Man), among others.[11] They all are, as Jahan Ramazani labels them, "planetary poems" in that they keep "figur[ing] the world as 'O,'" limning it as a complex unit, a "coloured," "singular, lucent O," as Heaney writes.[12] Not only a wooden globe but a planet, this "O" is a rounded letter and the letter of worldly roundness also, containing the entire alphabet, all characters, human and typographic, and all possible lines and lineaments of life: a world emphatically lettered and worded into worldedness. This worlding, this picturing of our common world as a relational space—albeit one in which the ethical content of relationality remains to be assessed—lies at the heart of the planetary imaginary. In poetry, fiction (as we shall see in part 2, II), and other genres, this imaginary is getting more and more culturally endemic on a world scale with the advent of the post-1989 period known as "accelerated," "strong," or "late globalization."[13]

A question, however, presents itself right away: What is it that we "know" about the world worlding itself faster and faster over the past two decades or so? The standard and by no means implausible answer is that this world has entered a qualitatively new phase of globalization. If this is true, then one could also claim, as I am, that, as a burgeoning world also brought about or more loosely "contextualized" or "occasioned" by worlding developments, and further, as a world vision, as an imaginary, and as a thematic-stylistic repertoire, "planet," "planetarity," and "planetarism" have emerged in an uneasy, concurrently symbiotic and oppositional association with "global" and the rest of the "globalization" cluster of terms and designated phenomena. Critics like David Held and Ramazani have in fact no qualms about defining globalization's interconnective arrangements as "the necessary condition for the lived experience of planetarity."[14] Likewise, one could suggest, and legitimately so, that planetary concerns are a global studies offshoot. What is less clear, though, is to what extent the hegemonic rhetoric of "globe," "globalism," and so on, irrespective of the political or moral construction—pro- or anti-neoliberal—it puts on globalization, *already construes* the world's worlding processes in a certain way and so ends up, oftentimes against its own critical agenda, further *globalizing* the world, that is, making it into a homogenous, conquerable, and commodifiable place rather than remaking it anew and allowing for its change. As couched in this uniformity-inducing rhetoric, globalization is treated, approvingly or not, as *the only way in which a worlding scenario has played out or as the only form of globalization possible*. This is not to say that globalization, as we "know" it, is pure "invention" of this rhetorical apparatus. Above, I do not write "construction" idly. "[D]debates over globalization are discursive"[15] *as* debates (form of discourse), but they would be pointless if they merely debated themselves. And yet the description or discourse in question has played up one way of looking at our world and, more broadly, one way of looking at the relation between culture and this world, so much so that seeing the world's face *in* literary-cultural artifacts, styles, and cultural practices has reached a serious impasse. To get out of it, we can begin by backing out of this rhetorical corner, and we should not let an otherwise understandable global babble fatigue get in the way. Lexical rigor and the distinctions it affords do provide, especially in times of terminological inflation, a foothold for serious critical action about and in the world.

Whether globalization, as articulated by its rhetoric, does justice to one dimension of worlding; whether, as the world's putatively sole modality of worlding, becoming-globe has more than one facet; or whether it means the same thing to all people and in all places—these are not minor concerns. They have been raised often too.[16] And yet, in my view, they are less important than this: planetarism and planetarity are well poised to supply another *worlding narrative*, an alternative—an alternate imagination of worlding and an alternate world altogether—over and against their own historical-genetic circumstances in general and counter to the more deleterious instantiations of post–Cold War geopolitics surveyed in this book's prologue (§1). As discourse, planetarism essentially points to, and encourages, we shall note, another worlding, other worlding vectors, and other worlding outcomes. But, to no negligible degree, this worldly otherness, this other to both the euphoric and the teratological world pictures painted by globalization scholars, cannot take hold as long as "globe," its phraseology, and worldview make up the default theoretical and linguistic conduit—and by the same token the foregone conclusion—for all sorts of world theorizations and pronouncements, be they "anti-globalization," anti-neoliberal, "altermondialist," and so forth. My first stop, then, has to be the naturalizing upshots of this rhetoric: what its terms have come to signify and perform rather than what they mean *in abstracto*, how their use shapes the world and the field, global studies, in which, willy-nilly, planetary studies had to lodge itself.

§6. Post–Cold War Globalization

Most political scientists and historians, and more and more critics would probably agree today that one need not be a hopeless "presentist" to accept that the fall of the Berlin Wall was a major milestone in modern world history. The post–Cold War crumbling and intensified porousness of all manner of walls, fences, borders, national sovereignties, and alliances worldwide, the wildfire spread of digital technologies, the previously unmatched circulation of people, capital, goods, ideas, and data are all symptoms of a world reaching a new world-systemic stage. By comparison, the pre-1989 period—virtually the entire twentieth century—had been moderately (if increasingly) connected. A *loose system*, the Cold War world was counterintuitively kept together by a Manichean template whose keystone was the nation-state. This conglomerate of nation-states and national subsystems ("blocs") was fractured along territorial, economic, and ideological fault lines within and without the East-West geography of divisiveness. Both conflictual and stabilizing in its repercussions, division was, in effect, the very logic of the Cold War-era geopolitical assemblage. If this was a world asunder, as some would insist, it was so because it was divided, carved out into more or less walled-in "influence zones" balancing each other out precariously yet, it turned out, efficiently, and functioning *centripetally*, under the jurisdiction of territorially secure, politically recognized, relatively sovereign, and reasonably operational political nodes, not because it was "fragmented" in a twenty-first-century, multicentric, centrifugal, trans- and postnational sort of way. Held in place by its mutually "deterring" antinomies of power, "common markets," pacts, and treaties, that world was nonetheless inferiorly worlded if not utterly "unworlded" in many of its aspects and regions.

That world largely ended with World War II's actual if protracted end, namely, the Cold War's conclusion. The new world professed to be rationally and beneficially worlded, viz., to grow more patently into a reassuring worldly togetherness, to evolve into a worldedness liable to close economic gaps and heal humanity's historical wounds. This is how the rising world liked to bill itself: as a postconflictual and even post-political, indeed, post-historical (à la Francis Fukuyama) state of affairs of a world decreasingly apart, in which the polarizing and disconnective impetus of the Cold War and of modernity overall took a back seat to a worldly connectedness that would allow more and more individuals—laypeople, artists, and academics—to see themselves "in relation," *sub specie coniunctionis*. This utopianism got big-time traction in sweeping, "new world order" pronouncements made by Mikhail Gorbachev and George H. W. Bush. Both were echoing Woodrow Wilson's 1918 "new world" rhetoric, and both were soon to be countered by Ken Jowitt's "new world disorder" and then by Zygmunt Bauman, Tzvetan Todorov, Amin Maalouf, Immanuel Wallerstein, and other chroniclers of "le Nouveau Désordre mondial."[17] If the latter often painted an entropic, world-scale pandemonium, the new world order enthusiasts, soon to be all but co-opted by neoliberalism, availed themselves of the by now classical, late 1980s–early 1990s roll call of postcommunist "achievements": the tearing down of the Iron Curtain and, with it, the greatest human-rights headway of the century; the 1993 signing of the North American Free Trade Agreement (NAFTA); the 1995 consolidation of the Bretton Woods institutions and agreements through the World Trade Organization (WTO); the new initiatives of the International Monetary Fund (IMF) and the World Bank; the expansion of the European Union and the North Atlantic Treaty Organization (NATO), which admitted most of the former members of the Warsaw Pact; new nongovernmental organizations (NGOs) cropping up all over the world while the older ones bolstered their activities inside and outside the United Nations; the Internet and other advances in communications, commerce, finance, and afferent digital technologies.

Are the quotation marks around such "accomplishments" warranted? Has the wish list of the 1970s turned out to be a dismayingly mixed bag? Does it also account for a "Balkanizing," ever-in-crisis world whose new, high-tech, economic, cultural, and geopolitical borders and fences replace the old ones? Does the same triumphalist enumeration register the spreading of regional conflicts, ethno-religious strife, and violent fundamentalism, the cyclical financial meltdowns, rising unemployment, pandemics, and the other bio-socioeconomic troubles making headlines after the breakup of former regimes, markets, barriers, and supranational and imperial entities such as the Eastern bloc, the Warsaw Pact, the USSR, and Yugoslavia? Even if we answer "yes" to the first two questions and "no" to the rest, as we probably should, it became undeniable around the mid-1990s that 1989 had been a tipping point in history. A new world had indeed been worlded into being. It was, and is, a messy one, no doubt, but many writers have responded to it. Analyzed in part 2, some of these responses showcase the kind of imaginary I call planetary.

I have explored this world in detail elsewhere and will go back to it a bit later. For now, I only wish to underscore its reverberations across the humanities, for this novelty was so sharply felt "out there in the world" that many concluded that, to deal with this new reality, a new interpretive apparatus and a new vocabulary were also needed. Before long, the top if highly controversial contender proved to be "global" along with "globalization," "globalism," "global age," and the rest of the "globe" family. The discourse coalescing around them sent shock waves across theory and the human sciences, which thus underwent a "global turn" comparable to the paradigm-changing, "linguistic," "postmodern," and "cultural" turns of decades past.[18] What I revisit, very succinctly, in this part's next section is this *discourse*, more to the point, what I take to be the prevailing trend inside it. Because, one more time, the planetary model of inquiry and attendant critical idiom arose as global subcategories and, as I venture, are on their way to establishing themselves as an undisciplined subdiscipline counter to globalization studies, I would like to think of the following overview of global terminology as requisite conceptual housecleaning. This is important not only because of global rhetoric's tendency to globalize itself across and at the expense of all the other ways of talking about and acting in the worlding world of the late twentieth century, but also because, more basically, "world," "globe," "planet," "earth," "transnational," and the like are *not* synonymous, and therefore they should not be used interchangeably, as they frequently are. My case for another critical paradigm and terminology must start out as a case for terminological discipline precisely because the differences between the discourses of "globe" and "planet," while not absolute, do not boil down to a paltry *querelle des mots* either. Otherwise, this is hardly the place for an exhaustive treatment of the multidisciplinary scholarship accumulated over decades. Unlike other dictionaries of the globalization debate, mine will be both more selective in rehashing some of the commonplaces of the literature and more tactical, in that the clearing of conceptual decks it seeks is preparatory to the subsequent articulation of the planetary alternative.[19]

§7. "World" into "Globe"

Borrowed by globalization enthusiasts from astronomy, geography, maritime navigation, and cartography, *globe* and *global* were the first to capture critics' imagination, essentially by subjecting the more generic "world" template to an ontologically, ecologically, and socioeconomically relational transformation or worlding process of which, conspicuously engrained in the word's etymology, geometry was already multiply symbolic. As most globalization scholars would point out, the process can be summed up as *totalization*. A rhetorically "perfect word" for the ideological purposes of globalization, "globe" and "global" are suggestive of a "frictionless," complete and completed, perfect world.[20] The large-scale multiplication and strengthening of relatedness—ties, connections, and barterings among people—reinscribe the world as globe by "rounding off" the latter's body, by setting in train a regularizing "agglomeration" (from the Latin *glomerō*, "to mass together") and "fashioning" of the polymorphic world into a "rounded," sphere-like (*globus*) totality whose "smooth surface allo[w] the unimpeded flow of capital, information[,] and language."[21]

Thus, *as* "globe," "world" is neither an open biocultural system nor our natural environment and elemental habitat, turf, or ground (this is [the] "earth") nor our cosmic address ("Earth"), but a mundane whole that flaunts its *totality*. Hardly dynamic or change-prone, this totality is also *achieved*, an immutability. The global world is, and purports to be, a well-rounded, integrated, definitive—and in that existentially and politically hopeless—closed system and happily confirmed teleology enforced from a political and economic if not geometrical center or centers and by a plethora of feedback loops, symmetries, parallels, and exchange procedures effectuated and conveyed across a relational web progressively overlapping with the world itself. The world worlds into globe, goes global, once the infinite, the unlimited, the multitudinous, the boundless, and the boundlessly different—the unqualified potentiality of worldly ontology—have been "qualified" and repurposed materially and conceptually as domains of the one, the homogeneous, the circular, the repetitive, and the selfsame. Topologically, both the world (the empirical world, at least) and the globe are measurable, even though, metaphorically and, I would argue, ontologically also, the world remains a resilient trope and space of the variegated, mysterious, and illimitable and thus considerably more complex as structure than the globe, whose terrestrial (or "library") variety was designed not only to represent the world more accurately but also to measure it, to fix, pin down ("position"), and *hold* it. The difference between them does not lie in volume, scope, or geometry but in ontology, culture, and politics; not in magnitude but in what this does or makes possible inside its bulk. Redolent of the "centering" and "smoothing" technology of control, command, and monitoring that went into its making, the globe is, again, a controlled and controlling system, and thus a containment fantasy also, a disciplined panopticon and a limit—a terminus not only, and perhaps not in the first place, to the world as journey, complexity, and meaning, to where the world can be spatially, but to what one can see and "envision" in it, to what the world and those inside it can be socially, culturally, and otherwise. The globe is or rather becomes, through the very rhetoric presuming to critique it in a number of disciplines, a multitude, a multiplicity, and a potentiality shrunk down to the measurable and the measured, to the classifiable, the charted, and the known or the seemingly known: an ontology of relational possibilities rationalized into a limited and limiting ontic setup. The world and the globe are both immensities; both boggle the mind quantitatively. But, unlike the world and insofar as it results from relationally totalizing reinscriptions of the world, the globe is no longer a worldly *opera aperta*, an open-ended boundlessness or *project*. Once it has been brought under the regime of rational calculability as globe, largely on economic, administrative, and technological grounds—whether, once more, through truly occurring worldly developments such as neo-imperial geopolitics and unification of financial markets or through rhetorical overadjudications—"world" is "reduced" ontologically and does not function as an endless space of qualitative leaps, as a playground of being any more. Fairly or not, this ontological reduction marks globe's entire kin, beginning with "(the) global."

The latter has been used more often, in fact, and more pejoratively, both as a modifier and independently. As an adjective, and along the lines of the same loaded—rather than "abstract"—geometry, it is descriptive of a form, state, situation, status, purview, capability, hyperconnective drive, and at-distance reach of a certain sociodemographical, geopolitical, economic, and technocultural megastructure capable or deemed capable to order, oversee, and otherwise bear on its *microdomains*.[22] These are specific, hitherto more or less isolated, sufficiently well delimited, and reasonably autonomous venues and communities of race, citizenship, ethnicity, language, and religious and aesthetic custom, which all have traditionally been beholden to the *territorially defined and politically reinforced epistemological authority of nation-states*. As a noun, but participating in the same family semantics as the globe, the global stresses the macro makeup and definitional leverage of the macrostructure. It engages its correlative, the local, in a whole spectrum of relationships, interchanges, transformations, and syntheses from the more nocuous to the more auspicious. Because these dynamics have been described by the students of globalization in their various fields quasi exhaustively, here I will only list the main categories. They include sheer substitution of indigenous practices; their displacement or dislocation; more thorough de-localization (in the extreme situation of globalization-as-homogenization) and its variety, dis-localization (which, according to Sarika Chandra, results in "dislocalism"); on the more positive side, "heterogenizing" interplays à la Roland Robertson's famous "glocalization" and more pronounced "creolizations" where the global is further customized, blends into native mixtures more aggressively, and even goes "slumming" (when it does not go native or local—is Milan's Vittorio Emanuele Gallery McDonald's a McDonald's any more, one wonders).[23]

§8. The Global Paradigm

Globality. It is the global's abstract cousin. It "means," according to Ulrich Beck, "that we have been living for a long time in a world society, in the sense that the notion of closed spaces has become illusory." "No country or group," the German sociologist goes on, "can shut itself off from others" any longer. As a globally reached historical situation or new human condition, globality also implies "that from now on nothing which happens on our planet is only a local and limited event; all inventions, victories and catastrophes affect the whole world."[24] Otherwise treading carefully, Beck is getting here on a slippery slope toward a "one-worldist" grand narrative of the world as wholly integrated "totality." Like Anthony Giddens and other risk theorists, Beck is an unrepentant modernist. Not very much taken with postmodern claims, he is a Habermasian keen, if not on rationality's questionable track record, then on its unfulfilled dreams, and this accounts for the somewhat unchecked pathos of his holist-totalist rhetoric.

Globalized vs. Globalizing. We live on a globe that has not gone wholly global despite blanket statements to the contrary and the "global agendas" presumably pursued by various economic and political actors. That explains some critics' preference to refer to a "globalizing" rather than (fully) "globalized" world, thus highlighting the continuative, fluid aspect of the global state of affairs, stage, or morphology while toning down the perfective "globalized." To many, myself included, the latter smacks of a *fait accompli*, which strikes me as both historically inaccurate and politically disabling. It is precisely because the world is still worlding, coming together—*because the world is (also) "planetarizing" rather than (only) globalizing*—that one can take a critical-"progressive" look at it and possibly "perfect" it along these lines, that is, not hone it into utopic perfection but complete it by harnessing it to a vision more inspiring and empowering than that at work in many of today's corporatist and neoimperialist-territorialist adventures.

To do so, however, globalization must be either de-completed or, more likely, reclassified as an "incomplete project." As I detail below, my hope is that the project will be carried through under the aegis of the planetary.

Globalism. In response to the "terminological quandary" evident in the interchangeable use of "globalization," "globality," and "globalism," Marshall Brown specifies that "[b]y globalism I understand an idea, an image, a potential; by globalization a process, a material phenomenon, a destiny."[25] Mentioning the "age-old phenomenon" of "globalism" in an obvious reference to globalization, Brown does not make the distinction consistently, though.[26] However, as more than one critic has suggested, globalism is to globality and globalization what modernism is to modernity and modernization and postmodernism is to postmodernity and postmodernization, respectively. My preference, then, is to look at globalism first mainly as a *cosa mentale*. To me, it represents, more than any other member of the global series, primarily a subjective, reflexive-evaluative position, possibly the rudiments of another "ism." It denotes an attitude or mode of perceiving things "in global perspective," a life philosophy and an epistemological stance toward a *global* conglomerate wherein the parts communicate and must face up to their interdependence. In the last sentence's italicized word, some stress the adjective as referencing a thoroughly solidified totality—a globally "saturated" world—whereas others, of the localist, anti-, and alter-globalist (*altermondialiste*) persuasion, point up the noun's dynamism and how the possibilities harbored therein are hampered by the world *qua* globe. In Robertson's middle-of-the-road assessment, this philosophy and epistemology would leave room both for globalist "relativism"—a sense that cultures are "bound-up"—and for "worldism," which he sums up as "the claim that it is possible and, indeed, desirable to grasp the world as a whole analytically" while keeping in mind that no "reference t[o] the dynamics of the entire 'world-system'" can afford to lose sight of the complexities, contradictions, and other asystemic features that might leap at us whenever we do not ground the analysis too strictly in a "world-systemic, economic realm."[27]

Globalization. If "globe" is a systemic, world totality and "globalism" the "vision thing" underpinning and overlaying, promoting, and conceptualizing this ensemble, globalization is the historical evolution through which both have come into existence. Lopsided, scarcely affecting all people and places with the same force or in the same fashion, its benefits unevenly distributed, darkly ambiguous and self-contradictory, globalization is both structurally and historically controversial, and, since the "how" and "what" of globalization—how it has come about and evolved across time and what it signifies today—are impossible to tackle separately, some discussion of globalization history and historiography is in order.

Here, the main split is between those who take a Braudelian "long view" of the phenomenon and those who deem it more recent. The divide roughly corresponds to, and therefore bears addressing alongside, another schism among global studies critics, which pits those who see globalization negatively against those who look at it, also with some approximation, positively. There are, I might add, some who have trouble noticing it at all. In Allan Cochrane and Kathy Pain's taxonomy, the "pessimistic globalists" are also sometimes "traditionalists" like Paul Q. Hirst and Grahame Thompson,[28] who "believe that globalization is a myth, or at any rate is much exaggerated as a distinctively new phenomenon."[29] I will touch on such differentiations very briefly not because the pessimists/traditionalists' participation in globalization rhetoric has had entirely nugatory effects but because such categorizations further this discussion as long as they help demarcate the developments said rhetoric inherently ascribes to the described world, regardless of the description's optimism or pessimism, from the worldly transformations the same rhetoric makes allowances for, beyond the construing purview of its core terminology.

Unsurprisingly, historians too have resorted to this nomenclature as a kind of lexical placeholder, which has often disabled those discriminations that would bring into play, inside, outside, across, and possibly against globalization as defined earlier—"totalist" globalization—other globalizing scenarios or different worlding categories altogether. If such alternatives or worlding histories are still awaiting their historians, their cultural historians in particular, the history of globalization of the totalist sort is better known, all the more so that, in line with the placeholder logic, it has come to be known by and large *as* globalization history *tout court*. This logic's moves remain both questionable and undisclosed. In turn, its lack of disclosure, its covert semantics, sets up a discursive apparatus in which "globe," "globalization," and the rest operate rhetorically as abusive synecdoches, namely, by routinely claiming more than what they account for in reality, by encroaching on other semantic vicinities ("planet," "world," "ecumene"/"ecumenical," "universal"), or by tacitly annexing them altogether: as used ordinarily, the global paradigm is intent on monopolizing all worlding phenomena and their description, in the humanities in particular.

On the other hand, abusive and deceptive as they may be, the paradigm's components are not solely hopeless misnomers either, for they are not purely fictional. They are not inventions but, as I say, "constructions," and they are so in mainstream criticism as well as in historical scholarship. So, while going over various histories of globalization—"globalization," one is tempted to write—I for one would like to keep in mind that these narratives are neither fictions nor factual reports, that they produce, in a quasi-theatrical sense, globalization as they narrate its historical course, and that such productions tell as much as they "un-tell," bring the world's worlding record into the historiographical focus as much as they obscure it and keep it in the wings. Not only are "world history" ("polycentric," less teleological) and "global[ization] history" ("economistic," narratively shaped by Western standards of progress, and in that both ethnocentric and teleological) not the same thing, as historians like Bo Stråth rightly insist, but, even if we accept that world history is a history of worlding, this history can be written in more than one way.[30] This is what planetarity as a "world theory" and the fictions of planetarity taken up in part 2's second half strive to accomplish.

And yet, not unlike most critics, many historians have lumped together the wide range of worlding mutations under the heading of "globalization," which, as some argue, has been in full swing for a while now, if not for ages. Thus, the *longue durée* perspective of a number of authors influenced by the French Annales school stresses that modernity had been "globalizing" since late medieval–early Renaissance times and that it only became *conspicuously* "global" and thereby lent itself more readily to a "globalist" interpretation after World War II. These critics' broad-compass approach spans geographical and geopolitical units (countries, regions, continents) as much as historical units (centuries, epochs, periods). Its main concepts are Wallerstein's "world-system" and its "stagist" biography. In Wallerstein—and this gets overlooked frequently—the world-system and the global are not equivalent initially; they would become so in the nineteenth century. Modeled on the Mediterranean world investigated by Fernand Braudel, the world-system may have "originated," as Wallerstein submits in *Geopolitics and Geoculture*, "in Europe in the 16th century," but it gets truly global hundreds of years later, following several globalizing stages.[31]

Even critics who reject world-systems theory have tacitly or overtly adopted Wallerstein's perspective and, selectively or entirely, his "phases." This has resulted in the mildly divergent "timings of globalization" offered, at one end, by historians who push its advent centuries if not millennia further back, and, at the other, by those who do little more than modify Wallerstein's phase brakedown even though they seem aware of the flaws of the long-view narrative. I spare the reader a rundown of their complaints. I will only say that, unlike Martin Albrow, I believe our current world situation—global, planetary, or otherwise—does constitute a "culmination" of events past. However, and this time in agreement with him, I do not equate those events nor their remote past of many centuries or even millennia prior to our modern era with globalization itself, no matter how one defines it, let alone with globalization in a "strong," "webbed," or contemporary sense. Like Albrow, I do think the process is more recent and, in any case, our immediate present opens an original chapter in it. I would retain, therefore, Albrow's hypothesis of a "Global Age" closer to us and distinguishable in its traits. Yet again, I would also place its uniqueness within an ampler time framework because this balances issues of continuity and discontinuity more effectively.[32]

"Global Age": "Thick" or "Late" Globalization. Our worldly makeup is not entirely new. It is new overall. This novelty does have a history, albeit shorter than some might think, and even a prehistory, possibly longer than others might fancy. To my mind, the *longue durée* tack uncovers the latter. The long view becomes less helpful, though, if, while laying disproportionate emphasis on occurrences like the Big Bang or the great migrations of the first centuries AD, it shortchanges the paradigm-setting and epoch-making role of late twentieth-century genuinely *world events*—events or event, rather, the kind that reveals its Foucauldian "extreme point of singularity" or unique "presence" across the phantasmatic cycle of repetitive occurrences and, in so doing, marks off a present moment from other presents, past or future.[33]

In this "eventful" and singularizing sense, numerous historians have concluded that the "global era" or "age" proper begins, with some approximation, after 1989 and is the stage of "thick" globalization. The latter arrives on the heels of a set of quantitatively and qualitatively largely unprecedented developments. What came before 1989 was, we are told, "looser," less technologized and webbed, less conspicuous, slower, more region-focused—in a nutshell, "thin" globalization. What goes on after is increasingly, if far from completely, systemic, more technology-driven and networked, growingly cross-regional, more fast-paced, "in-your-face," and superiorly marked by the cultural, economic, and military presence of the United States in the world. With these historians, and setting philosophical and terminological differences aside once again, I place the transition from a less to a notably more worlded if inevitably messier world in the geopolitically and techno-culturally determining interval between the late 1980s and the early 1990s, to be more exact, between late fall 1989 and late December 1991, when the former USSR officially expired. Thus, 1989 is, to me also, what "mondialization" critic Jean-Pierre Warnier would call *une année charnière*. Two centuries after the 1789 French Revolution, arguably modernity's political kickoff, 1989 is the "hinge" on which turns the door opening onto "thick," "revved-up," or late globalization.[34] This year marks our entering the later phase of a momentous shift away from a world, by comparison, still "cubicular"—Pierre Chaunu's *univers cloisonné*—to one experienced and conceptualized as an incrementally all-pervasive "network."[35]

§9. The Rise of the Netosphere

> I am emphasizing a new reality that can be summarized in very simple terms: *In the age of globalization the relationship with the Other has become more fundamental than ever.*
>
> —DOMINIQUE MOÏSI, *The Geopolitics of Emotion: How Cultures of Fear, Humiliation, and Hope Are Reshaping the World*

> Our newly interdependent global society, with its remarkable possibilities for linking people around the planet, gives us the material basis for a new ethic.
>
> —PETER SINGER, *One World: The Ethics of Globalization*

"20 Years of Collapse" reads the title of the op-ed Slavoj Žižek published in the November 9, 2009, issue of the *New York Times*, on the twentieth anniversary of the collapse *of* the Berlin Wall. A cynical headline, to say the least. No matter how critical one is of what has followed 1989, the year signals, in Berlin and worldwide—*urbi et orbi*—a radical reshuffling of time, space, and life across a world less and less held back and compartmentalized by the disassociative logic of the Cold War and modernity generally and more and more pulled together by a logic of connectiveness,[36] and it is in this sense that, as Jameson writes, "[r]adical alternatives, systemic transformations, cannot be theorized or even imagined within the conceptual field governed by the word 'modern.'"[37] On many levels, the Berlin Wall's fall—an eminently world-systemic, transforming event—heralds both the world's "fall into relation" and the relation's fall into the world. The ensuing "postlapsarian" regime of existence *ontologizes* relation, and this ontology gets more ecumenical in scope every day. Under the sway of this ontology, being in the world reveals itself as being-with-an-other—*Miteinandersein*, in Heidegger's *Sein und Zeit*—more powerfully than ever.[38] The human *is*, fully, as relational embodiment. In what they do, in how they respond to the world, in how they see it and themselves, people behave, willingly or less so, as vehicles, receptacles, agents, and objects of a highly complex, existential, cultural, and intellectual relationality. They think relationally, correlatively, "in context," with the world as that context or cogitative framework, and act relationally too, steadily using, testing, and building up the world's relational structure and way of being—the *netosphere*.[39] The "networked" imagination and behavior—the netospherical—is now officially part and parcel of the "human phenomenon," to recall Pierre Teilhard de Chardin.[40]

Slightly paronymous to Teilhard de Chardin's Neoplatonist-Thomist "noosphere" (from *nóos*, the Ancient Greek for "mind," "understanding," and "reason"), the netosphere designates a complex reality, also somewhat parallel to Teilhard's treatment of the noospherical as a sign of planetary integration or "planetarization" (*planétisation*).[41] A technological and biocultural incorporation of world-systemic rationality, *relationality become world*, this is more than a state of mind although its sphericalness—ominously suggestive, as we know, of physical and political completion—is metaphorical rather than indicative of the existence of an actual "global public sphere."[42] But the netosphere's unevenness does not exclude a material actuality. This accrues across a relational spectrum that includes both the "hard," geocommunicational and commercial kind known to humanity for millennia, as well as "softer" varieties consisting of recent, visibly and invisibly routed, wired, "knotted," "clouded," and otherwise digitalized, traced, and politically and economically mapped cyberspace, complete with its connections, itineraries, channels, languages, encoding systems, and the novel forms of sociality they enable. However, what we are talking about when we talk about the new world in a netospherical sense is essentially unparalleled density and extensiveness of connectedness, of *what relates*, joins, and binds together often above, across, and, as I have said, against ordinary, nation-state- territorialized and akin administrative-epistemological units, bonds, ties, and allegiances. Classical relations work predominantly in the immediate vicinity of those thus related (typically by blood, location, and language) and connected, woven together, and oftentimes tied down into a *Gemeinschaft* type of collective. Primarily world-systemic, netospherical relations function through and over space, from a distance. Relationally, our world still has to reach a saturation point; this is why the "sphere" in the netospherical is an approximation, a trope more than anything else. In its imperfection, it is nonetheless rendering the world, day in and day out, a cultural geography of distance management, a spectacle of orchestrated intervals and charting vectors across and by which people position and reposition themselves in relation with one another.

Absolutely vital to freedom, to difference, and to genuine pluralism, the interval, the limit, and the singularities effectively or allegedly protected this or that side of various borders and fences prior to the collapse lamented by Žižek are, indisputably, as important if not more important in a world whose continuum is much less interrupted by divides like the Berlin Wall and in which the connection, the nexus, the relay, and the intermeshing of lives and human expressions over all sorts of gaps have become the onto-cultural norm. "You wonder," writes Mukherjee in *The Tree Bride*, "if everyone and everything in the world is intimately related. . . . You pluck a thread and it leads to . . . everywhere." And she goes on to ask: "Is there a limit to relatedness?"[43]

Yes, would reply Bish, *The Tree Bride*'s telecommunication "mystic," there is one: "death." And this is where it gets tricky. This is also where planetary studies and the planetary paradigm, fluid and disciplinarily unstructured as they are, come in: as a reaction to the rather unconvincing effort within globalization criticism to get a handle on relation, more specifically, not on its presence as such in the worldly, netospherical sense, but on what it does or, better still, on what it can and should do, on what it could mean beyond the commonplaces piling up in the gargantuan bibliography already available. For, it became pretty evident, to the point of banality, that the global, its "age," and world-changing processes were quintessentially and intensely relational, that, one way or the other, from finance and economics to travel, leisure, research, and online education, they come down to a high-density, steadily widening phenomenology of relations. Relatedness had been indeed pivotal to our world, and it had been looking the part too, with a vengeance. And so, to many, it had been perhaps too obvious, too intimately embroidered in the world's netospherical girdle not to be taken for granted and dealt with as a matter of course, at the level of the superficial mechanics easily available, one might think, to the naked eye. Thus, the favorite approach to it had been *technical* and *economic* (not to say "economistic"). This means less that its students had focused exclusively on technological relations and more that they had been happy to give an account of its nuts-and-bolts workings in industrial, commercial, and entertainment sites, in the light style of the celebratory jet-setting reportage whose market niche had been quickly claimed by Pico Iyer, Thomas L. Friedman, and other global writers of neoliberal persuasion.[44]

The case against their uncritical enthusiasms has been made. I have made it too, and I do not think repeating myself here would be a good time investment.[45] I will say, though, that, if authors like Iyer and Friedman became very controversial very fast, it also happened because their narratives seldom cut through the technical to the political and, more generally, to the ethical. It is not that all their reports were ill-informed or disingenuous. They were incomplete, and not merely because they did not have the wherewithal to look around patiently or impartially enough and thus do justice to the omnipresence of the relational in the world's life, but because they seemed less sensitive to relationality's hand in the world's life *and* death. Bish's answer hardly holds up to scrutiny, in fact. Relation and death do not make up a clear-cut dichotomy. Relation is not opposite to death the way life is in their more hackneyed accounts. "Limited" by death and its deleterious manifestations in the world—destruction, fanaticism, exploitation, environmental degradation, trade inequities and other chronic forms of violence and injustice—relation is inherently shaped both by life and death. Relation, one's link to another place, one's ties and access to other worlds can be equally life-giving and life-threatening, nurturing and baleful, empowering and disenfranchising. Instituting a fundamental ethical amphibology, this "can," this potentiality, is or has the capacity of being at once emboldening and forbidding. It bodes well for the future as much as invites harangues of the "20 Years of Collapse" sort if not outright Stalinist nostalgias (unsurprisingly, also featured in Žižek's repertoire). In opening up the global play of connective rationality, this *potenza* destabilizes and multiplies the meaning of relation and, by the same movement, challenges us to stabilize, to construe relational ontosemantics—what relationality does or may be able to do and stand for in the netospherical world—into an *ethical reading*, namely, into an interpretation at once descriptive and prescriptive, sound analytically as well as indicative of a vision for the world commons and of an authentic commitment to that worldview.[46] Hyperrelational in its unstable and highly ambivalent phenomenology, the netosphere is thus both a reality and a provocation.

II

§10. Planetary Studies

> [L]iterature and literary studies now have one basis and goal: to nurture our common bonds to the planet.
>
> —MASAO MIYOSHI, "Turn to the Planet: Literature, Diversity, and Totality"

Responding to this provocation, planetary criticism brings us to a crossroads in the history of critical theory. It is noteworthy, though, that when, in his 1994 *Théorèmes poétiques*, French polymath Basarab Nicolescu pressed into service his planetarily and cosmically minded "vision of the world"[47] to open up the modern concept of territorially- politically and culturally-disciplinarily circumscribed discourse, the "planetary" series ("planetarized," "planetarization," etc.) had been part of the conversation in the arts and the humanities for some time but not as an approach- or field-specific vocabulary. Thus, "planet" was a cosmo-theological and mystic-esoteric concept à la Teilhard de Chardin and Jean D'Argoun, who also talks about a "planetary transformation" (*mutation planétaire*);[48] another name for Gaia and thus part of a spiritual-environmentalist movement that later, in alliance with a spectacularly resurgent cosmopolitanism, will take up "terrapolitan" forms;[49] or, most frequently, and inside global studies, a variously qualified synonym to "cosmos," "cosmopolitan," "earth," "ecumene" and "ecumenical," "world" and "world-systemic," and so on. More frequently, globalization studies conflated "planet" and "globe," a confusion that persists today.

Among Nicolescu's more influential precursors, albeit not in his area, Wallerstein has not been keen on the distinction either. Neither "planet" nor "globe" appeals to him. In *The Modern World-System*,""globe" is barely used, the author's disclaimer notwithstanding. Likewise, *World-Systems Analysis* mentions "globalization" just once, at the end, and, characteristically of worlds-systems rhetoric itself, only to dismiss the term offhand as a rhetorical maneuver of neoliberalism.[50] As early as the first volume of *The Modern World-System* (1974), the economics historian seemed particular to "world" instead and, to a much lesser degree, "cosmos" and "cosmology," which he described as "the study of the functioning of the system as a whole" and deployed to work out a geoeconomic framework, a hermeneutic "totality distinguished" from "completeness,"[51] and a political "utopistics" or future, world-scale, material-affective arrangements in which particularisms would restore "the universal reality of liberty and equality."[52] However, "cosmos" and its family, far from running out of steam, gained significant momentum with Yi-Fu Tuan's *Cosmos and Hearth*, Gérard Raulet's *Critical Cosmology*, which counters Americanizing "neo-universalism" with a citizenship notion intersecting multiple national traditions, Félix Guattari's "chaosmotic," "ethico-aesthetic paradigm" (*Chaosmose*), Anne Phillips's valiant endeavor to rebuild multiculturalism according to a "cosmic" rather than "discrete-cultures" scheme (*Multiculturalism without Culture*), and other similar, late 1990s–early 2000s interventions.[53]

In hindsight, this looks like a significant and logical transition. For, on the one hand, the planetary is a celestial subheading as Earth, a cosmic body and part of a megasystem whose systematicity the planet carries over into its own, intra-planetary constitution. On the other hand, some literary and cultural theorists felt that the cosmos remained an exceedingly broad, fuzzy category: too "physicalist" as an astronomical notion, too spiritualist, aestheticist ("cosmetic"), too "mechanicist" as (logical) "Order" and therefore too "timeless" (even when compared to "globe"), too "unspecific" from the standpoint of an "intermediate" (Nicolescu), anthropologically and historically meaningful scalarity, and so too nebulous semantically not to lend itself both to disembodied metaphysical speculation and scientific-rationalist colonization.[54] Thus, Elias is right to note that "the planetary model" and the new "chronotope" it has provided to the arts and their interpretation were "opposed to the dehumanizing context of cosmic space constructed by science and then, as a metaphor for the cybernetic, to scientific rationality."[55]

"Cosmos" has somewhat stabilized semantically in two emerging paradigms, both of them outgrowths of global studies. One is cosmopolitanism, which is not so much an "ism" but the social, political, and moral philosophy built around a cosmopolite's view of the world and the scholarship sponsored by this philosophy, namely, (neo)cosmopolitan studies. As is well known, the cosmopolitan has, in the West and elsewhere, a long and contested biography. This is the multimillennial life story of a highly complex, metaphysical, moral, and cosmological idea; of a set of sociocultural and aesthetic practices; and, lately, of a full-blown critical methodology with ethical, political, and anthropological ramifications. One way or the other, all these still feed off and communicate with older and broader concepts, ideologies, moments, and movements such as classical or more recent humanism, the Enlightenment, modernity, modernization, urbanization, colonization, decolonization, and globalization. With some of these or with darker episodes thereof like Nazism and Communism—Soviet- and Chinese-style alike, pre- and post–World War II, when people would be sent to various gulags and *laogai* camps on "cosmopolitan" charges—cosmopolitanism's basic tenets have been openly and commendably at loggerheads. However, in other instances, old and new, one can pinpoint embarrassing, "culturocentric," and hence ironically "provincializing" complicities, which no longer warrant an unqualified use of the term. Consequently, what distinguishes overall post–Cold War cosmopolitan criticism from an earlier scholarship centered on the notion is that the former has gone out of its way to localize, pluralize, and "culturalize" the cosmopolitan paradigm.[56] As a result, these days we are talking about cosmopolitanism*s*, most of which are "committed," ready to acknowledge cosmopolitanism's variations and contradictions across centuries and places but also to reenergize it politically through revisionary and eclectic approaches that absorb inventively elements of cultural, identity, and postcolonial studies. The cosmopolitan has thus indeed proven recyclable into a critical model. (Neo)cosmopolitan scholars have found the model empowering analytically in a contemporary world that, in spite of its incongruities, disparities, incomplete national projects, and fundamentalist nostalgias, does make available a stage for new cosmopolitan venues, sodalities, worldviews, and discourses. It must be said also, though, that, outside the circle of true cosmopolitan believers (most of them sociologists), a great deal of skepticism about the language, methodology, concrete outcomes, and even about the timing of their undertaking persists. Never in short supply, anti-cosmopolitan rebuttals feature, now as in decades past, references to elitism, classism, ethnocentrism, utopianism, a-topianism (the old "view from nowhere" charge), snobbism, non- and even anti-communitarianism, universalism, and so forth. On the whole, Robert Fine is right on target: "Even if cosmopolitanism becomes stuck at the level of conceptual thinking, it remains superior to a criticism that has no understanding of the concept and sees in world history nothing but power, self-interest[,] and contingency."[57] The comment does allow, however, that even if most of cosmopolitanism's rap sheet evinces the prosecution's ignorance in the matter, today's cosmopolitan critics are nonetheless struggling to come up with the most effective ways of presenting themselves and their project.

The other paradigm is planetary studies. As a philosophically and astronomically informed concept, the cosmos also appealed to certain critics, who, despite its abstractness, mined it for fertile, ecological-culturological and even political-ethical tropes, which in turn paved the way to "planet," its lexical constellation, and the more theoretically individualizing claims made around them.[58] Among those scholars, Masao Miyoshi was probably the first to ground programmatic, manifestly "epochalist," and epistemological contentions in what he saw as a veritable and inevitable planetary *Paradigmenwechsel*. In his 2001 article "Turn to the Planet: Literature, Diversity, and Totality," he observes that a change of historical proportions had been afoot since the mid-1980s. Further, as Neil Turnbull would venture in his own Copernican pronouncements five years thereafter, this change had "heighten[ed] the conceptual importance of the earth" across all forms and arenas of material and cultural practice.[59] Turnbull rightly reminds us that "[t]he premodern idea of the earth as 'the centre' of the cosmos did not, contrary to popular belief, suggest that 'the earth' was an important concept, either spiritually or politically. In medieval cosmology, the earth was given this position, not because [the earth] was the most, but because it was the least significant entity."[60]

The shift has been described often in terms of high-gear globalization and global age. Both are "exclusionist," Miyoshi propounds, insofar as the interconnectedness driving them is underpinned by global economics. In his opinion, to be genuinely global is to be inclusive, which the global is not. Actually, globalism falls short of its own, stated agenda. Its problem or paradoxical excess, says Miyoshi, is a structural insufficiency, and so the global world is found wanting; it is indeed global—shared in, lucrative, accessible, enjoyable—but only for those for whom relatedness operates beneficially. Thus, the globalized world is not, nor is likely to beget, a "true totality that includes everyone." Neither is, for the purpose of this inclusiveness, "the return to the nation-state" a realistic solution. "There is," however, according to Miyoshi, "one such core site for organizing such an inclusiveness, though entirely negative at present: the future of the global environment. For the first time in human history, one single commonality involves all those living on the planet: environmental deterioration as a result of the human consumption of natural resources. Whether rich or poor, in the East or the West, progressive or conservative, religious or atheist, none of us can escape from the all-encompassing process of air pollution, ozone layer depletion, ocean contamination, toxic accumulation, and global warming."[61] Acknowledging this "total commonality" as the premise for "map[ping] out our world and [for] engag[ing] in research and scholarship" leads to the recognition that

> literature and literary studies now have one basis and goal: to nurture our common bonds to the planet—to replace the imaginaries of exclusionary familialism, communitarianism, nationhood, ethnic culture, regionalism, "globalization," or even humanism, with the ideal of planetarianism. Once we accept this planet-based totality, we might for once agree in humility to devise a way to share with all the rest our only true public space and resources.[62]

As one can notice, the global is concurrently ascertained (as "environment") and rebuffed. It is, we saw, an assuming totality—a *pseudototality*, more bluntly put—whose flaw is not, thinks Miyosi, its inherent totalism but, to the contrary, the failure to achieve a real totality, an "allness" in which all could equally participate. Should that achievement occur, it would happen in a future whose seeds can be sown once we have "reimagine[d] our common and universal culture, as we have never done in our common history."[63]

Totality and universalism; humanism; ethno-national identitarianism; and, more generally, cultural difference seized, ironically enough, not unlike the global itself, that is, as "exclusionary," a wrench jamming the works of the internationalism required by the daunting job at hand: this is the kind of language Spivak and other planetary studies proponents are not very comfortable with. Also intent on "us[ing] the planetary—if such a thing can be used!—to control globalization interruptively, to locate the imperative in the indefinite radical alterity of the other space of [the] planet[,] to deflect the rational imperative of capitalist globalization," and thus "to displace dialogics into this set of contradictions," Spivak had already made clear, two years before Miyoshi's article, her uneasiness with the leveling, totalist-universalist legacy of Western rationalism whether in economic globalism or in cultural analysis.[64] In her view, life on the planet is or must be "lived as the call of the wholly other." If we lead it that way, then "we must also think" of our living "Space" or "individual home as written on the planet as planet," in other words, across a "cosmopolitheia" in which the planet as astronomical body and astronomy more broadly are no more than a "defracted view of ethics" and where, accordingly, "Space" must be capitalized because it is another name for "alterity."[65]

Highlighting planetary studies' reorientation inside, against, and eventually away from global studies, the emphasis on ethics will remain characteristically crucial to the planetarity project. To quote Spivak's 1999 essay title, "the Imperative to Re-imagine the Planet" is profoundly ethical—and, I might add, inevitably ethical insofar as the reorientation in question activates relationality and, subsequently, the problematic of otherness. An upshot of the "planet-as-planet" notion, the Spivakian "imperative" is, unlike Miyoshi's, non-totalist because the ontologized relatedness built into it and its ontology largely conceived stand on, and reaffirm, a Levinasian, nonrationalizing ethics of alterity. In warranting descriptions of relational arrangements, planetary ontology *by the same token* calls—this time around, like in Miyoshi and deliberately at variance with globalist arrogance—for humility, sharing, and other ways of owning up to the otherness that made relationality possible in the first place. Also in indirect reaction to Miyoshi, specifically to his admission that a planetarily minded research is still a nebulous concept,[66] Spivak's 2003 *Death of a Discipline* takes the next step by offering up, farther and farther away from the epistemologically patronizing and analytically confusing proximity of "global" and "globalization," the "planetary" as a remedy to the protracted crisis in comparative literature and cultural studies generally. To this day, this slim volume has remained a milestone in planetary studies. While below (§11 and §12) I take exception to some of the implications of *Death of a Discipline*'s argument, I find the book's emphasis on ethics quite salutary.

Since Spivak's turn-of-the-millennium interventions, the planet, planetary, and their lexical-methodological cognates have made inroads into disciplines and debates old and new: globalization studies with various foci and political-theoretical leanings from neoliberalism to antiglobalization; trans- and postnationalism; ecocriticism, (neo)cosmopolitanism, their "eco-cosmopolitan" cross (Ursula K. Heise), and related, systems-theory-based studies of "planetary autopoiesis" that, according to Bruce Clarke, pays attention to both "micro" and "macro" systemic modalities, a critical sensitivity also instrumental to my project;[67] "planetary thought" (*Planetendenken*) inquiries of the kind pursued by the late Sonja A. J. Neef in her fascinating yet unfinished 2013 study *Der babylonische Planet* (The Babylonian planet) at the intersection of cosmopolitanism, translation studies, and Spivak's ethical distinction between global totality (*Globus*) and the planet (*Planet*) understood as world committed to its "others" (*Welt-Anderen*);[68] "world risk society sociology" (Beck) and "network society" economics and communication theory (Manuel Castells); human rights, ethics, and world governance; the "empire"/"new commons" critique of Deleuzian-Guattarian persuasion in the Michael Hardt and Antonio Negri vein; studies of (post)ethnicity and "voluntary affiliation" à la David Hollinger; some approaches within postcolonialism, drawn by the challenge a planetary scope of discussion poses to the old colony/metropolis binary (Paul Gilroy); new comparatism, world literature (David Damrosch, John Pizer, Pascale Casanova, Apter, Hayot), "planetary literary history" (Frances Ferguson), studies of genre as a world-system formation (Franco Moretti, Wai Chee Dimock), and "global modernism." Speaking directly to the growing role played by the planetary as an analytic metaphor are also the rise of larger topo-interpretive units, fields, and concerns in comparative cultural studies and the advent of geocriticism as a whole. Just a few examples from a recent and much longer list in which vaster spaces, world spatiality itself as a critical problem, liminal zones, and critical grids take center stage would include Christopher Schedler's *Border Modernism* (2002); Stephen Clingman's *The Grammar of Identity: Transnational Fiction and the Nature of the Boundary* (2009); Gilroy's *The Black Atlantic* (1993) and especially *Postcolonial Melancholia* (2004), and the transatlantic cosmopolitanism reconstituted by Susan Manning and Andrew Taylor in their *Transatlantic Literary Studies* (2007) and by Kwame Anthony Appiah in *Cosmopolitanism: Ethics in a World of Strangers* (2006) and elsewhere; the contributions to *Hemispheric American Studies* edited by Caroline Field Levander and Robert S. Levine (2008); Yunte Huang's books, chiefly *Transpacific Displacement* (2002), Apter's *The Translation Zone* (2006), and Julio Ortega's 2003 article "Transatlantic Translations"; Paul Jay's *Global Matters: The Transnational Turn in Literary Studies* (2010); the Spring 2003 *Modern Fiction Studies* special-topic issue on the "trans-American imaginary," guest-edited by Paula M. L. Moya and Ramón Saldivar. On geocriticism, topocultural spatiality, and the geopolitical interpretation of literature and art, worth calling attention to are Jameson's earlier book *The Geopolitical Aesthetic: Cinema and Space in the World System* (1992), Gearóid Ó Tuathail, Simon Dalby, and Paul Routledge's *The Geopolitics Reader* (1998), Laura Doyle and Laura Winkiel's anthology *Geomodernisms: Race, Modernism, Modernity* (2005), Caren Irr's *Toward the Geopolitical Novel: U.S. Fiction in the Twenty-First Century* (2014), Paul Giles's *Antipodean America: Australasia and the Constitution of U.S. Literature* (2014), Dominique Moïsi, *La Géopolitique de l'émotion* (2009), and Robert T. Tally Jr.'s *Geocritical Explorations: Space, Place, and Mapping in Literary and Cultural Studies* (2011). Tally is also the English translator of Bertrand Westphal's *La Géocritique: Réel, Fiction, Espace* (2007), the field's founding text. Peter Sloterdijk's *Spheres* series is part of this trend too. I would also list here scholars such as Peter Singer, Lawrence Buell, Susan Stanford Friedman, Elias, Mary Louise Pratt, Leerom Medovoi, Mary Lou Emery, Tariq Jazeel, Joni Adamson, Mark Poster, and Min Hyoung Song. Over the last decade, these "planetary critics" have been relying consistently and characteristically on the planet as a platform for fresh analysis.[69] With them, in particular with the work put out recently by Dimock, Heise, Apter, Moretti, Westphal, Irr, Hayot, and Susan Stanford Friedman, planetary criticism has reached critical mass. Indeed, we may be witnessing at this point a sweeping "planetary turn."[70]

§11. "World" Reloaded

This means that, historically co-articulated with the global lexicon and concerns as it has been, the planet model may be, at last, well positioned to fulfill Spivak's dream and "interrupt" or "overwrite the globe" across disciplines. Such critical operation would supplant, throughout the humanities, globalization and globality by planetarization and planetarity, the global world-system by the planet's own system—"which," Spivak underscores, "we inhabit . . . on loan"—"global agents" by "planetary subjects,"[71] and globalism's rationality by planetary relationality[72] or "planet-thought."[73]

I propose that, to complete this sequence of terminological-rhetorical, epistemological, and ethical-political displacements, renegotiate if not sever altogether its ties with the discourse of globalization, and possibly usher in a planetary, "postglobal age"[74] in literary-cultural analysis, this thought first must formulate a planetary paradigm sufficiently emancipated rhetorically and theoretically from the global. The latter's tutelage is still visible in Spivak, who routinely couches the planetary project in a language of cumbersome derivativeness. In her work, the global supplies the ground and the continuum, the metaphysical *Grund* and the sociocultural surface. Even when they are "written over" and "interrupted," or perhaps especially when they are so, these tend to render such "oppositional" gestures mere accretions, accidents, and exceptions to an otherwise minimally impacted, and hence reconfirmed, status quo whose "overwriting" turns out to underwrite it. Now, unable neither to step outside the historical context that made it possible in the first place nor, more specifically, to unwrite its own relational genealogy, the planetary is not likely to shed its derivative skin completely either. This guilt by association, this onto-conceptual *hubris*, should be recognized too. To the extent that it also rests on the relational, the planetary both critiques and gives the global, or at least a part or aspect of it, a new lease on life: reminiscent of deconstruction's innermost aporia, this has been and will ever be its double bind. While the objective of the planetary with respect to the global remains emancipatory and even oppositional, the planet and the globe do not make up a crude opposition other than rhetorically, despite the impression critics like Spivak might leave. As Emery admits, the "planetary" is "[n]either equivalent to the global nor opposed to it."[75] The global-planetary connection is somewhat symbiotic, and the idea is to revamp it critically, to remake it into a truly *critical* symbiosis. Like postmodernism, which, in its best aesthetic, theoretical, and philosophical instantiations, did manage to speak against the dominant languages it had to speak (mimic, parody, creolize) in order to speak at all, planetarism can *and has to* ransom itself conceptually while rescuing the global, wholly or partly, from itself in the bargain.

To do so, "planet-thought" needs to *"reload" (rethink) the world planetarily*. That is, along the lines of my argument thus far, planetarism must appropriate the global's netospheric idiom of relationality so as to re-reinscribe critically—more precisely, ethically—the world *qua* reality, descriptive language thereof, and project. I attempt this appropriation, this ethical conceptualization of the planetary and, by the same movement, reworlding of the world as planet, in the remainder of this part by fleshing out "planetarism" and the rest of the planet paradigm. Similarly sketchy, the outline of the "planet" and its cognates following right below parallels roughly the item-by-item presentation of the global set of terms so as to create a starker contrast and thus weave philosophical-historical issues and interpretive considerations into a better-defined and more productive theoretical-analytic model. Of course, such theorizations, if meaningful, have to pass the test of critical practice. To that end, thinking of planetary persuasion must come up with an apposite interpretive methodology, with a modality of *reading* aesthetic and cultural "symptoms" of planetarity. As I show in this book's second half, the workings of this modality or critical apparatus are germane to the planetary ethics of relationality.

§12. "Globe" into "Planet"

> [A]n interlude of togetherness . . .
> —JOSEPH O'NEILL, *Netherland*

Introducing the key concepts of *Postcolonial Melancholia*, Gilroy confesses in the book's preface that he has "opted for . . . 'planetarity' over the more familiar notion of 'globalization' because those regularly confused terms, 'planetary' and 'global'—which do point to some of the same varieties of social phenomena—resonate quite differently." In his estimation, *planet* and its adjective, *the planetary*, "sugges[t] both contingency and movement." They "specif[y] a smaller scale than the global, which transmits all the triumphalism and complacency of ever-expanding imperial universals."[76] Drawing from *Postcolonial Melancholia*, Carl Schmitt's controversial *The* Nomos *of the Earth*, and Hardt and Negri's three-volume opus on global-era multitudes, Min Hyoung Song concurs that "[t]here is . . . something sovereign about what gets signified by globalization, a *nomos* that divides, restricts, hierarchizes, and criminalizes. It is a royal epistemology, a striation." "Planetarity, then," Song concludes, "might be thought of as a different order of connection, an interrelatedness that runs along smooth surfaces, comprises multitudes, and manifests movement."[77]

Tentative in certain places, arbitrary elsewhere, passages like these capture the dominant tone in a field still struggling to set its conceptual boundaries. The critics presume that the planetary "suggests" this while the global "transmits" that (the opposite). The actual demonstration is, here and in other commentators, by and large lacking (why and how exactly does the planetary "specif[y] a smaller scale than the global"?). Instead, it outsources its reasoning labor to cavalier speculations on the supposedly self-evident global semantics gelled in the global discourse that otherwise planetary criticism professes to displace. Drawing from global phenomena or aspects of global phenomena whose critique proved incontrovertibly legitimate, this discourse's rhetoric of ominous totality has virtually condemned the global, in the sense, if you will, in which neglect or abuse might condemn a building. Unredeemingly compromised as both object and language, as what it can represent in the transnational world and as critical representation thereof, the global *as such*, construed so uniformly "monological" despite protests by Ramazani and others, has nonetheless all but globalized discursively if not ontologically.[78] Rejected *in toto* and as a maleficent *totum*, the global has returned the compliment by casting the shadow of its rhetorical "totality" onto the whole field. Via critics' work, and—supreme irony—against this work's anti-neoliberal and antiglobalization grain, it has taken over the world of globalization studies if not over the world itself, homogenizing both the discourse of the world (by indirectly validating a single worlding narrative) and the world of discourse (by assigning, also indirectly, a single, totalist signified to "globe" and its relatives). Understandably enough under such circumstances, Gilroy, Song, Spivak, and others think they have no choice but to write the global off altogether. It is not on its terrain, we are told, not on this compromised ground, on the ruins of the condemned dwelling, that the planetary project can be founded, even though the very ambition to "overwrite" the planetary, to lay, palimpsest-like, the critical writing of planetarity over globality, practically predicates the former on the latter.

The palimpsest trope might help elucidate and perhaps work out the predicament. Wish as it may to start from a clean slate, "planet-thought" will always be an overlay: historically, it makes, as we have seen, for a global studies development; ontologically, the planetary, its central concept, is, *like* the global, a worlding possibility, a netospherical formation, although a nascent one, *unlike* the global, whose histories, contentious and schematic as many of them are, span centuries if not millennia. To my mind, an acknowledgment of both ties, as well as of the antecedences and filiations woven into them, is more fruitful than a vainglorious attempt to start from scratch. Or, to put it differently, the planetary project can try and scrape the global ontology off the sheet on which it strives to reinscribe the world, but it should embark on this operation fully aware that the relational, the very woof and warp of that ontology, will stick and eventually show through, rendering any planetary reinscription of the world an onto-intertextual affair. Furthermore, the world's un-scription as globe and reinscription as planet—the world's "deglobalization" and subsequent "planetarization"—is possible, in fact becomes even more feasible once it recognizes its palimpsestic condition, namely, the preexisting language, the *relational idiom* it has to speak so it can speak, and write, the world differently, into new relational arrangements and consequences. As argued previously, "globe" and "planet" are both relational scripts. These scripts set in motion relational processes through which the world is "worlding," but, depending on the relationality type they ultimately afford in the rising "worlded" world, they can bring about either "globalization" as defined (and indicted) by prevalent rhetoric or "planetarization."

This relational type, the actual content and outcome of being-in-relation—otherwise a very abstract notion—hinges on *relatedness management*. Under the auspices of "globalization," this management is indeed quasi managerial quite often and, more broadly, falls under the purview of economics, finance, technology (primarily informatics), media, and communication. Driven by profit-taking, this handling of relation is orchestrated and understood in terms that rationalize the relational by subordinating it to a lucrative rationality interested—we are informed either appreciatively or depreciatively, as the case may be—in the non-lucrative, the (apparently) gratuitous, the nonpareil, the exception, the idiomatic, the ambiguous, the elusive, and ultimately in the cultural itself just as long as they can be co-opted into the computing scheme that totals as much as it totalizes, squeezing the world's face into the unethical—simplifying, reductively explanatory—framework, chart, diagram, or any other data analysis format.

If the whole point is, as *Reading for the Planet* basically contends, to scrutinize this face—to work out the worlding world's aspects and expressions—then another relational concept, and approach thereto, is required, which would re-world the world into planet by *resetting the netosphere ethically* rather than by discarding it. But how can we rethink being-in-relation beyond the nationalist, imperialist, and, of late, globalist nexus, beyond the relational logos that, for such a long time, has underlain the main form of linking up here and there, self and other, ours and theirs? And how are we, artists and critics, to embark on such a radical rebuilding of our epistemologies and deontologies so as to deal with the surging availability of the imaginary museum, of the planetary archive, of sites of life and culture suddenly handy, vulnerable, ready to be annexed, googled, disembedded and disemboweled, exposed, toured, and sampled, intertextually used and commercially abused? Can we even "stop and think" when confronted with the world's overwhelming and hyperexposed Heideggerian *Bestand*? And, if so, for how long can we put our response off—for how long can we not look the world squarely in the face? To my mind, neither the old nor the delayed responses will do.

Proof that the world's totalizing worlding is not irreversible and that the globe's closed geometry is not geoculture's destiny, the world's relational reset as planet and, by the same token, fresh answers to the questions just raised are indeed possible. What makes them so, I maintain, is a planetary counterdiscourse susceptible to rethinking the rationalization of relationality into its contrary, that is, into, or as, a relationalization of rationality. Once ethicized, the impersonal, defacing, and equivalence-engendering relatedness of the netosphere becomes *nethospherical* and in that particularly sensitive to formations, workings, and implications of world relationality that escape or are disadvantaged by the co-opting fury of corporations, markets, and empires, by the serial, the formulaic, the routine, the "universal," the easily or apparently classifiable and profitable. Thus, in counterdistinction to the "globe" and "global," I define the "planet" and "(the) planetary" as a noun and an attribute, respectively, signifying and qualifying *a fluid, multicentric, plural, and pluralizing worldly structure of relatedness unfolding in the triple dimension of a geocultural space, discourse modality, and critical-imaginative framework or episteme, all of which are keyed to non-totalist, non-homogenizing, and anti-hegemonic operations existentially as well as culturally cognitive in nature*. As such, wherever and whatever the planet is structurally or ontologically in the world—for it is not the world's synonym, as we shall see immediately—it is "in the species of alterity," viz., underpinned and warranted by an ethical infrastructure.[79] Deflecting the equalizing-totalist thrust of a globalization that is both focused on and theorized, even critiqued, predominantly, disproportionately perhaps, *qua* market, profit, and finance apparatus that "impos[es] the same system of exchange everywhere,"[80] the planetary, *because* it pivots on otherness, on a phenomenology of individuation generally, is of necessity neither solely economic nor simplistically deterministic in its actual links to capital, trade, and market share nor monological culturally, aesthetically, and otherwise. As Elias has aptly stressed, its relationality is, nurtures, and, critically speaking, prompts dialogism, and a multiple one at that.[81]

This also explains why some critics prefer, alongside "planet," "planetarity," and their like, the Jean-Luc Nancy–Derrida-backed *monde* (cf. Latin *mundus*), *mondiale*, and *mondialisation*. As Apter comments, "Nancy's philosophical worlding asks," indeed, "to be read with Gayatri Chakravorty Spivak's notion of 'planetarity.'"[82] I will not elaborate on what this entails because I have done so elsewhere.[83] Reinforcing an important point also made by Apter, I will only repeat that we are not simply dealing with terminological squabbles, and I will also add that this is not a case of ethnolinguistic bias either. Major semantic differences are here in play, and they all follow from the ethos of the planetary "superscript"—from how the planet reworks relations *à rebours*, over and against global rhetoric's inscriptions of relatedness. Endorsing the mundane concept present in the French philosophers of *mondialité*, this ethos makes the planet a *relationalized* rather than a rationalized system. This has seven major implications.

First, the planet is not an accomplished oneness, an entity *accompli* (completed and irrevocably so), a structured, coherently administered, and measured geopolitical expanse, but a relational world-system at once "calculable and beyond reckoning," as Herman Rapaport echoes Alain Badiou's *Being and Event* and *Logics of Worlds*.[84]

Second, and on this very ground, this system is characterized, both geoculturally and epistemologically, by multiplicity, open-endedness, and sociocultural and political potentialities, as Rapaport also glosses.[85] The planet is not a "closed system" properly speaking. Its spatial, shareable finitude only begins to reveal itself gradually to humans, from outer space or on the ground, in the second half of the twentieth century. This system is mutating, and its architecture and meaning do remain exceptionally complex, multifarious, topoculturally shifty, and thus "necessarily . . . difficult to define."[86]

Third, our world is not a complete system. "The literature around us" is not already and "unmistakably a planetary system" either, as Moretti claims.[87] But they are both evolving into one. Neither closed nor finished, neither an attained finitude nor a teleology, the planet is a *soft* system: young (surely younger than the global, no matter how one writes globalization's biography), evolving and expanding, *a* world but not *the* world, a "webbed interrelatedness"[88] covering most of the world but not overlapping with the world itself. If it is a world-system, the planet is so under the aegis of the toposystemic "relativity" Wallerstein foregrounds when he draws attention to the spelling of his celebrated catchphrase. "Putting in the hyphen was intended," he avers, "to underline that we are talking not about systems, economies, empires *of the* (whole) world, but about systems, economies, empires *that are* a world (but quite possibly, and indeed usually, not encompassing the entire globe)."[89] Not a globality, the planet is not the (whole) world. Ontologically and philosophically, it is not coextensive with our existential and cognitional gamut as humans, with all we can be and envisage. We are and dream of being and doing things, as philosophers from Heidegger to Maurice Merleau-Ponty and from the existential phenomenologists to thinkers like Gilles Deleuze and Félix Guattari keep repeating, always within a world's "with" and "and" relational ambiance.[90] It is inside the latter that the *Dasein* pursues its potential. Neither does the planet span the entire world understood, in a more Wallersteinean sense, as geophysical earth, which is only the planet's cosmic background, physical foundation, and natural stage. As a world-system, the planet looks like a "spatial/temporal zone which cuts across many political and cultural units."[91] The planetary system is, then, "relative," that is to say, approximate, *partially* systematic in its extensity and *loosely* systematic in its intensity (functioning), and so only somewhat "worldly" from a scalar standpoint; it does warrant a quasi-holistic perspective on cultural representation, but, in and of itself, it is not a "wholism."

Fourth, because it is not a whole even though—or precisely because—it pieces together parts and features of many geocultural units (actual or presumed "wholes"), the planet geomodel is not of one piece, and in that it is not one, or in one place, or the same in all places either. It can be, geographically, culturally, and philosophically, many worlds or parts of worlds, "nested" inside each other at once rather than hierarchically ("vertically") organized, and it can be so in one spot no matter how little, as we shall see later (§21–§31). This spatial deployment of the planetary—this re- or cross-spatialization and, of course, re- and cross-historicization of the world—entails a geometry and, relatedly, an ontological distribution of life very different from the global. Correspondingly, the planetary mind-set or the individual committed to a planetary *Weltanschauung* may be or see himself or herself, not unlike the Greek and Roman Stoics, as participating in a number of worlds and world orders in the cosmos while physically located in a particular *polis*.[92] *The planet is thus a geodiscursive projection athwart—across, astride, and sometimes against—the one fixed on modern world maps.* In fact, spearheading as it does a cultural-imaginary remapping of the empirical world, the planetary often messes with the world's official cartography by opening up, de-limiting, and rearranging the topographic and geopolitical distribution of space on our road atlases, print and digital maps, and GPSs so as to challenge, as noted in the prologue (§4), the worldviews of such spatial encodings. In that, Pheng Cheah is right to point out below that what we ordinarily mean when we talk about the world's mapping is not "world" but "globe." If this is true, then postmodern fiction's notorious cartographic plays in authors from Pynchon, Guy Davenport, David Foster Wallace, and Michael Chabon to Jorge Luis Borges, Italo Calvino, Georges Perec, and Milorad Pavić anticipate the more decidedly deglobalizing, planetary recharting of world spaces, boundaries, and itineraries.[93]

Fifth, relativism as a measure of how much the system covers and how it works and relationalism as an index of the system's makeup go hand in hand. The latter indicates that, as netosphere, the planetary consists of relations, but these are *of the kind afforded by the former*, which in turn is built into the ethos of the planetary superscript.

Sixth, retrofitting the relational "underscript" ethically, the planetary ethos unyokes the world as foundational-totalistic *ground*—centered, self-reproductive, rationally developed and managed—from the world as relational, onto-culturally productive playground. As Cheah has shown, Goethe's *Weltliteratur* theory had already differentiated between the two world models and, by the same movement, set the stage for a planetary decoupling of the globe and the world. The German thinker, Cheah comments, "distinguishes between two different senses of the world: the world as an object of great physical extensiveness (that is, the expanse of the mundane or the diffusion of what is pleasing to the crowd [*der Menge*]), and the world as a normative phenomenon, a higher intellectual community that opens up a new universal horizon." "Goethe's distinction between two senses of the world," the critic continues, "is significant for us today because it cautions us from obscuring the normative dimension of worldhood by conflating worldliness with globalization. The world in the higher sense is spiritual intercourse, transaction, and exchange aimed at bringing out universal humanity. It does not abolish national differences but takes place and is to be found in the intervals, mediations, passages, and crossings between national borders." The world, then, can be understood as "a form of relating or being with. The globe, on the other hand, the totality produced by processes of globalization, is a bounded object or entity in Mercatorian space. When we say 'map of the world,' we really mean 'map of the globe.' It is assumed that the spatial diffusion and extensiveness achieved through global media and markets give rise to a sense of belonging to a shared world, when one might argue that such developments lead instead to greater polarization and division of nations and regions. The globe is not the world."[94]

Seventh, the world is not enough, however; not this one, at any rate. I determine it—the world as we know it—as pre-planetary or potentially planetary because what occurs in and through said "intervals, mediations, passages, and crossings" is netospherical but not yet or not necessarily nethospherical. Again, world relations, their venues, and technologies are not the point. Or, they are just the starting point, the palimpsest-like canvas and pre-textual premise of the planetary superscript. The actual point has to do with the pragmatics and, derived from it, the ethics of relations: what they all perform in and on the world, how they reword it, and how the ensuing script reworlds the world; how it makes "world" into a transitive verb with "world" itself as its object, by "salvaging" mundane relatedness for a worldly relational constellation in which sharing, belonging, and togetherness are more than heart-warming "assumptions."[95] Neocosmopolitan projects of demotic world togetherness have also met, as most critics agree, with modest success. Nor have anti-cosmopolitan (Stalinist or postcolonial) and, more recently, "postcosmopolitan" counterprojects fared any better. They have failed, more exactly, have been failed either by their own ideologies of fetishized, individual and collective identity—and more resoundingly still by history—or by their inability to grasp "cosmos," "globe," "planet" as separate and subsequently to realize that looking for the same "practices of planetary interrelation" across these categories is no less misleading.[96]

§13. The Planetary Paradigm

> We are no longer going towards postmodernity. Or rather, we have gone beyond all the "post," we are in contemporaneity.
>
> —ANTONIO NEGRI, *Art and Multitude*

Planetary-Becoming, Planetarization, Planetarized. Spurred by such practices, world- and planetary-becoming—becoming-world and becoming-planet—are not identical either.[97] As mentioned earlier, these developments are not parallel. Nor do they run on the same level. The world's worlding can yield, as specified previously, divergent relational configurations. Planetarity is only one of them. Its onset is a function of the *nethosperical reframing of the netosphere.* I call this transformation planetary-becoming or planetarization. Again, the world is not "always-already" a planet, as some think. It may fall, "devolve," or "unworld" into "globe," as so many others fear today, but it can also rise again by reworlding itself into "planet." This world-globe-planet sequence traces not only the dialectical deglobalization-cum-planetarization of the world or, as Song puts it, the world's "perpetual and implacable planetary-becoming"[98] over and against globalist injunctions, but also another twofold process, in which the ethical and the cultural dovetail, sustain, and illuminate each other. If, on one side, the world is "worlding" into the *ethical,* "diversal," and thus "worlded" relational ensemble of the planet, on the other side, the natural and cosmological world—the world as earth and Earth, as geographical and astronomical entity—starts infiltrating the culturally and aesthetically oriented humanities far beyond the by now "classical" area of ecology.

I am indeed weary, as noted before, of "one-world" declarations, some of which did come out of environmentalism. But I am so only to the degree that their language risks erasing, paradoxically enough, the "diversality," the multi-worldedness so vital to the blossoming world commons. Otherwise, the ecological world and ecocriticism definitely remain, in spite of their shortcomings, among the most significant precursors of the planet model and planetary studies, especially where the unit of analysis is concerned. Having run head-on into the "epistemology of state-centrism,"[99] ecocritics have gone to great lengths to develop, within their field, an alternate model of critical aggregation of the world against the nation-state territorialist knowledge claims and beyond the theoretical and political dead end where rudimentary oppositions such as those between local and global, particular and general, country and world, place and planet, and so forth are certain to take us. In this vein, it is hardly surprising that Heise's *Sense of Place and Sense of Planet,* which compellingly reterritorializes place as planetary site to offer a solution to the "theoretical stalemate" embedded in such dyads, stands out as a trailblazing contribution to planetary and environmental scholarship alike.[100]

It bears reaffirming, though, that, insofar as this worldedness is evolving in time ("defers" its "hard" oneness), there is no fully constituted "planetarized" order or spatial planetarity. What we have instead is an ongoing, polydirectional, and uncoordinated planetarization process whose twin *axis* is spatial and temporal *depth*: "deep space" and scope, scale, and spatiality overall, and Dimock's "deep time," both unfolding over and against globalization's compression of cultural spaces and temporalities, respectively. But this process's phenomenology is one of world-scale cultural *debt*, a living, evolving, transgressively disseminating culture driven, as suggested in part 2 (§20), by an ecumenical logic of ceaselessly mounting, mutual indebtedness. If "globalized" activates a rhetoric of developmental Messianism and thereby an *ad quem*, a teleology, and a material finalism ossified into a painstakingly calculated, all-too-symmetric world *de facto* tilted to the benefit of some, "planetarized" is an accomplished objective, endpoint, ultimate state of affairs, or fulfilled utopia neither temporally nor spatially. In having made their peace, apparently, with the incompleteness of the world-system, Wallerstein and his followers continue to be helpful in understanding "planetarized," counterintuitive as this may be, in a non-perfective and thus non-global mode. At the same time, and much as they publicly shun "global," its rhetoric, and *longue durée* narrative, the story of the world's system-becoming reads like a linear, popular globalization history turned on its head. "Developmentalism," the center-periphery, three-tier world model, a catastrophist teleology ignoring events that do not fit the story or tell an entirely different one—1989, to which Wallerstein and others conveniently substitute the geopolitically quasi-inconsequential 1968 (unless it is Prague, not Paris), the rise of China and further consolidation, rather than crisis, of world capitalism, etc.—then an economic determinism absolutely disabling analytically (and *world*-analytically too) insofar as it has no place for culture and even for geoculture no matter how often it refers to it: not only do all these make Wallersteinian narrative "grand" (its author acknowledges that much), but they also render it obsolete as a plausible account of the world-becoming historical process.[101] Stuck in the 1970s, more exactly in a version of them, itself anachronistic, Wallerstein's worlding scenario is indelibly dated doctrinally by an orthodox Marxism's view of the world and world history. Imputable to that dogmatic outlook are a skewed worlding story and the *partial worldliness* of the world with which that story culminates, predictably anticlimactic as that culmination turns out to be. This partiality is a historical, Cold War-era half-worldedness with an untold tale of two worlds in subtext that compounds the "hyphenal" ("natural") incompleteness addressed under §12. Developmentalist and yet in all actuality a fable of regression, gladly registering change as long as it is a change for worse, as Bruce Robbins astutely notes, that story is not the pathway we can walk to what below I describe as a "planetary age."[102] Planetarization follows a different trajectory. The world-system concept, however, remains useful to *Reading for the Planet* as well, provided we consider, as I will momentarily, its cultural retrofitting—provided we take geoculture seriously, in fact more seriously than most Wallersteinians themselves.[103] Indeed, and with another paradox, the more you look at world-systems theory, the more you come to appreciate what it can do today for the system's Cinderella, namely, for cultural representation. The theory itself hardly shows any appreciation of this sort, but its premises are there for the critic careful enough not to throw out the cultural baby with the bathwater of a "culturalist" critique of Wallerstein's worlding model, a critique this part will put forth in its conclusion.[104]

Planetarity and the "Planetary Condition." What reaches quasi-planetary proportions and gets roughly planetarized—what becomes *a* world, in, over, and across the empirical one without being *one* world itself, whether as a paranoid-globalist "oneworldedness" (Apter), as the already existing world, or as *the* (ideal, utopian) world[105]—is both a biomaterial netospherical setup, the world of linkages and interchanges of the network society, and a penchant, an eagerness, in brief, a netospherical *intentionality*: not only the inevitability to be in relation, which critic after critic deems a planetary hallmark, but also the will to "only connect" nethospherically so as to "counteract" the sometimes "spurious and perverse" kind of "interconnectedness" of the "global condition."[106] I see this as a tendency, "predisposition," or condition of world relatedness to foster certain configurations of sociality on the "planet-as-planet" and more broadly to frame the human at the dawn at the twenty-first century. "Tendency" is here paramount. The "condition" does not condition, actually; it only exhibits a yearning, a structural leaning, albeit a vigorous one. A core planetary prerogative and shaping force of cultural discourse on the threshold of the third millennium, this "netho-propensity" or world condition of relationality must be accounted for—explored, historicized, and theorized—as thoroughly as postmodern thinkers such as Jean-François Lyotard, Ihab Hassan, Brian McHale, Matei Calinescu, Theo D'Haen, Steven Best, Douglass Kellner, Linda Hutcheon, Jameson, and Harvey did decades ago with the "postmodern condition." Alongside interventions in planetary criticism by Spivak, Dimock, Heise, and others, this book takes the initial steps in this direction.

The first and decisive one co-articulates the ontological and the political ethically. Indeed, the ethical is the keystone of the maneuver. In performing it, the planetary theorist both takes stock of the present world and, by laying down a *relational decorum*, a code of netospherical conduct, as it were, imagines a world yet to come. Because the lucid assessment of the world and its imaginative transformation are the two faces of the same coin, one should probably start out in a realistic mode, with the recognition that the condition and, as we will see, the cultural dominant corroborating it, planetary culture, are *in statu nascendi*. We are fortunate to witness their birth much as we are baffled by what we are seeing or maybe are only beginning to see, and not very clearly either. As critics, we are diagnosing signs of new life. But the cultural diagnostician, deontologically honest as he or she must stay in the world field, can and perhaps should be a dreamer, a thinker who takes chances and thinks big, even "fantastic," like one of O'Neill characters, as we will learn in part 2. Run through the world-engendering, prismatic iridescence of such thinking, diagnosis—the diagnosis of planetarity—accrues a prognosis dimension where *the ethical (what one should do in the world as described) acts as a hinge joint or behavioral conduit between the descriptive (what this world is) and the normative (the planet this world should be)*. In other words, one reads the planet's future, and one can—one should—conjure this future up in the world's cultural present. For cultural manifestations of planetarity are more than epiphenomena. They are so not only because culture *is* life-giving, because it spawns life—and therefore it is structurally world-making rather than "superstructurally" world-reflecting—but also because they are demonstrably grounded ontologically as they paint the picture of a burgeoning world, more precisely, of something existing in that world, within it and in genetic tension with it, and planetary in essence and potential. At the same time, they are aspirational. I say "aspirational" and *not* "utopian," for they do capture a reality, or at least its seeds, and, critical of its world context, point concurrently to a different world in the offing.

With another vocabulary, planetarity is both a historical situation and a critique; a conceptualization (of this world), poised for a critical intervention (*in* the world also); an intellectual elaboration and a worlding gesture itself. It is in this complex, empirical and conceptual, associative and dissociative, descriptive and prescriptive, present and continuous, contemporary and futural sense that planetary terminology will be employed here. It is in this sense also that what I label our "geocultural matrix" is—is *and* is becoming—the planet itself, that the ontology of the dreams, visions, and stories underpinned by this matrix is one of planetarity, and that the time these images and projections measure more and more as they are couched at this juncture in literature, in the humanities, and in everyday private and communal routines is planetary. Of this world, brought about, as we will see, by certain world mutations, planetarity underlies those processes, intervenes in them culturally and thus reprocesses them politically, coordinates their production, and supplies their interpretive framework.

The Planetary Age. Similarly to postmodernity and postmodernism during the Cold War, neither planetarity nor planetarism has sprung, like battle-gear-clad Athena from Zeus's skull, from post-Cold War globalization as a neatly recognizable moment or full-dress cultural movement, imagination protocol, or style. We need to keep this in mind while also insisting, as I do, that, ontologically, planetarity is *in* this world already. It may not be a completely crystallized ontological structures but is moving—by leaps and bounds or just inching along sometimes—in that direction by actively making and remaking, worlding and reworlding the world according to its nethospherical *Zeitgeist*. This is another way of saying that the planetary era has largely arrived *and* is to be expected—is in the cards, texts, and discourses of planetarism—if we understand it as the temporality in which this gradual, both occurring and forthcoming making-cum-remaking plays out.

As Stevens's Ariel helped us observe in §5, the latter process was not culturally "remarkable," did not make for the bulk of aesthetic "makings" and "markings" of Cold War literature and art. I maintain that it is and does now, and more and more so every day. Limning what the next pages refer to as planetary culture, this abundance fleshes out this culture's "deep structure," the planetary imaginary or planetarism. In parallel with some mainstream stories of globalization, if at odds with some of their morals, this cultural dominant or "aesthetic majority" has been on the rise after 1989. Having suddenly expanded and thickened in the post–Cold War world, the netospherical reaches the ethically tipping point where its nethospherical retooling and with it another worlding model become imaginable in spite of worlding trends, tragedies, crises, and relapses that, in Pynchon's words, adding "late-capitalist planetary insults" to older injuries, seem to veer off course when they do not backpedal straight into the past.[107] I too am concerned that, as Derrida allows in his spectral reading of Marxism and Marxist regimes' demise in Central and Eastern Europe, the ghost of the Cold War and its ideologies might return in repetitive rather than progressive ways.[108] And yet, I underscore, the cautionary tone of Derridean hauntolology should not prevent us from seeing the demolition of the Berlin Wall for what it is: a true event, an "event-world" (*événement-monde*) in the strongest sense of the term. This development is unique, far from predictable, and a-serial, as post-Heideggerian thinkers of eventfulness from Michel

Foucault to Žižek, Badiou, Negri, and Ernesto Laclau have theorized it. But, in the same vein, it is also *world-eventful*—an *Ereignis* (event) and an *Anfang* (new beginning) in the world.[109] Where *a* history (not History) "ends," another gets under way *worldwide* under the auspices of this occurrence. "Regional" or localized (better still, "localizable") as it originally was in space and time (in East Germany's Berlin and in a certain November 1989), the Berlin Wall's fall had the typical worldwide impact of a "universal singular." As such, it marked a radical break with the past all over the world, proving not only capable of re-eventing the world as a set of sequential events but also of re-inventing, re-worlding it into a new "world-culture."[110]

Thus, at the risk of painting the last one hundred years or so of cultural history with some exceedingly epochalist and broad brushstrokes, I propose that this period has coalesced around three pivotal moments or paradigms. The first was the modern, which extended into the early 1960s; then came the postmodern, which lasted, in its strongest and best-marked configuration, for the next thirty odd years and way past its *années folles* (the 1970s and 1980s); and the postmodern was—is being—succeeded by the cosmodern and, on the world scale, by the planetary—the cultural or paradigmatic dominant on the rise since 1989 and picking up speed more saliently after 9/11.[111] *Practiced*, no doubt, *urbi et orbi*, the first two stages and their respective "conditions," modernity and postmodernity, have been *conceptualized* primarily in Western, Euro-American, and chiefly North Atlantic discourse forms and sites, with the nation-state assuming the role of axial epistemological trope, venue, and sponsor across disciplines. Anticipated and, to some extent, even made possible by the protracted critique of imperialism in postcolonial venues around the world, the third—the planetary—no longer revolves around the West's geopolitical center, methodologies, and vocabularies, which goes to show not only that planetarization and globalization are different kettles of fish but that planetary literature may well be the kind of "literature after globalization" some critics are already looking for.[112] Under the impact of various trans- and postnationalizing trends during but especially after the Cold War, former centers do not hold any more or, at the very least, they no longer do as they used to. Demonstrably, they have been weakened, broken up, disseminated, and otherwise transformed and displaced at the hands of various postcolonial discourses. The ensuing, countless creolizations, recyclings, and overhauls of the postmodern have no doubt played a role in laying the groundwork for a new condition, planetarity, and for a new, planetary epoch.[113] The postcolonial itself has made room for its "beyond," namely, for the condition of planetarity, in a process that entailed not only the post-postmodernizing tenor of postcolonial critique but also the post-postcolonialization of the postcolonial vehicle itself. Thus, as Simon Gikandi remarked in a 2001 article, while the vocabulary of postcolonial theory has not been cast aside,[114] a whole range of mutations have occurred, and with them an overall transition—surely incomplete, uneven, often imperceptible, and yet no less real for that—out of the postcolonial and the cultural-epistemological paradigm associated with it. These include the "worlding" of diaspora, by which this community formation spread and became a socio-ethnocultural structure of life worldwide; the complication of the classical margin-periphery and "dependency" dynamic, by which the (post)colony-metropolis give-and-take highway's traffic, previously controlled by the mimesis-mimicry/imitation-resistance model of creativity-as-subversion, got too congested not to be rerouted into a world maze of itineraries, trajectories, way stations, and "driving styles"; the at-distance, networked interaction that, as Poster suggested, begins to compete with the typically colonial and postcolonial "proximal" modality of exchanges between the parties involved;[115] the ebb of the nation-state as "controlling" framework of cultural production and reception in postcoloniality under the dissolving action of transnational flows of human subjects, symbolic objects, and data generally; and, following from all this—and to take only the British Empire/Commonwealth and English as examples—the turning of "postcolonial literature in English" into "World Englishes literature."[116]

If planetarity is, as I think, indeed epochal in the United States and elsewhere, then cultural historians will have sooner or later to reconsider their periodizations. Most basically, I submit that contemporaneity no longer means what it did forty or even thirty years ago. Up until the 1990s, the contemporary covered the entire post–World War II era, with postmodernity, chiefly in the West, spanning that period's last two decades. This is not the case any more. To resort to another cultural traffic analogy, we are seeing that present in the rearview mirror of today's planetary culture. Thus, I redefine the contemporary as the time elapsed since the Cold War's end, with postmodernism halfheartedly spilling over the 1989 mark and only to open an early twenty-first-century passageway to a new stage and, possibly, cultural paradigm: the cosmodern and, more broadly, the planetary.

Planetary Culture and Planetarism. Not, or not yet, a "period" in the classically literary-historical sense of a sufficiently discrete and stylistically marked period, planetary culture gets under way in the Cold War's aftermath as an incipient, loosely structured moment and scene of aesthetic output. The various discourse-engendering and conceptual functions, frames, and tools of the nation-state model are now tested out, used up, refurbished, or discarded, and a more wide-ranging formation—the planet—is arising as a dominant environment, means, and onto-ethical ground of socioaesthetic and critical expressions. Insufficiently—but more and more—world-systemic, these developments have not given birth to a coherent, well-defined world culture yet. While our world is neither netospherically saturated nor nethospherically governed at this point, such processes have already led to a conspicuous and consequential set of planetary themes and cross-discursive protocols of culture—to planetarism. However, befitting its epoch, planetarism is not your typical "ism" either. An incrementally consistent way of picturing the worlded world, planetarism is a planetarily minded world picture or imaginary that is taking shape before our eyes.

Neither entirely new nor everywhere identical in terms of its meaning, material embodiment, and effects, planetary geoculture looks to be the hotbed of a powerful paradigm leaving, ever more visibly, its daily imprint on how people imagine themselves and the world in the third millennium. With rising frequency, the planet is, as argued earlier under §3, the decisive dimension in which writers and artists perceive themselves, their histories, and spaces. On this ground, a thorough analysis of the planet as shaping context of twenty-first-century life, affect, and creativity should be able to yield a reasonably functional, plausibly laid-out model of planetary poetics. The issue is not so much that planetarity as a new site, formal operator of culture, and *episteme* must be given pride of place by any rigorous, historically minded effort to come to grips with the twenty-first-century arts. To me, this is no longer up for debate. *The rise of netospherical objectuality, complete with its expanding, cultural as well as material nethospherical rethematization, is, I offer, the event horizon of the contemporary* as defined above. Both a space and a structure, a relationally structured space, today's planet consists—and this is surely a truism by now—in ever-denser relations among people, cultures, and locales. Therefore, to comprehend the planetary, one must "get" the relationality worked into it.

On the other hand, I cannot emphasize enough that planetary culture should be taken as heuristic rather than deterministic. The function I assign it for now is cautiously exploratory. I do not posit the planetary as an absolute and sole context for culture and cultural analysis. In contrast to well-known theories of globalization, planetarization is not geared toward a one-world, genetic, homogenous and homogenizing totality. Forging, in some of the more optimistic and ahead-looking assessments, a culture of sharing, the planet itself has not yet provided a stable and wholly structured platform for an ecumenically and equitably enjoyed economic or cultural commonwealth. A full ethical configuration of planetarity awaits its building in the "real world," one reason a thoroughly formed planetary culture is, befittingly enough, still on the horizon. The second part of *Reading for the Planet* takes steps to theorize and deepen this critical understanding, with the addendum that, at least for now, the geoaesthetic commons of planetary culture is primarily an aspirational construct at once necessary and necessarily provisional. Yet aspirational does not mean unrealistic or ahistorical. As I will underscore momentarily, *planetarism, as planetary culture's individualizing imaginary mode, is not an idealism, aestheticized or not, but a materialism*. It is a world imaginary that faces up to the materiality of the world's cultures.

In taking globalism in a culturological direction aesthetically and interpretively, planetarism and the geomethodology dealing with it incorporate some of the earlier resistance, within global studies itself, to the reductive and undoubtedly self-defeating treatment of the role in which culture has been cast on the global scene. Some critics have insistently and rightly "cautioned against such frequently used formulations as 'the impact of globalization on culture' or 'the cultural consequences of globalization.'" These "phrases," they hold, "are, no doubt, often used casually as a reference to the way in which the connectivity and fluidity of globalization make [themselves] felt within the sphere of culture. Yet the trouble with these phrases is that, taken literally, they imply globalization to be a process which somehow has its sources and its sphere of operation outside of culture."[117] Insufficiently acknowledged for what it does to the global world, culture is, to most globalization commentators, *in* that world and hopelessly "constructed" by it, a (by)product, a "consequence," and a dire one to boot. Even when it gets more than a few lines in the global high drama, culture is still not viewed as a producer, a mover and shaker, but as traded product, and by the same token "produced" in sites and by agents external to it. At the receiving end of "true" global actors and the realignments these determine, culture, it is routinely suggested, does not prompt globalization but bears it, does "globalize" yet primarily as a "patient" of other forces rather then transitively—it does not globalize the world. And so where most critics employ "the culture *of* globalization" phrase as a subjective/possessive genitive, I insist—in a planetary, further culturalizing setting—on a more descriptive-interpretive and ontologically performative usage, with the planet as (a) *context* for culture's planetarizing impetus; (b) *object* of this process; and (c) episteme encapsulated by said process as well as guiding its critical reception. I see planetarization as a property culture shares with capital, data, and migration, as much as I acknowledge culture as a driving force behind planetarization, a vector sometimes weaker than economics, informatics, and demographics, sometimes stronger, sometimes on a par with them, and working across, alongside, or against them, as the case may be. And again, if this culture "planetarizes," that means that cultures around the world call out to each other and interact in the planetary forum faster and more substantially than ever. It does not mean that these cultures have become or are becoming *one* culture, although this risk should not be played down either.

If, as Warnier says bluntly, "speaking of the 'globalization of culture' is abusive," the abuse is even more egregious in the case of planetary culture.[118] True, one has witnessed the flourishing of certain regional and cross-regional lifestyles, tastes, hobbies, interests, cultural codes and rites, some of them now already on the wane, others still expanding. But none of these has integrated world cultures, and thus the world, into one culture and world, respectively. Cultures go planetary in that, building on their genetic multiculturalism, they enter in even more complexly multicultural, that is, cross-cultural discursive alloys. But world cultures have not merged; they have only been interacting in the post–Berlin Wall era more vivaciously than before. What is occurring under planetarity, in other words, is not cultures' fusion into one megaculture, but a *worlding* of cultures, a range of geopolitical and aesthetic transgressions, delocalizations, migrations, and other forms of motility and mixing leading to an astounding intensification of cultural contacts and amalgamations. Without question, there are still some privileged cultural hubs, agents, circuits, and styles—there are *Dallas*, the never-ending (and increasingly transnational) *Die Hard* series, and fast food, as there are, let us not forget, telenovelas, the "slow-food" movement, Japanese fashion design, and the steady expansion of Bollywood, Iranian, and Romanian cinema outside their historical markets. Still, critical culturalism of a planetary bent tends to point to an ongoing transculturation of the world, to a new acculturation or, as Jacques Demorgon words it, "interculturation of the world" into a body of culture, a rewriting of the world archive into an overall flexible system of cultural relations where what counts and occurs most is that once-separated cultural producers and discourses are now able to interrelate instead of simply fading into one another.[119]

Thus, cultures do not come together in the planetary theater to plunge into standardization and uniformity. Neither is planetarization an "Americanization." Globalization itself is not either, even though the world consolidation and dissemination of U.S. influence, military-economic power, popular culture, lifestyle, and values overall—including Benjamin Barber's notorious "McWorld," Updike's "deep-fried homogenization," and other forms of "Coca-colonization"[120]—were and are pretty hard to ignore. Fortunately, scholars no longer hesitate to take to task the paradoxically "standardizing"/"Americanizing" effects of such one-sided interpretations. Pierre Rigoulot is just one of the French critics who have disparaged it as a "pre-thought," *prêt-à-penser* doxa or "ready-to-wear," uncritical "hand-me-down" itself in urgent need of examination.[121] If the "actually existing" globalizing world is not as "flat" as Thomas L. Friedman reports, the planetary world for whose building we are breaking ground should be even less so. In either case, extrapolating, unawares or not, from unacknowledged positions of critical authority can be as problematic a proposition as making broad claims from privileged centers and headquarters of political and military authority. As I see it, planetarization is less an ecumenization or generalizing of certain national cultural contents and more a widening, thickening, and intertwining of the *links* among those contents. Danish linguist Louis Hjelmslev's distinction between *relatum*, that which is connected to something else within a structure, and the connecting *relatio*, is helpful here: what planetarizes one's self, one's place, others, and the world ultimately is not so much particular *relata* or elements as the linkages, processes, and venues relating these units and thus getting them to "interrelate." It is in this sense that cultures planetarize and a planetary culture is in the making.

Not a monologue but an echo, speaking to us not through a mouthpiece but as through a sonar, cultural discourse and identity either form or position themselves to take shape in the planetary age nethospherically. They surface more and more relationally and dialogically, according to the logic of the Ancient Greek *dià*, that is, always belatedly, by a detour through the world's distant or just "different" places, intervals, and styles. So conceived, both discourse and identity, and the whole culture concept alongside them, fly in the face of dogmatic and oppressive politics—it wonders about the political—as it wanders geopolitically. Their anthropological matchlessness, that which makes "my" discourse and the identity resting on it so assumingly and exclusively "mine," supervenes in the strong sense of the word. It too "comes after." Characteristically, it ensues from a "wayward" narrative of oblique addition, filtering, and refracting, thus expanding—

"worlding"—the intertextual poetics of postmodernity rather than completely discarding it. Identity is thus a "fraud," if you think about it, insofar as what makes it (in)authentic is a transcultural chain of deviations, divagations, borrowings, importations, and interpolations, in short, spatializations. Adrift in space and meaning, an ongoing uprooting, this route, this dromo-genesis of culture and subjectivity, is a routine of derivation that splices together diachronic ("vertical") filiation and synchronic, lateral affiliation or, more likely, maps the former onto the latter, time and again. Thus, culture or author X, over here, may adopt and follow as its or his/her "past" tradition culture or author Y, over there, a "there"—a location, aesthetic repository, stylistic arsenal, or artistic pattern—that can be either from the past or from the immediate present. Therefore, planetary culture seldom overlaps with the nation, ethnos, and their territories, with which both culture and identity have been associated routinely. However, its presence, consistency, makeup, and symbolic leverage oscillate across countries.

This is also probably the place to admit, and, as some would be quick to add, hope, that, like the world itself, no culture is or will probably ever be wholly worlded. Resistance to cultural planetarization should not be ignored, nor should one be oblivious to the nation-state as the geographical, administrative, and linguistic venue inside which cultural expression physically—institutionally, locationally—still comes about and where, by the same token, it must cope with tremendous territorializing pressures. But, increasingly faster after 1989, virtually no culture can opt out of the world's worlding narrative. And, since a worlding culture's transactions and meanings perforce overflow the territorial-historical extension of one polity, tradition, or language, this narrative, the world epic into which more and more of the world's stories feed, should be understood as an inter- or cross-cultural aggregate.

§14. Politics, Poetics, Epistemology

I prefer "planetary imaginary" over Gilroy's "planetary mentality"[122] because what I want to highlight in planetarism is an energy and an activity, an operation in and *on* the world rather than this world's effectively or presumably passive "imaging." My decision has notable bearings on world-making, text-making, as well as text-understanding, and so it pertains to politics, poetics, and epistemology alike. I wrap up this part by going over the most significant among these consequences.

From a political standpoint, to begin with, planetarism makes for an ontologically unhappy culturalism. World-transforming, it is a world-picturing with re-worlding ambitions because it is both forward looking (forward picturing) and eager to "overshoot" itself, to transcend the cultural-aesthetic as well as the imaginary and thus plug itself into the world's existential nitty-gritty. As an activity of the conscious mind and, insofar as it sets off imaginative mechanisms, of the unconscious too, planetarism can be viewed as an "activist" and effectively historicized ("always historicize!") version of the Jamesonian "geopolitical unconscious." It is activist in that the acts it performs—Jameson's "(sub)cognitive" mappings—not only map the "new world system" and "our new being-in-the-world" but also redraw the existing boundaries, distributions, and Baedekers of affect, discourse, power, national sovereignty, territory, and capital according to a world order still to arrive;[123] and it is historicized insofar as, *qua* geopolitical cartography of the contemporary, it actually accounts for the nebulous, tactically unqualified "newness" in Jameson's "new world-system" reference, that is, for the eventful 1989 and the ensuing post-Soviet bankruptcy of Wallerstein's and Jameson's notoriously schematic three-tier "worldism." As is well known, neither the tearing down of the Berlin Wall nor the breakup of the USSR and its client bloc shows up in any meaningful way on either critic's world-system maps, pre- or post-1989. *The Geopolitical Aesthetic* came out in 1992, a mere few months after the Soviet Union ceased to exist, and this world-shattering event remains the elephant in the china store of Jamesonian teleology, a sort of epistemological dirty secret that renders said maps, along with the historical and critical narratives behind them, if not altogether useless to any venture in the territory, then far more obsolete today than they already were twenty-three years ago.

This world picture falls short epistemologically not only because it has always been oversimplifying or because it has become geopolitically antiquated but also because of its aforementioned "economism." As with global analysis in general, the conclusions of this approach predictably and quasi invariably replay the premise of an all-present, all-defining, uniformly operating and yet somehow Protean Capital with capital "C." This is, we learn, the true Network running underneath all networks à la the Wachowskis' *The Matrix* and whose "reloading" hiccups spark a real (Real) crisis (Žižek dixit) the silver lining of which inheres in the opportunity to "get" the Symbolic—to understand, finally, that all world phenomenology camouflages an ontology of cash. The demonic market is almost always the depressingly foretold message, the gist of the conspiratorial narrative both uncovered and reinforced, as I have said, over and over again by critics who, following in the Wallersteinian line of "nomothetic" inquiry, understandably miss out, much like their master, on the "idiographic," namely, on the idiomatic "social phenomena" and their "uniqueness."[124] Of course, in response to this doxa, the idea here is not to play back the message but to fight back; not to rehearse the world's knee-jerk descriptions but to change the world, to redescribe or reimagine it into another structure of worldedness; and surely not to ignore the "corporatist mediation" of literature, culture, and the world either, but to take conceptually and critically remediative action.[125]

If, at least in its ordinary accounts, the global is a nomothetic environment in which the selfsame reinscribes itself according to rewriting laws (*nómoi*) passed in advantageously positioned, legislative, administrative, and managerial hubs, the planetary is primarily an idiography or, better still, an ideography—world figuration and writing—of the idiomatic as an "other" badge of the world's people, emotions, and places. Neither short-circuiting financial relays and the economic generally nor mimicking their configuration, planetary culture's nethospherical imaginary sidesteps the logic of the selfsame, of the repetitive, and the equivalent by remapping the world otherwise. Planetarism is not a reaction, a reflex, and a confirmation of the status quo, but, once more, an action in which the imagining of the present, fictional as this imagining's arena may be, has a reworlding and futural vector to it.[126] The ethos planetarism affirms is world-making and world-remaking in that the mental maps the planetary sanctions connect the planet's dots in ways that make visible new configurations, allotments, and hierarchies of space, discourse, community, and power.

While "globe" implies an "imaginary"—a "one-world"[127] master picture—globalism is surely not just a matter of culture or of the imagination. Nor does planetarism perform its "act" in a sphere of its own outside the material world, for it retraces, and traces over, routes, relations, and onto-political possibilities in that world. As Robbins suggests in critiquing Wallerstein and agreeing, up to a point, with Arjun Appadurai's "culturalist" stance, if there is a system in the world in question, "then culture ipso facto cannot be excluded from what makes [the system] systematic"[128] and hence, I would add immediately, from *what makes the world a world*. To reverse the syntax of Cheah's *Weltliteratur* considerations, world-imagining activities are those that enable us to make a world.[129] Thus, *culturalism, the cultural approach to our worlding world*, for which I am arguing here, *is not an aestheticism but a "worldism."* It is in this sense and in this sense only that planetarism, pace Wallerstein, is a culturalism, and so will have to be, as we shall discover before long, the geomethodology applied to it. As an imaginative formalization and reformalization of the relational world, planetarism articulates the systematic, is both a mimetic and a visionary model of the world and thus an axis on which pivots the turnstile between the present and the future, the world "as mapped" and the map of the world to come. A Foucauldian thought-event and an imagination-event at once, planetarism is more concrete and more engaged in the world than the "cosmopolitan imaginary." Described as "an aesthetic of openness that engenders a global sense of interconnectedness,"[130] cosmopolitanism may take up the form of an "imaginative supplement," but the "figuration of ethical territories" so inaugurated remaps and may well end up supplanting, as Claire Colebrook posits, "whatever the world is here and now, with all its global networks, markets, and power structures."[131]

Planetarism's imaginative mobilization in the world carries over into planetary poetics. As specified in the prologue (§3), planetarism is the "Prevailing Operating System" on which planetary literature and culture's nethospherical enunciations run thematically and, with less conspicuous effect, formally. Critics like Pratt were right, about a decade ago, to alert us to the pell-mell "proliferation" of "global objects" of "all kinds and shapes: viruses (cybernetic and biologic), evangelical Christianity and Islam, satellite television and the cellphone, hip-hop and rock, transnational feminism, the sweatshop, the anti-sweatshop movement, ecology, the T-shirt and rubber flip-flops, the traffic in human organs and the drug trade, vampires, and migrant communities."[132] No longer a novelty at this point, the global bazaar of logos, trinkets, commodities, opportunities, and fanaticisms has come under the discriminating sway of a post-global, meta-objectual planetary ethoscopy that screens, assesses, and classifies them into a critical thematics that is both analytic and evaluative. Planetarism's basic infrastructure, this thematic poetics deploys certain recurring images, motifs, and, especially, a sheaf of typical *metathemes* or nethospherical allegories. These are clustered around the "worlded world" spatial arch-theme—planetarity's "primal scene"—with its various *mise-en- scènes*: the worldly elsewhere and the planet itself as that elsewhere's palpable rather than abstract inscription into "here," inside and astride the traditional habitats of indigeneity, autochthony, nativity, homeliness, homeyness, *Heimat*, and nation-state territorialism, an inscription or wording that worlds those locales, emotions, and sociopolitical entities, opening up their ethno-national narratives, mythologies, and epistemologies; remote sites, habits of those habitats, customs, and their "others," which the narrative eye perceives, typically, as intrinsic or internal to closer ("our") places, groups, and their ways of seeing the world and comporting in it; a whole gamut of time-space constriction games, the nethospherical imaginings they spawn, and the new sense of proximity, adjacency, with-feeling, and the togetherness the resulting planetary ethoscopy in turn endorses.

Further, while a distinctively planetary stylistics is yet to come about, homologous to this geothematics is also a certain poetics of form, with the proviso that "form" here is never solely a formalist matter, an issue of mere craftsmanship and aesthetic ploy, but also a rewording-reworlding algorithm, a procedure pertaining to the discursive interface of the word and the world. Planetary poetics features a range of elements and characteristics. Usually present together, in different constellations and varieties, they all boil down, in my view, to three sets of textual traits and literary instantiations.

i. Dramatizing the "connectability" of the worlding world, the first is a wide spectrum of worlded, sometimes Internet-assisted intertextual formations. Genuinely compatible with Castells's socioeconomic and cultural network, on one side, and with the venerable cosmological trope of the Bibliotheca Universalis, on the other, intertextuality continues to consolidate its seminal *poietic* status across literatures in the twenty-first century.[133] "Planetary culture" is not just a matter of "transculturation," but this transculturation—a more complex, intertextual-intercultural process in which spatial and textual crosses and crossings dovetail—is a core feature and mechanism of planetarization and, as such, also postmodern intertextuality's planetary avatar.[134] In fact, more emphatically than under postmodernism, *planetarization affords a cultural ontology qua world anthology*.[135] Furthermore, and also more substantially than in the postmodern arts, planetary "quotationalism" is transterritorial, and politically so. "Quotations," Dimock reminds us in her search for a "literature for the planet," "do not have to be foreign, but they can be. No border patrol can stop them. This breach of territorial sovereignty is the starting point for a global continuum of words. It is the point where temporal and spatial distances break down, where chronological jumbles and jurisdictional jumbles produce weird offsprings."[136]
ii. The second set documents the multiplying of these inscription-cum-reinscription protocols of discourse across aesthetic and transaesthetic practices. These protocols reach far beyond the literary, the textual, and the analog. If an older, postmodern-Gérard Genettian category of intertextuality lives on in its Wikipedian reembodiments,

the latter spread, via such operations, not only across countries and traditions but also across discourses, representations, and media. In reality, the "new media" is, with a term hardly new either, "intermediality," both a multi- and an inter-media, despite renewed nationalist-authoritarian attempts to circle the wagons around communities, cultures, customs, and party lines, to limit the circulation of people, ideas, and even goods, to corral, control, censor, and monitor Internet users inside statal territories (China and its "Great Firewall," Iran, Turkey, Cuba, Russia) or even outside them (the never-ending National Security Agency scandals).

iii. The last category consists of certain types of literature and literary forms ranging from woollier aesthetic categories, morphologies, techniques, and enterprises to somewhat better described literary movements, "genres," and "species": "world poetry" (Dimock);[137] "World Bank Literature" (Amitava Kumar, Philip E. Wegner) and "world-system literature" (Medovoi); *littérature mondiale* (Jérôme David);[138] "'comparison literature,' and the emerging genre of world literature for which global comparison is a formal as well as thematic preoccupation" (Rebecca L. Walkowitz);[139] Susan Stanford Friedman's all-embracing "modernism," which is multicentric rather than West-centered, and thus planetary, plural in its spatial extension, temporality, and formal configuration; "planetary postmodernity" (W. Lawrence Hogue); nomadic, rhizomatic, "archipelago"-like, or "trajectorial" form—"trajectories have become form" in "altermodernism," claims Nicolas Bourriaud;[140] "transcultural narrative" (Maurizio Ascari); the "planetary poem" (Ramazani); "the post-9/11 novel" (Ascari), the "cosmopolitan novel" (Berthold Schoene), "the world novel," and the "geopolitical novel" (Irr) either of the more postmodern kind (DeLillo, later Pynchon) or of the even more geopolitically, cross-historically, and narratively networked sort (David Mitchell, Colum McCann, Roberto Bolaño); more radically perhaps, historically speaking, the novel itself—with Moretti's title, "the modern epic"—as inherently world-systemic, a "world genre" successively redefined by Moretti himself, by Dimock's critique of Moretti's "distant" approach, and by Spivak's "creolization" of Dimock's planetary model of genre and genre reading; "fractal" stylistics and "grainy," exogenous lexicon (Dimock).[141] More and more critics deem these forms, formations, and discourse modalities "planetary" in terms of origin, circulation, and even structural patterns. In essence, such productions document thematically and enact

> formally the sharp, post-1989 upswing in worldedness. They soak in, mark, and critique the contextual clashes, movement, and intermingling of worlds, peoples, and values; they capture *the wide world-as-world* textually, "topically" (subject matter-wise), as well as topologically, namely, within texts highly sensitive to the world's worlding and, inside those works' fictional space, within "little worlds," communities, and locations less and less immune to the worlding pull of planetarization.

Largely underpinning planetarism's poetics, then, is the notion that formerly separate, territorially and nationally bound and categorized cultures can and, in reality, cannot but borrow from each other according to a transactional *ethos beyond, or rather across, ethnos*: "horizontally," following a rhizomatic growth scenario, as if they were drawing "organically" from their own patrimony and in conformity with the standard, one-track, "root" diagram of intra-national, ethno-endogenous historical evolution. Consequently, "digimodernism," "hypermodernism," "altermodernism," "metamodernism," and other transvaluating, epoch-making events and trends capable of couching earnest questions about postmodernism in past tense and thus lead up to planetarism can be grasped as exercises in a new traditionalism—as symptoms of a cross-national, world commons *posttraditionalism.*[142] Part of larger cultural-economic transformations, the shift such symptoms pinpoint is constructed mainly in the aesthetic-theoretical lexicon of a post-postmodern avant-garde. The global's "over-" and "counterwriting" into planet signals insistently and programmatically an ethicization of a cultural—now decidedly cross-cultural—dynamic at the production as well as the reception end and presents itself as a complex, transcultural-transtopological phenomenon whose ramifications are economic, political, and, more notably still, ethical.

For "planetarity" is neither merely cultural nor solely epistemological, simply an inquisitive *forma mentis* molding the world, as some contend;[143] at once a material (ontological, generative, *poietic*) *and* a cognitive-analytic (epistemic) master framework, the planetary is *also* an episteme, and part 2 will tackle planetary epistemology at length. Epistemologically speaking, the planetary is capacious and integrative. It has its ebbs and flows. It transforms and surprises. In keeping with its etymology, the planetary "wanders," remains shifty, cannot help turning, literally and otherwise, and so it is neither an ontological nor a hermeneutic given, let alone, as I have said, a completed project. Therefore, it does not stamp all art objects or all artworks entirely, nor does it elucidate them completely. To repeat, planetarity is a relationality, not a totality. While thinking "totality relationally" may reproject the global planetarily, viewing "relationality in a totalizing fashion," as some advise, is risky business politically, culturally, and epistemologically.[144] The planet is not only a new and fluid cultural landscape throughout which people and their sustaining fantasies wander, connect, and reproduce, but, along the same liquid and blurry lines, a clarifying and interrogative domain simultaneously, a *poietic* matrix spawning wonders and ambiguities and, by the same genetic gesture, a germane, "soft" epistemology. It wanders and makes us—helps us—wonder. Not so much a doxology, the arrogant cousin of "totality," but a heuristics, the planetary setup presents us with a historical occasion and cultural site for travel, exploration, communication, and interaction, as well as for cognitive "wondering," for methodical perplexity and principled discussion about a literary-artistic aesthetics and hermeneutics that, at the end of the day, may remain a rough critical construct. Loose and loosely invoked, heteroclite, still uncharted, the planetary nevertheless intrigues. Its presence and bearings on everyday life as well as its reflections in the life of the arts await comprehensive yet prudent articulation. In a nutshell, the planetary is more generous, more permissive with what one can be and mean than the prevailing constructions of globality, which posit—quite positivistically at times—an all-embracing context of living and meaning indomitably drowned, existentially and semiotically, in liquidities.

To summarize, defining planetarity epistemology are chiefly an emblematic mind-set, *Weltanschauung*, or world picture sponsored by the insight that fewer and fewer separate or presumably discrete places, groups, and undertakings are sitting out the transnational and transcultural protocols that link up, intertwine, and inflect things, people, and cultural iconologies on a steadily widening scale; a rare sensitivity to the planetary articulations and problematics, which supply increasingly central, formal metaphors and foci to artists and critics alike; national traditionalism's posttraditionalist, "worldly" sublation, which fosters something analogous to Amin Maalouf's "horizontal tradition"—the planet's "other" places and inhabitants, along with their heritages and fantasies, to which "we" turn and which we mine as if they were "from around here," "ours";[145] a new, at-distance, "endless," non-patrilineal and cross-patrimonial "planetary feeling" or sense of closeness, kinship, and ties, which designates posttraditionalism's utmost affective upshot and supplements textually—and usually intertextually also—our inherited ("genetic") familiarity with the kin type of relations or relatives and with the orthodox (not to say "traditional") idea and praxis of relatedness.[146]

Built into the cultural-aesthetic expressions underwritten by the planetary imaginary, the planetary episteme testifies to a *téchne poietiké* that does double duty as *téchne hermeneutiké*, to a world-making art pregnant with its own hermeneutics. If "the rational ordering of the global" projects a figure that dis-figures,[147] planetarism refigures the world into an imaginary ordering that both guides and beckons another mapping, a critical order. In the livid figures, lifeless numbers, and computational pantomime of the mercantile universe, the world's face is, at best, blurred, serialized, and rendered anonymous, a complexion without complexity, without its "idiographic" wrinkles and other signs of history and life underneath its skin; at worst, this face is here defaced, made unreadable by the very gesture—decreasingly analog and increasingly digital—that purports to figure and contour it. With planetarism, however, the world becomes legible again according to a reading (de-wording) scenario encoded (worlded), as I say, in planetary figuration itself.

The first step of *reading planetarily is, then, reading for this figure*, reading for the planet's declension—for the worlding world—in planetary writing, in writing that "writes for the planet.[148] Specifically, what this means is *reading for the nethospherical carved into* poems, novels, plays, or screenplays, scanning discourse for fictional *spatializations* of ethical relationality. Even if it was a solely thematic procedure—reading "the world-system as a theme; the world-system 'inside' literature"—this kind of work is still ahead of us.[149]

What we do know already—and what Goethe himself knew almost two hundred years ago—is that a truly worlded literature circulates on a world scale; we know, too, that the "world republic of letters" across whose territory this circulation has taken place for centuries is hardly "an enchanted world, a kingdom of pure creation, the best of all possible worlds where universality reigns through liberty and equality";[150] and we are certainly aware that, like everything else, books are not traveling at the beginning of the twenty-first century how they were when Goethe was talking to Johann Peter Eckermann about world literature. Therefore, "circulation" is not the issue, or not the most pressing one, especially since we are getting better and better at tracking it technologically, financially, and so forth. What we lack, instead, is an understanding of how circulation, the netospherical (of which dissemination, distribution, and so on are key components), and planetarity (of which the netospherical is part and parcel) are engraved in literature, how literature takes them in. Both thematically and formally, as an imaginary exercise, literature *knows* the worlding world of the new millennium, hence planetarism's epistemological value; *what we do not know is how we can learn what and how literature knows*. There has been no systematic attempt thus far to put together a critical apparatus for showing how the planetary and its condition are actually inscribed into the texts, styles, and artifacts symptomatic of this epoch-making development, So, to rephrase the question Colin MacCabe raises apropos of Jameson's cognitive mapping—a question Jameson fails to ask—what do the thematic-formal "mechanisms" of such an inscription look like?[151] More to the point, how exactly does planetarity translate into planetary literature? How does the former's Prevailing Operating System actually operate? And, if the planet is framing artists' imagination, how is the critical imagination responding? With what framework? How are we facing the "face of the earth" in its planetary portrayals? How do we read it, and, when we do, what does that entail critically, epistemologically, and ethically? How does *planetary criticism* work, and what might its workings mean beyond literary-cultural criticism? The book's second half provides the answers.

PART 2 GEOMETHODOLOGY

Theory and Practice

Everything begins with Houses, each of which must join up its sections and hold up compounds—Combray, the Guermantes' house, the Verdurins' salon—and the houses are themselves joined together according to interfaces, but a planetary Cosmos is already there, visible through the telescope, which ruins or transforms them and absorbs them into an infinity of the patch of uniform color.

—GILLES DELEUZE AND FÉLIX GUATTARI, *What Is Philosophy?*

I feel that the academy has not yet developed the grid and the grammar to explore American works that are not quite "American" in a canonical sense. Such a literature possesses the one essential quality of all great writing: energy. And energy is released in the mangling and macerating of fused languages[,] in the reckless violation of outmoded forms, and in characters pinched and pulled into supernatural shapes.

—BHARATI MUKHERJEE, "Immigrant Writing: Changing the Contours of a National Literature"

I

§15. The Face of the Earth

"The face of the earth": let us tarry with the venerable idiom a little longer at this crossroads in the history of the world, the human, and the humanities. For, if thousands of years of use have worn the locution thin, the onset of the netospherical is prompting the phrase's semantic reset. One wonders, in fact, what the old expression might convey at a time when, tying some of us down to exploit, disenfranchise, and otherwise "expe[l] from the narratives of futurity,"[1] the earth's revved-up morphing into an increasingly integrated biocultural aggregate is also drawing more and more of its denizens—

the restless and the ruthless, the enterprising and the dispossessed, the doers and the knowers—farther and farther afield. It also bears asking, in this vein: how is our exponentially broadening familiarity with the beyond-the-familial rekindling the syntagm in casual conversation, popular media, classrooms, and scholarly analyses? How might we defamiliarize it privately and publicly, colloquially and academically, as we chat, fantasize, cuddle up with our favorite books, and write about them?

The point that galloping globalization forces us to take another look at the worlding world hardly needs any arguing. Nor is this just a matter of responsibility, although planetary obligation, care, and advocacy trace the contour lines of the ethical shores where this book will eventually land us. "Looking the other way" and thus bypassing the urgency of the problem are simply no longer an option nowadays, when fewer and fewer "other" ways, directions, and routes circumvent the ever-denser "dromology" of Castells's "network society."[2] A modality or, rather, countermodality of looking the worlding world in the face—a planetary ethoscopy—planetarism refuses to look the other way. In effect, we might think of it as a profound and multiple prosopopoeia. Unlike global surveys, mappings, and other similar rationalizations of the world's face, planetarism's prosopopoeial poetics literally ascribes, "makes"(see the Ancient Greek *poieīn*) by making out, by visualizing and representing a face (*prósopon*) for and to the world. This face is not a hocus pocus, an invention, but an invocation and an unveiling. The face preexists and only makes its appearance (or has its appearance, its "figure," made) via the *poiēsis*—the eloquently tautological "face-makings" or "facings"—of planetary imaginings. In the face, the world comes alive as if "personified." It moves, speaks, and looks at us from afar, over a distance (*prosō, porrō*), no matter where we may be hanging out. "Within the perceptible world," writes Georg Simmel in his famous essay "The Aesthetic Significance of the Face," "there is no other structure like the human face which merges such a great variety of shapes and surfaces into an absolute unity of meaning." But, as planet, the "perceptible world" itself flaunts its "wholeness."[3] Resonating to planetary displays, planetarism conveys aesthetically what we are experiencing existentially: the face of the earth is "in our face" now, and so the real question or questions are what we see and how prepared we are epistemologically to look at all when we do so. Therefore, what we should also ask ourselves is: While windows are opening wider and wider onto the world—whether in Microsoft or, no less innovatively, in Beigbeder's 2003 9/11 bestseller[4]—what kind of figure is the world cutting in our studious frames? How do we look, and what is it that we notice when we screen planetarism's figments and images? Do we see the netospherical in its full, unchecked, often furious swing? Do we see something else, a world motion of a different order? Do we see a globality, or do we see a nethospherical reordering of the world, a planetarity? And, if the latter truly is what we contemplate, how exactly is the planet's figure revealing us, in and across the very sites of its figuration, something that the discourse of globalism often obfuscates and stymies while planetarism forefronts and nourishes? How does one make sense of this face, of whatever its countenance may express, given, as Levinas teaches, our reflex reaction to rationalize it, to cover its "nudity" in the self-serving ratiocinations of our system-beholden gaze?[5]

Undoubtedly timely, these questions boil down, as the last one hints, to interpretation, specifically, to a critical act—and to an ethics—that has everything to do with today's "actually existing" world and so gets the critic "down and dirty in the trenches of reading, teaching, conferencing, publishing" in a very applied, non-"utopian," and "quotidian" kind of way.[6] Generally speaking, all these interrogations demand, in fairly practical terms, scrutiny of the world's fast-changing "look" in the aftermath of the world's latest, themselves multifaceted reconfigurations. More concretely yet, and thus more closely to our private homes and disciplinary abodes, the sheer existence of the netospherical setup, its socioeconomic layout, its saliently interconnective logic, the encounters, synergies, syntheses, and clashes in which this logic is instrumental, and the *courte* or *longue durée* etiology of the in-progress world-system are not the issue here, or not in the first place. The ever-more integrated world-as-world, the netospherical's utmost upshot, is a manifest reality both diachronically, as an evolutionary rationale, and synchronically, as a present world ontology or, more simply, as the form in which the world exists. Whereas the roots of this form, of this geocultural framework contextualizing the planetary visions—the primal scenes of planetarity—adduced in this part of the book, push deep into the early Renaissance's transcontinental travels, "discoveries," and redistributions of territory, community, affect, and capital, this framework or worldly armature of the contemporary remains no less unprecedented for that. The sociohistorical uniqueness of the context within which today's world physiognomy presents itself to us strikes me as hard to ignore. To repeat: what literary planetarism illuminates and helps us discern is a physiognomy of planetarity, a world that is worlding not only netospherically, by following globalism's instrumental rationality, but also nethospherically. The face that arises and shines in the fictional ethoscopies examined below does so according to an *ethical interface* (in the world) while calling for another, between the "diegetical" face (the face-in-the-text) and its spectator-reader.

§16. The Infinite and the Infinitesimal, Cosmos and Cosmetics

> Instead of upholding territorial sovereignty and enforcing a regime of simultaneity, literature, in my view, unsettles both. It holds out to its readers dimensions of space and time so far-flung and so deeply recessional that they can never be made to coincide with the synchronic plane of the geopolitical map.
>
> —WAI CHEE DIMOCK, "Literature for the Planet"

This physiognomy comes into play in two mutually constitutive and tightly imbricated dimensions. These are the macro and the micro, the vaster planet or planetary picture, which connects the world's dots, and this picture's pointillist flipside/inside with its little points and grains of life and expression, into which the worldly panorama funnels down. I call the appearance of the world-as-world, of planetarity as non-totalist totality, *macroscopic* when it breaks forth and appears accessible, not to say obvious, from above or afar, from technologically enabled, spatial-evaluative positions and postures, but also when its scope—its spatiality or distance understood both as horizontal extension (expanse) and vertical scopic reach—is literally planet-encompassing. The macroscopic or the world *qua* "macro" ensemble implies and often is a distant perception and a large-scale representation, image, or photo. This is the proverbial bird's- or, more accurately, astronaut's-eye view; the interval-conditioned approach and what this technologically or imaginatively assisted prosopopoeia yields from afar and above (*prosō*): the planet's face or the planet as Face, rather; what comes through, and what one makes out, from the physical and intellectual distance that presupposes without always bringing into sharp relief the many little shapes and faces in the planet's Archimboldian collage, the cross-local, integrative-interlinking, and world-systemic operations of planetarity.[7]

I throw my lot with those who wonder less if the macro, reluctantly "wholistic" picture of the world actually exists and more what the picture means and how it compares to available, sometimes officially endorsed depictions, images, and maps of territories, regions, and so on. The netosphere's marks on individuals, places, and artifacts are, to me at least, obvious. Instead, my concern is how such marks are to be read, and so our problem falls, I propose, chiefly under the *microscopic*. This problem is of the order of the infinitesimal. As I have said, even though it has larger repercussions, it is a practical one, and also the real test. This is where the critical rubber meets the road, although, as I have also made clear, and as the writers examined in this part's second half prove, the micro, its focus, and the reader's own attention to it do not involve an ontological, topological, or epistemological disjuncture with the world-as-world, a complete shift away from the macro, from the "cosmic" perspective of the NASA ("Apollonian") "gaze" and the "infinite" it gestures toward while paradoxically construing the earth as provisional one, limited "unit."[8] Indeed, the macro and the micro work—must work, of necessity—as the two arms of the analytic scissors.

As Robbins reminds us in a commentary on Spivak's resistance to notions of totality and totalist viewpoints that hark back to suspiciously coherent worlding paradigms,

> *Cosmos* (world) in *cosmopolitan* originally meant simply "order" or "adornment"—as in cosmetics—and was only later extended metaphorically to refer to "the world." Cosmetics preceded totality. Worlding, then, might be seen as "making up" the face of the planet—something that can be done in diverse ways. At the same time, the case for this modest cosmopolitanism is also a case for a certain professionalism—a professionalism that, without presumption of ultimately totalizing certainty, believes in its own intellectual powers of generalization, abstraction synthesis, and representation at a distance, and in the process of putting them to use—that believes, one might say, in its own *work*.[9]

Most critics would probably agree that cosmopolitanism, old and new, has not completed this work yet, and it may never do so. Under these circumstances, planetary criticism might do well to step in. For its approach befits planetarism's prosopopoeial poetics, whose "face-making" results in a configuration of form, color, and emotional content that neither implies an abstract scheme nor reinforces the one already supplied by the global cognitive order.

Reordering, remapping, and reworlding the world at the micro level, the cultural cosmetics of planetary ordering resists, however, not only global totalization but reading as well. It both founds and confounds the interpretation. Thus, in the era of the "big picture," of a picture taken by a see-it-all, and see-it-*as*-all, eye-in-the-sky, the challenge, the world's own provocation to the discerning observer, is not principally the big picture itself, the planet's "macrophysiognomy" or the Face as such, of which we have been given more and more detailed and accurate representations. This is not our toughest task. Macroscopically discernable thanks to the new technologies of digital and satellite photography, the Face becomes indiscernible in the micro, in planetarism's ever-multiplying facial ornaments and remappings, which violate recognized maps, boundaries, and distributions of space, culture, and power. Along all these, the Face gets blurred inside and among the planet's faces, and so it becomes the job—the tougher job—of the planetary critic to deal with the unsettlingly ambiguous encryptions of planetarity in the local, the tiny, and the humble, to listen for the macro's murmur in the vernacular of the micro. For, fraught with distinctions and codifications of planetarity, the indistinguishable is or looks so only at first glance. To really pick up the gauntlet, therefore, is to try and ascertain what it entails to work out cultures' fine print with this planetary configuration, figure, or face as master framing device; what it takes to attend geoaesthetically to the enduringly enticing arabesque of "small things" alongside and through their godly and human handlers, locales, and styles; in brief, what it means to us, now, to read "with" the planet: to read the planet itself but not as a reductively "global" totality—a wrongheaded, unethical, and, at the end of the day, futile undertaking—but, in reading against that ominous oneness, to read the planet with and ultimately for the myriad of places, archives, and artifacts of which its fragile, pluricentric, and makeshift whole consists.

§17. "A Single Embrace": Turn of the Planet, Turn to the Planet

> My personal hope for the coming decade is that we will look more deeply into the presence of the world within the nation, even as we continue to develop further our exploration of national traditions within the wider world.
>
> —DAVID DAMROSCH, "World Literature as Figure and as Ground"

> The world does not turn without moments of grace.
>
> —COLUM MCCANN, *TransAtlantic*

My premise, then, is that, at this point in history, the planet is swimming into the critic's ken. On a less Keatsian tone, the earth's face is coming into view as planet, in the planetary age and through planetarism's cultural projections, in its fully tangible dispensations and cultural-intellectual affordances complete with their sometimes uneven and contradictory offshoots. This development is controversially complex. Nevertheless, in bringing about a "discontinuity" in how we understand ourselves and others, it has all the makings of a major, game-changing "event"[10]—an event and, with it, as noted earlier under §13, an event horizon, namely, the planet's "registering" in our mental pictures but also planetarity as picture within which human creativity is reframed on the threshold of the twenty-first century.

As such, the event is an occasion not so much for uncritical cheering as for earnest and sustained inquiry. Does the planet—more accurately, does the earth—have a face to begin with? Has it ever had one? If so, how visible was or is that face? To answer, one might start out by specifying that this visibility need not be anthropomorphic and by the same token vulnerable to Deleuze and Guattari's critique of "faciality."[11] Further, one should point out that our earth does have a *surface*. It has had one all along, if not a solid one *ab ovo*. This is not what I am talking about, though. Primarily a matter of geometry, geodesy, and, more basically, geology—after all, "earth" supplies here a geological synecdoche for "planet"—the earth *qua* telluric-oceanic surface is, so to speak, sur-facial, hence culturally superficial, impassive. We have seen, the globe and its rhetoric are post-figurative, an anti-prosopopoeia that de-faces the earth at its developmentalist end, depleting its material and aesthetic resources and washing off the colorful "makeup." Instead, the earth's face is pre-figurative. Pre-facing the Face, this blank, faceless face is aesthetically "asleep," as Michael Ondaatje would put it.[12] Less an expression than sheer expanse, this unmarked flatness—this "undented" plane, Westphal might gloss—lacks in volume as it does in variety.[13] Thus, the mysteries it harbors are either hollow or redundant. Depthless, smooth, and uniform, this is not a face proper but a geographical façade, indifferent theater for the drama of cultural difference rather than the netospherical arena or "semiosphere" in which discourse is engendered and exchanged.[14] And, since this a- or proto-semiotic superficiality does not feature a topology, it makes no provisions for a typology or principle of classification either, that is, for a language, a locus-minded logos; the face of the earth so conceived is scarcely a site of meaning.[15]

However, it may turn into one, as planet. After all, turning is what the earth does as a planetary body, in both senses. Terra turns (*planā*, in Ancient Greek) to gyrate, concomitantly around other celestial objects and its own axis. But, by the same movement quite literally, it also turns *to* change, turning in order to change and thus into a world-change order itself, the earth's revolutions bound up with the twists and turns in anthropocene history, revolutionary or less so. On one side, then, the earth's whirling through space as the planet physically revolves and evolves and as space on earth itself stretches out, shrinks, is redistributed, and is mapped out in step with the systoles and diastoles of human civilization; on the other side, our own pirouettes, swerves, and about-faces, marking how we shuffle around the world, how we transform it, how we ourselves change in the wake of worldly changes, and, last but surely not least, how the latter call on us to revisit our *Anschauungen* of the spinning *Welt* and of ourselves in it: all these turns matter a great deal. What is more, they do so together, for they have been demonstrably intertwined through the ages. If geography—the earth's human writing into cartographic as well as topo-material visibility, the planet's life within and without *homo sapiens*'s scholarly disciplines and material-aesthetic practices—is subject to becoming, then "the becoming" of such fields, discourses, and the overall culture they speak to "is geographical" too, according to Deleuze's celebrated tribute to the "Superiority of Anglo-American Literature."[16] On this account, no anthropology or ethnography without a geophysical chapter is ever complete; no cultural history or paradigm shift account overlooking the earth's own motions, cycles, and crises passes muster; no posthumanism still treating the planetary as inert, anthropocene context or backdrop to the human text or figure fulfills its promise; and, more broadly, no philosophy that does not operate "geophilosophically" is worth its salt.[17]

As Deleuze and Guattari posit, not only is thought's measure the ability to "create" its concepts, but this creation also requires an "earth or deterritorialization" as its "foundation."[18] Note too that, for them, the earth and its historical de-, re-, and, we shall discover, under-territorializing dynamics are mere figures of speech neither ontologically, "out there" in the world, nor philosophically, inside the reasoning apparatus of the "Geophilosophy" chapter of *What Is Philosophy?* Or, they are figures etymologically, as it were, inasmuch as they designate "aspects" (*figurae*) in a fairly palpable, phenomenological fashion, ways in which the planet and thought *look and should be looked at*, once again, correlatively, together. Equally significant is that this togetherness, this mutuality of planetary complexion and thought's complications, fluctuates across time. True, Deleuze and Guattari observe that the illuminating codependence of the earthly as deterritorialization geoapparatus and of the philosophical has always been in play. In fact, as Rodolphe Gasché explains in his ample commentary on *What Is Philosophy?*, Greek democracy and philosophy are, according to the two thinkers, "both born of an earth and an existence that are self-foundational, autonomous, free from all attachment to particular territories, born, in short, of a fully immanent earth whose internal consistency is not diminished by the existence of an outside cause or reason."[19] Greek citizens and philosophers, one might say, are, or rebecame, *autochthonous* "not because they are of the land and the earth but because they have all by themselves and of themselves grounded themselves, deterritorializing the land and reterritorializing it into a politically" and philosophically "grounded community." The new concept of autochthony, then, Gasché concludes, is

> distinct from the one encoded by the official obsession with sameness and the fascination with the auto-referential, distinct from, in short, the myth of being born from the earth that dominated the official discourse, especially in Athens. Wrenched from the earth, the philosopher's earth as the deterritorialized par excellence is reterritorialized onto Greece as an earth that is constituted by the free and autochthonous citizens of the polis, an earth that, in practice, has also been much more open to foreigners than the official discourse would seem to allow, which thus also made it possible for a miracle to occur in Greece: the miracle of the birth of philosophy.[20]

On the other hand, the post–Cold War years have enhanced and foregrounded spectacularly the geopolitical, geophilosophical, and geocultural seesaw of the foundational de- and re-territorializations that promise to bring, as Deleuze and Guattari say, "all the elements within a single embrace" of the planetary earth,[21] of an ecumenical indigeneity that forgoes—when it does not explicitly upend—any *appellations d'origine contrôlée* by reaffirming the earth under the post-autochthonous auspices of planetarity. No other chapter in the world's history, I contend, has literalized the planet's figure so extensively, making it so ineludible in its ubiquitous physical immediacy, so non-figurative in its concrete, geocultural presence, and so productive conceptually, so consequential for how one thinks—for how "immanent" to thinking *thinking with the planet* has become across disciplines.

This "immanence," this philosophical operationality of the planet, derives, as Deleuze and Guattari also comment on Heidegger, from a planetary turn, given that "by virtue of its structure," Being "continually turns away when it turns toward," to the point that "the history of Being or of the earth is the history of its turning away."[22] For one thing, this movement is to no negligible degree trans- (and, some might add, post-) statal; arguably, Henri Lefebvre guessed wrong when, back in 1975, he assured his readers that planetarity—*la mondialité*—would be a "planetary extension of the State."[23] For another thing, this has been a turn away from, and has been accompanied by the subsequent opening up of, territories, polities, policies, patrimonies, canons, standards, and paradigms heretofore neatly circumscribed—"territorialized" in terms of administration, coverage, and meaning—by national jurisdictions, nationalist mythologies, and attendant epistemological claims and descriptive models, or just so advertised. These complex turns trace the ambivalently distancing or "deterritorializing" by which the planet *de facto* draws nearer to us, to the little places of our lives but also to that hub of human reflexivity where it becomes effectively "immanent" to thought, or becomes thought, pure and simple, so as to involve thought itself in the "double becoming" that would make it planet-like—"earth," write Deleuze and Guattari—and thereby transform it radically.[24]

In the multimillennial, interweaving histories of the world and thought, we stand, as Kostas Axelos would alert us, at the decisive juncture at which the coextension and co-implication of planetarity and thought—the *devenir-pensée du monde* and the *devenir-monde de la pensée*—render the worlding world's fashioning of representation and the latter's planetary scope, structure, and content two faces of the same coin.[25] For, if the planet turns away, it does so only to return, turning back toward us ontologically and analytically, as existential grit and interpretive grid, working itself into the everyday and its material heterologies at the same time that it turns into the pivot or "plane" around which thought and comprehension themselves gravitate. This way, the planet's turn lays out, still in Deleuze and Guattari's lingo, a "plane of immanence." "Clearly not a program, design, end, or means," this plane nonetheless "constitutes," today more than ever, "the absolute ground of philosophy," the foundation on which, in accord with the planet's cycles, thought warrants re-founding,[26] with the sciences and the arts also responding to these challenges, making similar moves on their own thinking planes and in their discourse-specific languages.[27] Thus, the planet serves, increasingly and with historically unrivaled force, as a level, matrix, or condition of possibility for a *forma mentis* whose purview covers the conceptual (philosophical), the referential (scientific), as well as the aesthetic (imaginative).

This is how the planet is turning to us to *concern* us all, thinkers and artists, specialists, and laypersons, irrespective of where and what we are, to sponsor novel forms of world writing and reading, of imagining, figuring, and figuring out the planetary world-as-world. Otherwise put, this concern works both ways. We are concerned, "looked at" by the planet as it is turning to us so we can see the earth's face. But this turn invites ours; we ourselves have to turn to the planet. The earth has—finally—entered the picture *qua* planet and, in the geocultural dimension of planetarity, shows its face to us. This face is meaningful, but it will not be *readable*—it will remain fairly meaningless to us—unless we too face the earth. Because the turn *of* the planet subsumes thought itself, it calls for an intellectual turn *to* the planet; the reciprocity of planetarization and thought—of thinking on the planet and of thinking of the planet as planet—presupposes apposite "concerns," a certain planetary consideration on *our* part. This is as much as saying that, besides the world cast variously identified as multitude (Negri), Crowd (Badiou), "global soul" (Pico Iyer), cosmopolitan (jet-setting or not), and, somewhat disconcerting, "nowhere man" (Iyer, Alexandar Hemon), the *planet affords itself a receptive consciousness.*[28] In turning to the planetary spectacle of meaning, this consciousness takes in the world homologically, by availing itself of a methodology germane to its planetary object, moment, and environment. This methodology is thus a *geomethodology*. In it, objective and subjective concerns, context and text dovetail. It features three major constitutive steps and closely interrelated thrusts.

i. The first is principally topological. As such, it latches onto planetarization as spatialization of the world and of aesthetic routines alike. It does so not at all because temporality is planetarily irrelevant; after all, Dimock's "deep time" (other, oftentimes longer histories than U.S. history) proves as instrumental to the planetary imaginary as "deep space" ("other continents"). But, in the imaginal economy of planetarism, planetarization and its relational mechanics are *with*nessed—put together, recognized, and accounted for—more extensively, more conspicuously, and more easily in the language of space, of places and surveys *other* and *of* others (from) elsewhere, mapped onto the fiefs of old-fashioned selfsameness, homogeneity, jurisdiction, ownership, and autochthony. In brief, if there is a spatial bias or penchant to planetarism, this has to do with its ethoscopic vector, with the unethical spatializations that make for the target of planetary ethoscopies.
ii. The second is, in the main, structural or relational. It homes in on a segment, locus, or facet of one or more artworks to tease out—to "decompress" analytically—their *planetary inscription*, namely, the "here"-"there," "we"-"they," "part"-"whole" relatedness structure folded into them. This "folding," I submit, is the strongest common denominator of emerging planetary culture. Otherwise, as I have acknowledged, "planetary culture*s*" is far more befitting because there is no one-size-fits-all folding or compressing mechanism but only folding or compressing codes, which differ a great deal from one cultural site, practice, or agent to another. In decoding cultures, in showing how "here" is *co-imagined*—pictured inside, alongside, and more

broadly "with" there, and vice versa—geomethodology proceeds as a reverse engineering of sorts, characteristically activating a *reading-with* or a *with-reading* as it reads these works and their subsequent topo-cultural "*part*ialities" *with* the planetary "whole." Geomethodology's modus operandi can be compared to the famous scene in DeLillo's *White Noise* where Jack Gladney undoes the work of his garbage compactor or—surely in the same vein—with Freudian dream interpretation's dealings with oneiric symbolizing mechanisms, particularly *Verdichtung* ("condensation").[29] In ways similar to DeLillo's archeologist of collective culture or to the analyst of private fantasies, the geomethodologist is a "de-composer," one who—incidentally, against the grain of E. M. Cioran's *Précis de décomposition*—decompacts or lays out the worlded world the planetary imaginary compresses into the nooks and crannies of smaller worlds.[30]

iii. The third thrust is predominantly ethical. It accentuates even more powerfully the nethospherical repercussions of relational compressions, condensations, and foldings. Building on the previous two, it reaches beyond the descriptive by retooling the "with" as a twofold critical-deontological "for": geomethodology is not only geared toward tracing symptoms of planetarity "in territory," in this place, film, or novel; it also reads *for* the planet, on its behalf. This is where planetary interpretation and planetary stewardship become one. Below, I will walk us through these three geomethodological components in this order.

§18. The Space of Method

This methodology is a *geomethodology* first and foremost insofar as the world's planetary becoming—the turn *of* the planet—is, in its most noticeable form, spatial. Planetary spatializations do affect time and its historical (and historiographical) construction also. More often than not, they touch off spectacular rehistoricizations, as we shall learn, for example, apropos of O'Neill's "Dutch America." However, by and large, as Lefebvre, Harvey, and others have suggested, one way or the other planetarization works through, brings about, and, once more, "appears" most saliently as a transterritorialization—dislocation, reallocation, and novel aggregation—of space and its meanings on earth. Felt by the world, carved into its body in the form of late twentieth–early twenty-first-century boundaries, passageways, itineraries, venues, and geopolitical units of exchange, discourse, communality, and contestation, this turn cannot be thought of independently from the planet's geophysical shifts even though its logistics remain largely anthropological. Seemingly a natural category, a given (to us, humans), space has been, in reality, as Lefebvre would also insist, subject to well-defined production technologies. Occurring in and through human history, the planet's turn is thus inseparable from our spatial footprint on earth.

As Westphal maintains in *Le monde plausible*, the historical scene of this turn is postmodernity[31] or, more likely, whatever postmodernity we got left after the Cold War. If the "spatial imagination"—across the humanities as well as in the world "out there"—is older than postmodernism, the "spatial turn" dramatically picked up speed during the Cold War's last years to culminate, inside the academy, with a "hyperspatialization" of literary history,[32] theory, and especially postmodern theory through interventions by topo-theorists, ecocritics, and literary cartographers such as Foucault, Harvey, Marc Augé, Edward W. Soja, Brian Jarvis, Buell, Heise, Moretti, and, outside, with a quasi-worldwide spatialization of the postmodern paradigm itself.[33] Now we know that the globalization of the postmodern was a Pyrrhic victory. More noteworthy here is what made it possible, what helped postmodernism go places in the first place: its "place fixation" itself (if you indulge the pun) or perhaps the opposite, that is, postmodernism's insatiable appetite for unfixing, loosening, and setting things adrift, for displacement and deferral, the transgressive, intertextually digressive *furor topologicus* that bows to neither center nor inside because the marginal and the outside, along with the "outside the text" (*hors-texte*), have lost their contours on its maps. In this light, postmodernism's anti-logocentrism is, apropos of its spatial "fury," a "lococentrism."[34] But the postmodern's insistent re-centering around space rests on a core-periphery dialectic redolent of Blaise Pascal's *Pensées*, where the stable, "rooted" center-circumference dichotomy gives way to multiple, ubiquitous, shifty, and rhizomorphe spatialities. This plural and fluid topology has been—*was*, some might rejoinder—postmodern, terminally postmodern perhaps, before becoming not only a theoretical-aesthetic but also a geocultural "dominant" of planetarity. It is in response to it that authors from DeLillo, Bolaño, Andrei Codrescu, Paul Auster, O'Neill, Iyer, Orhan Pamuk, Mircea Cărtărescu, Michel Houellebecq, Edwidge Danticat, Mohsin Hamid, and Teju Cole to David Hollinger, Thomas L. Friedman, Nancy, Jameson, Miyoshi, Hardt, and Negri—all fiction writers, critics, and philosophers representative for both paradigms or, more accurately, for the *transition* from one to another—extol, bewail, and otherwise dwell on the "disappearance of the outside" and of those "hiding" places where territory-bounded and culturally "cloistered" individuals and groups struggle to opt out of one of our time's sea change scenarios.[35]

Imperfectly accommodated by the spatial-discursive model of postmodernism, new kinds of painting, moviemaking, writing, reading, and thinking are made possible, and the world they conjure up becomes intellectually, ethically, and aesthetically "plausible" once the planetary turn has been completed or, more realistically for now, has reached a point of no return. As I have expounded at greater length in my book on cosmodernism, and as reiterated earlier under §13, in carrying us past this moment the contemporary is taking us beyond the postmodern,[36] for its nowness weaves the present and those present in it into a chronotopically novel fabric. Marking the fast-evolving structure of presentness temporally, this quasi-ecumenical *fuite en avant* shrinks the playground of "now" also known as contemporaneousness down to a more modest interval: the time lapsed since the end of the Cold War. This geohistorical process renders this now less generic. While the contemporary is, of course, always mutating, sliding out of its aging skin into new ones and into a perpetually self-updating newness, the immediate past bestows uniqueness on this "now," articulates it as post–Cold War presentness in very concrete and characteristic ways.

Spatially, one registers, at the same time, a compensatorily amplifying and juxtaposing "positional" pathos that, within and without the United States, unpacks the historically discontinuous category of "here" and the related notion of self so as to forefront the effective presence "in our midst," in the immediate proximity, or in the mediate, at-distance propinquity, of those once upon a time "out there," not "from around here," or not like "us."[37] My point is not simply that Harvey's chronotopological "compression" model covers just a slice of a more complex world reality subject to a range of simultaneous, spatio-temporal contractions and expansions, but that what sets our epoch apart is a radical geosocialization of places and of place generally. Even though its intensity and cultural markers shift from one place to another, this process obtains on a scale as conspicuous as it is planetary. In this respect, as a "trend," the cosmodern is, indeed, to the United States and most Euroatlantic cultures what the planetary is to the entire world, including the late postcolonial. Put differently, the Western cosmodernization of the postmodern represents a world-fractal phenomenon, is part and parcel of a development or transformation of planetary proportions, and, *because of that*, the change in question must be addressed from the "world's end," not from America's.

This shift or turn comes down to an undeniable worlding of world places. Granted, there are exceptions to a phenomenon that, again, can take up any number of forms, from the more heartening to the obstreperous and outright terrifying. But because what I want to point up is the worldwide, documentably topocultural dominant, it is worth stressing that this large-scale spatialization stands out as a defining reality of the third millennium. What our hyperconnected world has been "specializing" in, and also what distinguishes it, is worldly spatialization itself, which bears on how we are in this world, on what we do in it, and on what we make of it. A perennial attribute of Heidegger's *Dasein*, being-in-the-world, with others, has been heightened by the accelerated "de-distancing" of the world's places, sites, and cultural practices.[38] Thus, as previously disconnected or loosely connected regions have brought closer together modernity's world *en miettes*, the spatiality (*Räumlichkeit*) tied into Being *ab origine* has now become worlded spatiality. Already instituted—presented—by the Heideggerian *Welt*, presence sets itself forth and is legible in *spatial co-presence*. So characteristic of our age, this onto-topological condition of vicinity is not a planetary condition *a priori* because the management of the self-other, here-there nexus warranting it still has to become uniformly non-oppressive and non-exploitative. But planetarism's world-making, "normative" imaginary opens up, as we shall see, some interesting possibilities for this equation.

§19. Getting the Picture: Rationality, Relationality, Distance

> World literature that emerges from intensive lecture of a certain type, and remains—despite its global ambitions—compatible with close reading.
>
> —ERIC HAYOT, *On Literary Worlds*

Spatialization works by way of an ample repertoire of cultural sites, vectors, and materials; *world* spatialization operates via ever broader arenas and socioaesthetic rites and on a world scale. The unprecedented, ever-expanding contiguity and co-articulation of formerly stand-alone—or so imagined—agents, discourses, and settings are hallmarks of our worlding world.[39] But, to reemphasize, what "worlds" (*weltet*, in Heidegger) this world, and what "welds" its "independent" statements and clauses into a worldly syntax of subordinating, coordinating, of simply juxtaposing geoontology, is a world picture (*Weltbild*) that must be grasped both objectively—empirically, as what is—and subjectively—cognitively and ethically, as what it must eventually become. Reflective of the world's "worlded" form or "built," this *Weltbild* facilitates critical reflection *on* this world, helps us "get the picture" of the world.[40] It is in this multiple sense that the worlding world, and the planet with it, has entered the picture: topologically, as spatial extension of the human; historically, as a certain point in time when the world picture comes about—the Heideggerian "age of the world picture" or, more accurately still, the post–Cold War era, in which late globalization's netospherical *nomós* (in Schmitt's sense) "ventures" planetary spatiality as much as it "rules" against it;[41] and "spatiologically," in Lefebvre's terminology, or, in mine, geomethodologically, as a planetarily minded approach in the humanities and beyond.[42]

This approach's critical algorithm works out readings through strategies of *semiotic spatialization*, viz., through *telescoping* meaning-making associations that, besides the unavoidable, if cautious, at-distance ratiocinations, also enact, as we shall see momentarily, semantically microscopic *decompressions*—self-distancing interpretations—of local and proximal spaces and of their aesthetic renditions. The Heideggerian qualms about the modern attempts to reterritorialize our purchases on particular places and occurrences therein by bridging the distances and divides between them and otherwise transterritorializing their locations and significations are not completely unwarranted, and yet they do not capture our present historical circumstances. What Heidegger could not factor in is the crucial mutation distance as concept and world spatial habitus has undergone over the past half century: due to the planetary spatialization of places, distance itself has been so thoroughly displaced and placed, territorialized, *inside* places, territories, and cultural microdomains that dwelling on distance, on this kind of structural or structure-embedded distance, no longer means automatically subscribing to globalist-totalist ideologies. To the contrary—and on this ground—"distant" reading can play out *as* close reading of spatial and aesthetic distance-laden sites.[43] In effect, as we shall notice repeatedly later on, the distinction between "distant" and "close" all but disappears in the praxis of planetary interpretation.

In light of this tactical conflation, is bears remembering that, in "The Age of the World Picture" and elsewhere, the German philosopher is taken aback by the "wholist," anthropocentric arrogance behind wide-sweeping, culturally and politically co-opting, and technologically assisted "calculations" about remote objects, their positions, meanings, and our physical-intellectual access to them. No doubt, thinks Heidegger, there is something to be said about the "gigantism" ("Americanist" or not) of our "distant" topo-interpretive élans.[44] But, as I have observed under §11 and in other places in this book, Spivak, Neef, and others surmise that the planet—and implicitly any reading model based on it—may override "globe" and the globalist rhetoric that assimilates the far-flung and its beyond-reckoning others into the rational, one-size-fits-all selfsameness makeup of the world's political and cultural centers.[45] In most accounts, globality and even some world-systems-based comparative approaches *rationalize* to shrink the earth's topo-epistemological interspaces by a "top-heavy" comparison that "impos[es] the same system of exchange everywhere."[46] Instead, planetarity and the criticism built on its conceptual matrix *relationalize* to link up and read side by side the world's worldly insides, its non-interchangeable entities, thus, *and only now*, allowing for the Heideggerian "incalculable," the aesthetically immeasurable, and the culturally asymmetrical.[47] Typically geomethodological, this (cor)relational move crosses the gap of difference without annulling difference itself. Much like the planetarity that makes it both "necessary" and "impossible,"[48] the move delineates an analytic back and forth between either spatially distinct, though connectable, meaning units (works, genres, authors, movements) or from one meaning level to another *within* the same unit or cluster of adjacent, partially overlapping, or wholly coextensive units. Not infrequently, critics who have taken the former road have assumed that those units are not only external to each other but also organized into a self-evident hierarchy of space ("centers" and "peripheries"), culture ("origins"/"originals"/"sources" and "imitations"/"replicas"/"echoes"), and power ("capitals"/"metropolises" and "provinces"/ "colonies"). Rearing its head even in a more democratically run world republic of letters such as Casanova's, this geoaesthetic pecking order antedates the planetary turn.[49] With a long disciplinary history behind it, the methodology underpinning it has yielded notoriously mixed results especially within the "influence studies" variety of comparative literature. Driven by a "macro" kind of logic—in fact, excessively "macrological" at times—it risks shortchanging the micro; wielded from afar or above, and habitually from unacknowledged hubs and heights of political and cultural capital, this panoramic view of the faraway and the atypical provides for a "distant reading" that does remain distant. Here, distance is not only a "condition of knowledge" but, unfortunately, also its stumbling block,[50] for, historically, it has produced analogously "distant, abstracted knowledge" indicative of a cognitively suspicious "detachment."[51] If the cavalier dismissal of "close reading" is damaging and thereby license for playing fast and loose with the idiomatic richness of the infinitesimal, then whatever planetary picture the "distant" critical procedure paints may not differ significantly from the broad, totalizing, and "ideographically" insensitive brushstrokes of the Wallersteinian *and* of the globalist model.[52]

§20. The Telescopic, the Microscopic, and Planetary "Quilting Points"

More picturesque, from a planetary standpoint, is the latter road. Less traveled and more recently cut, it is better marked not only with the usual road signs but also with the planet's lush and variegated ontosemiotics—in short, with life. What with its high speed, uniformly designed ramps, exits, rest areas, express tollgates, and lookout points over distant if awe-inspiring scenery, the other road is an autobahn. The critical traffic it fosters remains keyed to covering the distance physically rather than uncovering the geocultural minutia of the in-between locales. The highway is just that, a high road to, and at times even a bypass of, the problematics of the planetary trivia, the horizontal counterpart of a telescopy exclusively and unambiguously sold on the ideology of *tēle* ("at distance," in Ancient Greek). No less necessary, it must be treaded carefully, as thinkers from Heidegger to Deleuze and Guattari to Paul Virilio counsel. At the very least, planetary critics, because they are adepts of a "dialectical" telescopy—a telescopy without a teleology, an art of looking without a foregone conclusion—must supplement it with the long-winded detour whose critical microscopy may help us better descry the planet's Face, the roar of the bigger world, in the faces and wrinkles of the apparently isolated, in the cultural grimaces, historical modes, and stylistic mood of unambitious, "cosmically" shy, or politically disenfranchised topographies.

As we have seen, planetarization works through, brings about, and "appears" to us phenomenologically as a transterritorialization—dislocation, reallocation, and novel aggregation—of space and its meanings on earth. Consequently, discrete places overlap, link up, or reterritorialize each other inside one another. What I dub the planetary "primal scene" is, in the writers summoned below from §20 on, a fictional episode typically bringing to life "little places"—neighborhoods, small towns, sport clubs, theater halls, family homes, intimate moments—that "telescope" the wider world. Here, telescoping integrates two spatial-optic and intellectual operations. To my mind, they do not make for a telescopic dilemma (*das Dilemma des Teleskops*), as Neef calls it after Hans Blumenberg,[53] but for a scopic-cognitive unit in the more Deleuzian and Guattarian sense in which "spatial registers" can "switch" so as to perform critically revealing microscopic and telescopic tasks capable of "showing us [both] the molecular and the super-molar," the world's smallness and the world's bigness.[54] One such operation "shrinks down" to size to compress and comprise something much bigger, quantitatively and qualitatively different: the over there, the otherwise, the greater world. The other "brings closer" so as to "develop" in a quasi-photographic sense, to render visible, but also to reach through and, in a way, beyond the visible, to its meaning, and thus to foster a new understanding of place and world alike. As a method, "reading for the planet" consists in retracing this telescoping protocol of writing by unfolding and making legible the world's picture rolled inside the humble pictures and snapshots of humanity, telescoping out and holding up to view the greater universe in its fragment, the planetary curled around or hidden *inside* the *omphalós* of the indigenous, the dialectal, and the place-bound. Thus, not only does this critical itinerary prove analytically safer sometimes—for we risk missing less as we stop by, look out the window, and take our mental pictures—but it also is more emphatically ethical because it encourages us to really "get to know"—to *relate* to—those we meet along the way. To continue in the same Frostian vein, this road can literally make all the difference. Here, the journey pulls the world together and draws out spatially and intellectually the planet's togetherness by zooming in on the different, the off-the-beaten path, the small, and their nuances. The understanding-enabling distance Hannah Arendt talks about in *Reading for the Planet*'s opening epigraph is neither absent nor purely figurative. Its geographical dimension is still in play. But this expanse has been encoded discursively, as the interstice between the work's outer and deeper layers, and then critically, as the scopic-interpretive gap between a first and second glance, between what we have in sight as we turn to look and as our gaze caresses the work's surface, and what comes into clearer focus as we complete our turn and inspect deeper, that is, the kind of planetary picture we might be able come away with as we develop the cultural negative of the novel or painting in question. Distance now is, and in planetary criticism promises to work, also in Arendt's words, as an "inner compass."

The highway, rooftop, the astronaut, the satellite, the GPS, and their maps and vistas are elevated both attitudinally and altitudinally. In their more mechanical applications, they betray a twofold hauteur of standpoint, a perspectival loftiness of geopositioning and topography as well as of judgment. Quite high on their macro agenda is the barely disguised ambition to corral the infinite into various distant readings, measurements, and conjectures. Instead, the back road is, less assumingly, a portal to the infinitesimal. A dromological version of the microscope, this route runs more emphatically—to paraphrase Gregory Bateson—through a geography of the mind, before trekking across the planet's terraqueous body. In other words, it is predicated on a geoaesthetic order, on a homological model of the world and the artwork, in which the Stoic, macro universe of ever-enlarging circles of belonging slide into one another and, together, into the particular, into the "located" work, and into the micro as their generic category.

It is in this sense that the micro telescopes—shrinks down to size to encapsulate—the macro, which makes the opposition far less cut-and-dried. For, in this sense too, the microscope is an epistemological telescope, a *meaning-making machine*. Harnessing its magnifying capabilities, the microscopic reading technique of critical planetoscopy subsequently decompresses meaning, spreads out the world's bigger canvas folded inside the little picture, exposes the whole in the fragment, the planetary curled around or nestling *inside* the *omphalós* of the indigenous, the dialectal, and the place-bound. The idea behind this compression-cum-decompression granulary reading optics so crucial to planetary criticism is not to abolish or transcend distance in order to annex the destination. If, as noted earlier, the classical telescope skips over places to cover (hoping to cancel out) great distances, the microscopic view connects vastly separated cultural dots by affirming and "working through" place after place, beginning with the starting point itself.

In attending to it diligently—in tracking the cultural specimen's Brownian motion closely—the critical microscope pursues the planetary spatialization of the geocultural sample under scrutiny. In so doing, it sets forth the "inherently relational" constitution of that place as intersectional communality or trans-communitarian *locus communis* in which, following in the footsteps of Georges Bataille and Maurice Blanchot, one "inoperative" community theorist after another locates and gives a chance to the world's singularities and to their idioms.[55] Instituted through planetarism's topoludic cartography, inscribed on a mind map still different from the world's, this sociocultural *haecceity* implies a communalist project, a "laboratory of the common" (Negri) and of a commons to come.[56] This is not the locus of an "illusory" or abstract (Augé) being-with, despite the "distancing" spatial games inevitably played in and across it.[57] On *closer* reading—the kind of reading distant interpretation, as remarked earlier, is not incompatible with—this site turns out instead to be a scene of many-sided cultural-historical situatedness, one on which, as the planetary readings proposed later in this part show, people's dreams and "knowledges" are localized because, like all locales, they are planetarily positioned. An aesthetic location where "here" and "ours" are spatialized into "distant kinship" with "there" and "theirs," this individual place or aesthetic venue and its *this-ness* itself are therefore no longer opposed to planetarity but apposite to it, a scaled-down *with-world*.[58] Characteristically, this site cites (telescopes) the planet spatially and intertextually, "sites" (situates) and quotes—with one word, embodies—worldly relationality in ways that may or may not be right away noticeable. Watermarked with the planet's figure, this "sitational" textual-spatial formation lends itself, accordingly, to a reading with this figure, across the panoply of local figurations serving as the figure's cipher and vehicle. This reading is, to invoke Westphal again, a *lecture du monde* in the strong sense of the world as worlded or relational *mundus*, in short, a with-reading poised to face and shed light on the "withness" makeup of this world.[59] To that effect, planetary reading turns to the latter's relational structure—to the planet's "mondiality"—microscopically, screening the micro for signs of the macro.

If the close reading handed down to us by the New Critics all-too-often purports to "resolve" the contradictory by simplifying the complex, planetary close (or micro)reading seeks to complicate the illusorily simple. This kind of interpretation does the planet's bidding epistemologically—and thus instantiates what Axelos pinpointed as the planet's "thought-becoming"—by spotting the worldly multiplicity of place, time, and discourse in the deceptively monistic, the distant relatives, the exogenous, and the incoherent genealogies placed under erasure by institutionalized culture and officially endorsed by the nation-state's endogenous reveries.

As a product *of* this endorsement, culture is a cover-up operation. What does this mean? It means that simulation is hardly the issue here, Jean Baudrillard's variously rehearsed case notwithstanding. To the contrary, dissimulation is the problem. "Streamlined," culture in general and national culture in particular do not so much simulate as they dissimulate, conceal, disregard, or short-shrift the many that have gone into the cobbling together of the one, of the same, of the "we," and ultimately of the nation, complete with its collective mythology, solipsist fantasies, and institutionalized territorialism. Countercultural *because* cross-cultural, reading with the planet is a relational form of analysis that exposes, first, the compilation itself, the outsourcing of nativist allegories, and the heteroclite underbelly of the putatively all-of-a-piece.[60] Second, this is a "proximate reading" eminently keen on the worldliness of the *bricolage*, on the nomadic, peripatetic, and "distant" archive settled "around here," as national literatures.[61] And, third, but in the same vein, reading with the planet shines light on the problematic, historically produced and oftentimes epistemologically counterproductive "state-centrism." According to planet-oriented reading, in aggressively territorializing—in limiting to statal territoriality—the genetic-interpretive play and overall domain of literary-cultural and humanistic discourse, "nation-[state]-based" disciplinarity jars with actual cross-cultural/cross-territorial scenarios through which this discourse comes into being, evolves, spreads, and is mapped by scholars.[62] As Neil Brenner maintains, the epistemological impasse one faces here has to do with a "jealous," culturally "possessive" institution as much as it does with political cartography and space. "The epistemology of state-centrism," Brenner says, can be understood in terms of a number of several "geographical assumptions," including the postulate "that social relations are organized at a national scale or are undergoing a process of nationalization," which, in turn, has "generate[d] a *methodical nationalism* in which the national scale is treated as the ontologically primary locus of social relations."[63] Oddly enough, Brenner does not credit, if not Anthony Giddens and Herminio Martins, then at least Beck. For the German is the sociologist who coined, in 2002, and then repeatedly refined the "methodological nationalism" concept and its critique, "methodological cosmopolitanism."[64] "Methodological nationalism," Beck expounds,

> assumes that the nation, state and society are the "natural" social and political forms of the modern world. It assumes that humanity is naturally divided into a limited number of nations, which on the inside, organize themselves as nation-states, and on the outside, set boundaries to distinguish themselves from other nation-states. It goes even further: this outer delimitation, as well as the competition between nation-states, presents the most fundamental category of political organization. Indeed, the social science stance is rooted in the concept of the nation-state. It is a nation-state outlook on society and politics, law, justice and history, that governs the sociological imagination.[65]

This outlook, Beck concludes, "prevents the social sciences from understanding and analysing the dynamics of the human condition in the twenty-first century."[66] The state may be well and alive rather than a "zombie categor[y]," but the nation-state as a descriptive unit and, organized around it, state-backed epistemology have arguably become overbearing, if not outright terroristic in their territorialism, and increasingly obsolete, as critics such as Paul Giles, Fine, Dimock, Spivak, Robbins, and Emery assert on various occasions.[67] Thus, "that a relevant literary history must challenge the national paradigm is no longer a provocative statement," points out Svend Erik Larsen. "Nevertheless," the Danish critic adds, "this paradigm still plays a dominant role, if not in the explicit theorising about literary historiography then at least in the actual writing of local histories."[68] As the narrator of Hamid's 2013 novel *How to Get Filthy Rich in Rising Asia* comments, the states and their "tireles[s efforts] to determine our orbits" are still "on the cosmic list of things that unite us."[69] But, also notes the narrator, this determination "tugs" at us, and its pulls, yanks, and calls to statal order are getting both overreaching and restrictive epistemologically.[70]

Gauging this undue pressure, planetary-era writers like Hamid, Cărtărescu, O'Neill, W. G. Sebald, Nicolas Bouvier, and Antonio Muñoz Molina discover that "[a]rt cannot be explained"—or comprehensively explained any more—"as a social activity that fulfills the stated goals of a national" or "[economic] agenda" and that "[t]he specific place of art is now increasingly located in networks that are both above and below the reach of the nation-state."[71] These authors do remain visibly, "thematically" weary of the persisting "tugs" of statality, sovereignty, national citizenship, and capital. At the same time, this thematics itself lays open, in their books, shifts away, on one side, from the national and the postcolonial, and, on the other, from the global. A novelist as Pakistani as he is American, Hamid would be here the perfect case study not only for tracking such imaginary reorientations but also for tracing the moves planetary reading would have to make in response: across and past the national territory and allegories that, for many, still designate the foreordained destination of postcolonial analysis; across and beyond the related, ethnicist-racialist allegory embedded in most cultural and comparative studies; and across and against the financial allegory to which mainstream global studies usually comes down one way or another. These moves across nations and discourse formations are not only spatial and semiotic. They are, I must stress, also political. Far from "not reading scale politically," they flaunt a flexible scalarity that affords political reading, namely, the pursuit of power, influence, and authority across their actual, statal *and* worldly encodings and geographies.[72] To be clear, the point of such simultaneously transterritorial and post-allegorical reading is not to brush aside the national, the ethnic, the racial, the global, the economic, and the injustices and conflicts swirling around them, nor to always "rea[d] beyond" ("against," "below," etc.) the nation, the local, or the ethnic, nor to search for "scales of belonging" necessarily or exclusively at variance with these categories' extension within the perimeter of the nation-state.[73] In fact, the point is just the opposite: the point—and my hope in *Reading for the Planet*—is *to see them for what they are and as they operate in today's worlding world, messy as this world is, to rediscover them afresh, in their true, worldly configurations, outside current hermeneutical teleologies and athwart the statal injunctions territorializing and making predictable such critical-theoretical predispositions.* If this world of ours is indeed messy, we can begin to sort it out politically, culturally, and so on by acknowledging how enmeshed in it, how entangled in each other's lives, turfs, and stories, in one another's "terri(s)tories," we all are.

Critical of the sociocultural aggregation model and "homeland security"-style of epistemology hawked by methodological nationalism especially in major moments of crisis (which, of course, is always "national"), epistemological planetarism cuts, therefore, in the literary and in the critical imaginary alike, across traditionally territorialized—territorially bounded or pictured—societies and socioformations such as race, ethnicity, class, and so forth. "[L]iterature" is not just "written as a defense of the dignity of the strange," as Julia Kristeva says.[74] Literature *is* strangeness. It "defamiliarizes" things, as we know too well. But, in order to do so, its making resorts most fundamentally to a prosopopoeial face-making of planetary mapping, to a "displacement"—a *Verschiebung* not very different from Freud's *Verdichtung*—that "moves" the strange, the afar, the "other," and the cosmic to the throbbing heart of culture, rendering the latter's putative egocentric hearth a paradoxically yet genetically necessarily *allocentric* zone.[75] In the process, planetary *poiēsis* denaturalizes the "national" in "national culture" and thereby helps cultural understanding, and ultimately culture itself, shed its national-*étatiste* epistemological straitjacket. Whistleblowers of sorts, planetary critics leak culturally classified information about the recycled material's planetary provenance or, conversely, about the worldly affiliation of presumably discrete traditions and autonomous identities by laying bare the worldly relationality that the fast-expanding planetary imaginary has threaded into descriptions of allegedly self-subsistent singularities.

What these critics promote, then, is a perusal protocol driven by a post-traditional, planetary logic of withnessing according to which cultural space's nationally legislated ("named") *nomos* is remapped heteronomously. In this space or intersection of spaces, this remapping relies on two intertwined critical and geopolitical rearrangements. One concerns classical statal spatiality; the other, the planetary paradigm and the world's Face this model of worldedness helps discern amid the world's faces.

The first permutation impacts the topocultural and political "centers" of world spatiality. Typically imagined as (rather than truly instantiating) an "organic" or "vertical" model of growing, such hubs are not surrounded, at least to the degree they used to be, by peripheries, semi-peripheries, circumferences, borders, and other "quilting points" through which centers link up with other centers of power and administration.[76] The center itself now fully is, as Derrida already theorized it at length in the late 1960s, a collection of quilting points. A "literature for the planet," Dimock similarly insists, is an "off-center set of vibrations, chaotic and tangential."[77] The "crisis of territoriality"[78] is thus not solely one of national frontiers, of "political sovereignty" and self-determination understood primarily as "peripheral" issues (pertaining to boundaries, margins, and so forth), but of centers themselves and of their very systems of centralization and control, of *state cultural apparatuses* and their aggressive *overdetermination* of culture's and cultural identity's meanings.

In its self-perceived, ethno-linguistically, territorially, and institutionally homogenous configuration, the state has set itself up as the post-Westphalian era's default aggregation unit and "scalar variety" of aesthetic production and analysis.[79] This arrogance, complete with the cultural-epistemological servitudes required of those buying into its premises, was already evident to Friedrich Nietzsche. In *Untimely Meditations*, he paints a famously disenchanted yet characteristically prescient picture of Western modernity and its fundamental institutions. "We live," writes the philosopher,

> in the age of atoms, of atomistic chaos. In the Middle Ages the hostile forces were held together by the church and, through the strong pressure it exerted, to some extent assimilated with one another. When the bond broke, the pressure relaxed, [and] they rebelled against one another. The Reformation declared many things to be *adiaphora*, domains where religion was not to hold sway; this was the price at which it purchased its existence: just as Christianity has already had to pay a similar price in face of the much more religiously inclined world of antiquity. From there on the division spread wider and wider. Nowadays the crudest and most evil forces, the egoism of the money-makers and the military despots, hold sway over almost everything on earth. In the hands of these despots and money-makers, the state certainly makes an attempt to organize everything anew out of itself to bind and constrain all those mutually hostile forces: that is to say, it wants men to render it the same idolatry they formerly rendered the church. With what success? We have still to learn; we are, in any case, even now still in the ice-filled

> stream of the Middle-Ages; it has thawed and is rushing on with devastating power. Ice-floe piles on ice-floe, all the banks have been inundated and are in danger of collapse. The revolution is absolutely unavoidable, and it will be the atomistic revolution: but what are the smallest individualistic basic constituents of human society?[80]

The picture is not only bleak but also critical in that it critiques a world picture, a certain cultural, hermeneutic, and geopolitical imaginary. This critique is as relevant today, after Nietzsche's "atomistic revolutions" have broken out and when, in a sense, they are still unfolding, as it was in 1874. Its main relevance is twofold. On one side, it speaks to the systematic efforts by various geoinstitutional apparatuses of modernity to aggregate the human domain into intelligible and manageable structures. The earlier Catholic Church, the Reformed Church after that, what with its partial "withdrawal" from the social, then capital, and, in the late post-Westphalian era—after 1848 rather than immediately after 1648—the nation-state have all scrambled, observes Nietzsche, to "organize" the human. Organize: read territorialize. Read: shape, contain, define, and rule; be recognized and even "worshipped." This territorialization, which some equate with modernity itself, posits a meaning for something—for human spatiality, sociality, and ultimately the human itself. This positing bespeaks the rather intellectually impatient decisional violence of paradigm-setting: this is the model, the paradigm for the human; this is what human society and the human mean.

On the other side, what humankind, the social, and the cultural signify—*what* they are—is a function of *where* they are. Here, territorialization gets quite literal. That is to say, ontology becomes topology and interpretation a geopositioning protocol, in a literal-statal sort of way that, we shall notice below, planetary criticism sets out to break wide open. Thus, the positing of meaning goes hand in hand with position, with the human's place, which is also paradigmatic; linguistically, ethnically, economically, politically, or culturally, the human is locational, assumed to play out *within* various "units." It is inside them, we are told, that the human makes sense, can be researched and described—inside them, or, more accurately, inside it, the nation-state geoapparatus of discourse-making and discourse-processing. For, in modern history overall and surely in Nietzsche's time, the latest and by far most enduring installment in this hegemonic narrative of political, cultural, and epistemological scalarity has been the nation-state. It is through the statal that the human, in its cultural expression, and the human world become intelligible to humanists for almost two hundred years. In fact, one founding assumption of modern Western humanism ever since the nationalist *trahison de clercs* exposed by Julien Benda is that one sees culture, and, with it, humankind and the world, through the nation-state—that the intelligibility model of the world is self-evidently and unassailably statal.[81] To go back to Nietzsche's liquid metaphor, culture is presumed to flow "paradigmatically"—and thus to be inevitably streamlined—within the "banks" of the nation-state, to be contained by it, so much so that it cannot but "internalize" the container, take it in and also take it up as its content.

Of course, modern culture has greatly overflown its statal-territorialist riverbanks worldwide. Furthermore, as Adrian Florea notes, new data shows that "nonstate territorial units" are more numerous than "sovereign states with often disputed, but fairly stable, borders." Under these circumstances, the "anachronistic view" of political or cultural authority "being monopolized by clearly demarcated states that exercise full control over their territory" has become a true "stumbling block" in political science as well as in cultural analysis and other humanities in which epistemological mapping of human expression is still dependent on traditional, state-centered world cartographies.[82] As with the post-Reformation Church, whatever spills over, whatever flows or falls outside statal jurisdiction, risks being ignored or downgraded culturally, that is, treated as less typical, less representative, with paradigmatic condescendence, if you will. To be representative, and therefore canonical, is to be representative *of* certain aggregation units privileged by modernity, of the nation-state first and foremost, and of classical identity formations such as race, ethnicity, and linguistic indigeneity, which have been usually associated with and situated within the master communal framework of the nation-state. What is not "representative" along these lines—the less "paradigmatic" phenomena—tends to register less on our radar screens: in our anthologies, in our sense of history, tradition, community, group membership, and the like. However, planetarity is forcing us to reconsider the "one-on-one correspondence between the geographic and ethno-linguistic origins of a text and its evolving radius of literary action." "We need," Dimock further argues, "to stop thinking of national literatures as the linguistic equivalents of territorial maps. . . . [H]andily outliv[ing] the finite scope of the nation, [literature] brings into play a different set of temporal and spatial coordinates. It urges on us the entire planet as a unit of analysis."[83]

The second geopolitical and geocultural rearrangement speaks to the paradigmatic energy of telescoping operations. The "quilting-point," allocentric model of centers and centered cultural spaces does not simply "open up" the local to the global, thereby "resolving," in its "glocalizing" fervor, the local-global (or national-global) aporia, as many critics purport to do by following Robertson's lead.[84] No "glocal" synthesis gels here. Nor should it, because it would still be a recipe for globalist homogeneity and for its implicit universalism, which both Robertson's and Beck's theoretical blueprints feature, another sign that Robertson's "middle position"—"methodological glocalism" as a correction of methodological localism or nationalism—is not entirely different from methodological cosmopolitanism.[85] What takes hold instead, with a spatial and material force and concreteness neither methodology handles effectively, is a telescopy of the worlding world curled up inside the local, within which "here" and "there," the face and Face, remain distinct and yet intimately co-present, *with* one another. Detached from themselves in order to reattach themselves to others according to novel, posttraditional and "postethnic" attachments, allegiances, and affiliations, they *are* thus a discontinuity, a self-displaced continuum that exists in an "interface" mode that neither obscures the other's face nor obviates the need, indeed, the duty to look into it.[86] Thus reterritorialized as "nested territorial units"[87] of space, culture, and subjectivity—all of them qualified in terms of gender, sexuality, race, ethnicity, class, and faith and, reciprocally, serving themselves as qualifiers of such identitarian parameters—cultural territory calls for a new, planetary cultural studies paradigm attuned to the mutual articulations and imbrications of the world's Face and face, of the tiny writ large in the planetary and of the planetary writ small in the tiny. For, as we shall see at great length in this part's next half, this is what planetarism's literary geo-graphy writes out, oftentimes against internationally recognized mental and territorial delineations of statehood, national borders, and statal sovereignty: a Face made up of the world's mosaic of many faces. Vice versa, the planet lies "condensed," "folded," "curled up," or "nested" inside the anonymous and the isolated. The swelling whole is "compacted," then taken apart, looked into, and put back together in its parts, fragments, and subsets; at the same time, each face's makeup is a planetary prosopopoeia, makes out the Face, paints *and* showcases its interfacial structure. The idiographic, then, does not redramatize the global *nomos* but reveals, under the magnifying glass of planetary critical autopsy—etymologically, "eye-witnessing"—a unique, asymmetrical, and yet powerful formulation of planetary withness, the worldly anatomy of elsewheres, multitudes, habits, and ways. The idiomatic here and there, the "world in a nutshell," is, in reality, a culturally and historically *trivial* site—from the Latin *trivium*, "intersection of three roads" and more generally "crossroads"—a "pointillist" point in space and time where the world's other ways, routes, places, and histories cross, and so concurrently a cross-section of everything meeting, touching, classifying, mixing, and passing in and through it.

So different from the rhetoric of global geometry, all these topological metaphors have been cropping up in twenty-first-century exchanges in the humanities, attesting to critics' growing and akin interests in a fractal notion of discourse, in issues of maps, scale, and aggregation unit, and in a *histoire croisée* model of cultural history. The planetary protocol of critical telescopy employed in part 2, II both incorporates and recalibrates four components of this fractal-intersectional "outlook" on literature and literary epistemology as follows:[88]

i. This analytic procedure retains, first, the post-global, post-Euclidian, Benoît Mandelbrot–inspired fractal model with a greater emphasis on the irregularity among fragments and between fragment and whole, which arrangement or mapping is, as Dimock comments, "what gets lost in a big picture."[89] In this light, planetarism—a picture of the bigger world—is anything but a "big picture" volume-wise. It captures a sociocultural phenomenology of fractality in which the trivial face or the fine print of the "minuscule" joins and documents the world's majuscules of the planetary large-print and thus a world, "endless," nonkind type of "kinship" that is, as Dimock allows, neither truly genetic nor, as I would stress, formally mimetic if by this we mean intentionally (and submissively) reproductive of the planetary ensemble. "The infinite," the critic explains, "is embedded in the [finite], coiled in the former, and can be released only when the former is broken down into fractional units. For it is only when the scale is smaller and the details get finer that previously hidden dimensions can come swirling out." "Scalar opposites," Dimock concludes, "here generate a dialectic that makes the global an effect of the grainy."[90] This dialectic, I hasten to remark, is what no longer makes the "grainy," the trivial face, and the micro a docile repository and mimesis of the global but the fine print in which the inscriptions and prescriptions of globality are unwritten and reinscribed planetarily. Either "over here" or "over there," the *planet*'s own footprint on "local" representations—the flipside of our ecological marks on the planet itself—becomes visible and thus lends itself to reading in those representations' fine print. Usually crystallizing at a deep level, that fine print is couched in the elusive language (allusions, connections, references, parallels, borrowings, puns and cognate playful associations) where the *relation with the geocultural other*—other texts, histories, places, and people—turns out to be so instrumental to the meaning-making process at the writer's as well as the critic's end.

ii. The second component of critical telescopy is comparative. If Moretti's "distant reading" is not quite fit, as Dimock suggests, for the crucial and urgent task of attending to planetary culture's fine print, fractal analysis is, with the proviso that my concern, also comparative in nature, is less morphological (a matter of planetary form) and more thematic-imaginary (a matter of the planetary imagination).[91] Otherwise, planetary reading is a comparative effort. What makes this endeavor comparative is, for one thing, the very makeup of the planetary ensemble. If comparison involves, according to the Latin *comparō*, "placing" the world's things "together," then comparatism is homologous to the worlding world itself, to the juxtapositions (*comparationes*) the world's coming together sets off. Planetary critics realize, maybe more than others, that we are living in an increasingly "comparative" or "(con-)pairing" world that demands an apposite, comparative reading. For another thing, a "comparative" ontology is not one in which things run or flow on or within separate tracks or "riverbeds." As I insist ever so often, the tracks, the "routes," are rerouted across other tracks and itineraries of commerce, exchange, influence, and derivation. All these weave a world circuitry of cultural debt. The "comparative," worlding world is, then, fundamentally subtended and ethically marked by a credit-debit nexus. The world *qua* planet is an *expanding geodomain of reciprocal indebtedness*. It goes without saying—or perhaps it needs to be said, given the growing turbulence in global finance—I am not talking about debt as a U.S. Department of Commerce official, a CEO, or an accountant might. My concern is planetary culture and planetarily minded cultural analysis, which, in this vein, is an account of the indebtedness that goes into the ecumenical manufacturing of originality. Along these lines, planetary theory and the studies built on it make for a major, quintessentially comparative subset of cultural theory and of the cultural studies swirling around it. What planetarity criticism attempts or should attempt, against the centuries-old *doxa* of morally "toxic" debt, is a revaluation of indebtedness, a reaccreditation of the discredited notions of credit and debt. I would contend, in effect, that rethinking these categories from a cultural standpoint is something of an urgency in the twenty-first-century world. Paraphrasing, apropos of this ethical, aesthetic, and epistemological reassessment, Gordon Gekko's infamous "greed is good" line (*Wall Street*), the planetary critic entertains the notion that debt, in an important sense, is hardly a sin. In fact, debt *is* good. Debt is *better*, actually, because, especially in a planetary context, it is foundational to doing good, designating the premise of ethics and moral conduct rather than their breach. Moreover, debt, that thing that we lack and need, that absence (*béance* in Jacques Lacan), has constitutive force. What we call "subject formation"—and certainly what we might some day call planetary subject formation—is nothing less that going into debt, to others, to the other than "self" and "here." Being is thus being indebted, for we would not be, particularly in our time, if it were not for that originating—and originality-spawning—deficit. This shortage, the stuff we do not have or are short of, is ontological. More accurately, it has ontological *potential*: we can be or become, make the "most of ourselves" if we live up to it. Otherwise, as Levinas says, its nature is ethical.[85] What that absence carves out inside ourselves is a space of otherness, and this has crucial implications: the debt accrues a duty, a responsibility in and to the world. In this light, it is important to realize—in the planetary age more than ever before—that this debt is originary rather than supplemental to being. Planetarily speaking, we do live on borrowed time *ab origine*. We do not incur debt after we have somehow made and spent our fortune or have blown our "inheritance." It is already there. *It* (*they*) must be in there before *we* set about being and expressing ourselves. Our "credentials" are predicated on this credit. In the planetary era, we "rise up" to our potential from the fertile abyss of alterity. This debt is a precondition to being human and to all that human beings can be. Giorgio Agamben says as much in *The Coming Community*. "The being most proper to humankind," he glosses, "is being one's own possibility or potentiality."[93] Our full humanity is something we achieve, something to come and to strive for. Being, at its fullest and "most proper," Agamben also notes, implies not being-there, a being "devoid of foundation."[94] But this missing foundation is, once more, foundational, for we embark on the human adventure, we enact our humanness, if you will, without being "in possession" of that ground.[95] And so, the Italian philosopher argues, "humans have and feel a debt," leading their lives by taking out an ontological loan without collateral.

"Humans, in their potentiality to be and to not-be, are, in other words," he concludes, "always already in debt; they always already have a bad conscience without having to commit any blameworthy act." Agamben's take on "the doctrine of original sin" pertains to theology as much as to ontology, ethics, and even to literature and its history.[96] In speaking, reading, and writing, in cultural practice generally, debt brings into play issues as linguistic and textual as ethical and political, an indebtedness—hence an accountability—beyond accounting, a debt-derived duty larger than words, figures, balances, and accounts. Granted, it is a different kind of incommensurable debt that, in his 1996 article "*Dette mondiale et univers parallèle*" (Global debt and parallel universe), Baudrillard zeroes in on to pinpoint a major challenge of contemporary economics: the financial sublime of the global age. This is world debt that further globalizes the world, for better or worse and everything in between. Incrementally shared one way or the other by the planet's population—although by some of us more than others—this debt is practically infinite because impossible to pay off while still mounting ad infinitum, "beyond counting," *au-delà de toute comptabilité*—beyond measuring and representation and without correspondence in reality, in "available capital." This is why, Baudrillard contends, it is financially meaningless. Its only value is symbolic because this debt speaks to a "symbolic credit system whereby people, corporations, nations are attached to one another by default."[97] But the symbolic value of globalized and globalizing debt, I would reply, is not immaterial or meaningless. It was not in 1996, and definitely it is not today, even though the discrediting narrative has since then somewhat changed. World insolvency points, in an admittedly twisted way, to the very meaning of symbolic values in general at the dawn of the new millennium, to the concrete "attachments," barterings, and exchanges underlying them, in brief, to the global formation and reach of a cultural capital that grows as it finances—funds and founds, credits and authorizes—rationales, tropes, stances, trends, and values transnationally, around the world and across traditional lines of indebtedness, influence, taxation, and jurisdiction. Non-referential as it may be, unevenly distributed as it certainly is, global monetary debt nonetheless supplies a serviceable model for coming to terms with the worldwide circulation of symbolic capital and the swelling planetary indebtedness derived from it. The indebtedness planetary analysis—or comparative analysis with a planetary bent—dwells on, *cultural indebtedness*, is neither "sinful" nor virtual. Setting aside for now the history of financial credit, the banking and political practices behind debt, how badly it sometimes hurts us, and how bad we feel about it, one must come to terms with its reality, namely, with what it does to us all: its "credit lines" tie us together in real or quasi-real time and space; it "worlds" us, sets us side by side, "pairs" us up, "com-pares" us as we are credited so that, in turn, we can also "compare" the world, *acquire* it (another meaning of *comparō*), get a purchase on it aesthetically, as representation. Most notably, in this material landscape the formation of cultural interconnectedness expands and becomes more and more visible. Here money, a signifier of value, is isomorphic to a worthier axiology, and accordingly, here too debt is the other name of all-pervasive influence and the cultural *métissage* coming on its heels. Here, self and other farm their discourse out to one another frenetically, so we are all becoming more indebted to others elsewhere than we have ever been. These others and their locations hold liens on our times and spaces, on what we do and say in them, on *our* discourse. And vice versa: we ourselves are jump-off points, investments, "seed money" for cultural ventures thus inevitably joint, coming to fruition somewhere else. This applies to individual authors as much as to communities and traditions now more than at any other point in history. In the compressed space and time of interweaving world cultures, authority is increasingly on loan, authenticity and originality intertextual affairs, and "individual talent" and "personal tone" often echoes from afar, ventriloquisms.

This is not an unprecedented paradox. The phenomenon does not pertain solely to the worlding world of planetarity either. It is in this world, though, that relatedness and, stemming from it, mix, "impurity," and the allogeneic have become staples of life around the world. The planet's cultural credit/debit arena is giving birth to a new, physical and non-physical (at-distance) proximity, to a culturally woven immediacy with "my" culture and "yours" intermingling and fostering new assemblages. It is within this exchange horizon that what I have called the offshoring of identity takes place, and it is within this world arena that planetary studies stakes out its territory.[98] Whatever I am or become comes about under the impact of remote, heterogeneous sources, places, and styles. The familiar is less and less a function of the familial. More and more *afforded* by the alien, it does not exclude—to the contrary, it entails—a remote sort of kinship. As a result, the economy of my being is hardly self-sufficient, depending as it does on others for "loans" and "parts"—myths, fantasies, stories, symbolic structures, and the like. Leaving behind a separatedness-based model shaped by the center/margin, "in here"/"out there," our culture/theirs, and other similar *disjunctions* typical of coloniality, postcoloniality, and the earlier stage of multicultural awareness, this economy is moving toward a *conjunctive* or *relational* model informed by cross-cultural, cross-geographical, indeed, world-scale contacts, juxtapositions, borrowings, and barterings. What this new, cross-territorial, cross-cultural, and cross-linguistic scalarity helps visualize cartographically and appreciate critically is how much culture—any culture—has borrowed from world cultures and, accordingly, how much of the nations' cultural fabric consists, as I have explained, of "credit lines," threads, strains, stanzas, quotes, and other similar investments from elsewhere.[99] It is therefore our job as planetary critics to take comparative literature into the planetary era and read, accordingly, between and across these lines so as to assess both the investments and their returns.

Thus, far from sounding the death knell of a "discipline" (Spivak's comparative studies), planetarity and its paradigm actually mark its rebirth: of the field and perhaps, around it, of the "ruined" university itself, which is, or should be, beholden to its statal sponsor and epistemological handler no longer.[100] For, to unpack a text's planetarity is to read that novel or novella as a bundle of relations in the sense previously defined, and unraveling this entangled relationality comes down to a comparative undertaking. Further, this comparatism ought to agree to revisit its own classifications, epistemological habits, and intellectual maps—to face the incomparable, the immeasurable, the asymmetrical, the non-repetitive, and other forms of a-serial representation, rough discursive conglomerates, and narratives less accommodated by the territorialist metanarrative of the nation-state. What the "asymmetrical" model of comparison/interpretation allows is, to recall Clifford Geertz, a "thick description" or critical telescoping of planetarity that, in integrating macro- and microanalysis, enables a reading of the larger world *en filigrane* ("in filigree"), as the French might say, that is, in the arabesque-like fabric of "idiomatic" textuality. Comparatists if not by trade then by necessity, planetary critics must look for the planetary quasi-*totum in parte*, contemplate the fragile, ever-self-reconstituting face of the "all" *in filigree*, in that which seems to be facing no one else but itself. Does this mean that, in reading the "grainy," they indulge too much in a reading against the grain, against how local and bounded the local and bounded seem to be and seem to tell us that they want to be seen? Not quite. In practice, their reading is also one *with* the grain. This reading often fleshes out the insights of worldedness turning up in U.S. and other literatures with symptomatically increased frequency since the late 1980s.

iii. The third element or maneuver of planetary telescopy highlights the codependence of the microscopic and the macroscopic. In accommodating "multiple scales"[101] and interpretive contexts spatially and temporally[102]—rather than forcing the comparatist to choose one over another, on the "internationalist" assumption that "[t]oday . . . the planetary scale trumps the smaller, national scale"[103]—fractal world maps "reorient us towards an axis of scale that runs from the microcosm to the microcosm."[104] But because the latter is *not* an independent, a priori "totality" socially (nationally) or internationally, as some think,[105] this reorientation also prompts a recursive feedback loop, a mutually illuminating ("cognitive") and transformative back and forth between micro and macro, a successive chain of reciprocal remappings. What these are likely to uncover is the singular as a cross of singularities, a particular world as an encoding site and passageway for other worlds, world channels, paths, and cultural codes.

iv. The fourth and last telescopic procedure is germane to *histoire croisée*. While unconvincing in its anti-comparatist bias—which seems so counterintuitive, given the objectives of "intersectional" historiography—this historical mode of inquiry is well equipped to assist the planetary critic. Not unlike "new cosmopolitanism" in sociology,[106] this (neo)neo-historicism is a brainchild of the post-1989 cross-disciplinary paradigmatic revisionism. Accordingly, it deploys a methodological apparatus also self-described as "relational" and transnational, one functioning by virtue of a cross-historical worlding mechanics in which the resulting world, society, or time period is entwined with other worlds, societies, moments, discourses, and categories, and therefore pluriscalar, a multiple cross in terms of structure, location, and genetics. Most importantly, the *histoire croisée* approach treats the cultural-engendering "intercrossings" as "intrinsic" to the object of study, with historical microscopy unearthing, in an "inextricable connectio[n]" with the macro and with its macroscopy, previously unnoticed, distorted, rationalized, played down, or censored macrorealities.[107] As we shall discover in the last sections of this part, post–Cold War narratives stage a world so deeply akin to the *croisé* sociohistorical model that geomethodology cannot afford to ignore what this new trend in historiography has to offer. Insistently refocusing the gaze on the planetary "all" and on its histories and places crisscrossing inside the apparently second-fiddle, cloistral, ingrown, and otherwise "unworldly," some of the most emblematic fictions of our time can be read as geomethodological blueprints.

II

§21. Cosmology and Cosm*all*ogy

> Yet what is any ocean but a multitude of drops?
> —DAVID MITCHELL, *Cloud Atlas*

> This nobody contains multitudes.
> —JAHAN RAMAZANI, "Poetry, Modernity, and Globalization"

Mircea Cărtărescu's *oeuvre* is a case in point. If Hungarian author George Konrád confesses in his 1984 book *Antipolitics* that "[t]he world is one; and it is more interesting than Budapest,"[109] the Romanian writer feels, around the same time and a few hundred miles east of Konrád's Budapest, the pull of planetarity *in situ*: not only does the planet exist, but it can be *lived out* locally, in and *as* his hometown. "I truly love my world, the world of Bucharest," he declares elsewhere, "yet I am fully aware that Bucharest is concomitantly *all*, the Aleph."[109] To get a grip on the Borgesian allusion, it is important to remember that, at the time, the Communist rulers were seeking to expunge Romania's capital from the world's cultural and political script and turn it, along with the rest of the country, into what the dissidents were calling "internal exile." Pushing back against this agenda, the "cultural resistance" movement (*rezistența prin cultură*) of the Romanian 1980s marked one of the most cosmopolitan periods in East European history.

In the vanguard of this battle, Cărtărescu fights off the twin incarceration of his beloved city and of himself in it by opening it out onto what his 1985 poetry volume calls the "All" (*Totul*).[110] Drawing from this and other earlier works, his 1993 novel *Nostalgia* sketches an astounding vision of planetarity.[111] Forlorn and dilapidated, plagued by shortages and blackouts, late Cold War Bucharest is, literally and allegorically, worlded, written by the book back into the wider world and thereby made "interesting," into a site of and argument for worldly belonging. The city may be "airtight" in the regime's paranoid delusions of "territorial sovereignty," as Dimock notes apropos of Osip Mandelstam's Soviet Union, but, in Cărtărescu's worlded imaginary, it reclaims its seat in the bigger world.[112] To turn one of the cynical ruminations of Jamaica Kincaid's narrator in *A Small Place* on its head, Bucharest and its people, "small" as their city may be, "ca[n]" and do "see themselves in a larger picture, . . . see that they might be part of a chain of something."[113] They are, we gather, part and parcel of this world; they live in its nurturing embrace, although not out in the open, for politics and policies of cultural lockdown have all but deterritorialized the greater outside—or, more exactly, have *under*territorialized it. But, from beneath the defaced surface of Nicolae Ceaușescu's "golden-age" Bucharest, the writer summons strange faces and the very face of worldly strangeness: the Face—the face of the planet—the figure of that hesitant, incoherent and raucous, totality-shy and yet appealing cosmos further and unduly fractured by the country's heavily militarized borders and more generally by the disjunctive geopolitics of the Cold War. From within the maze of concrete housing projects, the author conjures up cosmic panoramas by bridging physical and metaphysical gaps. In dialogue with E. T. A. Hoffmann, Franz Kafka, Gabriel García Márquez, Borges, Pynchon, and other modern and postmodern masters of the fantastic, the absurd, and magical realism, Cărtărescu unearths a maimed metropolis whose heart throbs in the world's wider body and whose idiosyncratic mix of squalor and "Paris of the Balkans" charm he flips over to display unsuspected depths and gateways into the hidden, the elsewhere, and the otherwise—into the world's larger assemblage. Where the Western mind-set relegates his city to an alien geography overrun by strays and ruled by vampiric dictators razing entire neighborhoods to make room for their sepulchral headquarters, Cărtărescu unfolds a borderless dreamland.

The oneiric politics of *Nostalgia*'s urban imaginary was lost on Cărtărescu's readers neither when the book first came out in spring 1989, under the title *Visul* (The Dream) and butchered by censorship, nor a few years later, when it was reissued in unabridged form. Its staggeringly world-relational toposophy went head-on against officially upheld "tradition," an exceptionalist-solipsistic notion redolent of early twentieth-century, agrarian-Orthodox and nationalist-chauvinist doctrines, on which the Communist Party was falling back in the late 1980s to ward off perestroika. The novel symbolically liberates the city's bodies and body politic by linking them, à la Pynchon, Hamid, and Ian McEwan, with other urban bodies and bodies of work, with bigger and better-networked places and with geopolitical events, with older and vaster *topoi*, styles, texts, and contexts. An *other* to the city and its institutionally sanctioned corporeality thus coalesces beyond the closed-off self, community, and place, an other into whose capaciously agglutinating texture *Nostalgia*'s main first-person narrator weaves himself and his kin.

The weaving spider is, in fact, Cărtărescu's signature *mise en abyme*. A motif *in* the story, it also designates, metafictionally, the novel's multiply intertextual fabric and, inside it, the web of Kabbalah-like copulas between stages and layers of existence where the individual brain is plugged into other brains and their projections of other worlds and the worlds behind those, *ad infinitum*. As in one of the novel's sections, the narrating writer-in-the-novel plays the spider sliding up and down the threads of various plot lines. He gets in and out of his dramatis personae's minds, transforming into his characters while telling us about their own changes into others. At the same time, he shows how the phylogeny of these metamorphoses (another Cărtărescu trademark) rehearses cosmic ontogeny by recapitulating a whole cosmology—an entire cosm*all*ogy. Indeed, what he ultimately puts up is a spectacle of the planetary All and of those without whom this provisional, non-totalistic whole's wholeness would fall short, a performance of self and—and as necessarily *with*—others (*álloi* in Ancient Greek).[114]

People's bodies; Bucharest's crumbling body; the nation's hyperterritorialized bulk; and the world's geocultural corpus: these are *Nostalgia*'s concentric circles, its network-mundus or pre-Internet version of the netospherical. Whatever takes place in this planetary web must take place first topologically and, we will learn before long, ethically, to wit, must take *its* place from another place and place-giver "not here." For, explains Agamben, no matter where it happens, what ontological seat in the planetary amphitheater gets assigned to it, this place-taking occurs as one "eases" into a place, into a residential "easement" that is both one's own lawfully and "always-already" an adjacency *within* the private property in which the proprietorial and the exclusive are consequently premised on an other's presence, on the shared, and the right-of-way. Owners and the finite space where their ownership is exercised are predicated, as Levinas, Derrida, and other thinkers press home ever so often, on hospitality (*hostipitalité*, writes Derrida), its guests (others), and the luminous infinity bathing the face-to-face of hosting. Innately *ek-static*, beings thus depend on—they rest on and have "always-already" internalized—a literally vital exterior. Their realm *and* modality are a horizontally as well as vertically spatialized relation. A priori adjacent, traversed by visible and invisible "easements," here-ness only apparently takes hold just "here," on one level of existence.[115] What occurs on one level unfolds or can unfold Kabbalistically on the rest as a drama of planetary All-ness, of quasi-mystical partaking of the planet's All. Everything—this very All—is a matter of multiple, overlapping scales, scopes, and perspectives. Matter itself is no exception because what defines it is extension and "situation" in a space where all locations communicate and so make up a continuum. How and what things are hinges, as noted earlier, on where they are, but they can mutate abruptly because their places are (or are not) theirs insofar as these are spliced together or border on other places across, near, inside, beneath, or above them.

Ontology *is* topology, then; position, an inherently relational spatial coordinate, ultimately turns into an ontological category while ontology too becomes, as Soja would say, spatialized.[116] Therefore, one can shuttle back and forth between different levels of life. One can "overcome" ontological difference, run the whole gamut of being and thus be in "other" ways and worlds topologically: here, one changes by simply changing one's place, status, or classification. By the same token, this ontology is political. *Nostalgia*'s planetary imagination marshals beings polemically by reshuffling the segregationist-autonomist biogeography of Cold War Romania along the lines of flight of a two-pronged onto-spatial rhetoric. On one side, this rhetoric is metonymic. It sets people and objects next to people and objects in whose vicinity they have neither been nor are supposed to be. On the other side, it is synecdochic. Treating individuals and locales as headings of greater units stretching above and athwart the Party-State's immediate, totalitarian totality and ossified taxonomies, this *pars pro toto* planetary figuration only reformulates, from the vantage point of the part, the *totum in parte* of fractal reading. Thus, either way, Cărtărescu's characters act out a drama of being—they *are*—as they are in relation to others, thence determined, at the same time bounded and freed by the proximity to others and their modes of being in culture and history. Propinquity, the terminus that both limits and assigns the self a contiguous meaning, also liberates it, brings it forth and across.

Political through and through, topological and cultural relatedness is thus *Nostalgia*'s *modus essendi*. Bucharest's "little context'" reflects the shape of bigger places and units or feeds into them without warning. The micro and macro worlds are similarly built but neither repetitious of nor opposed to each other. In broader bodies, venues, and sequences, the self does not run into versions of itself but into others. An ontological alloy—made of *álloi*—the planetary All's structure is not a global cosmology but non-*allergic*, cosm*allo*gical. This constitution features others and calls upon the self to acknowledge them both outside and inside itself. Further, if the planetary All is the Alpha and Omega of "little" existential forms, and, further, if these forms mirror the whole's own form, then they are its microcosm; further still, because the levels of this ontology interface and overlap, the microcosm is not only formally unique, but, in its very uniqueness, it is also isoform and juxtaposed to the macrocosm, and a portal to it too, an *Aleph*.

§22. "Mondializing" the City: Blueprints and Constellations

> [T]he inextinguishable longing for elsewheres.
>
> —JUNOT DÍAZ, *The Brief Wondrous Life of Oscar Wao*

In calling the small, the finite, the shut-in, the incarcerated, the city and its bodies Alephs, the Romanian writer also calls out to Borges, interpellates and interpolates his "Aleph."[117] Another homology comes into play here via the Argentine author's planetarily holistic ("*All*istic") model of intertextuality: the Babel Library. In it, literature and place are limitless in number, extent, form, and content, and so they also are coextensive, one. Therefore, the universal library and the universe overlap. In "The Library of Babel," "The Book of Sand," "The Total Library," and other Borgesian *ficciones*, the library, the book, and the textual show off the universe qualitatively, best illustrate its fabric, its "textile" makeup. Conversely, they also hint that, if the cosmos is like a book, all books are infinite. That means that every book holds the rest of the holdings, is an Aleph, "one of the points in space that contains all points."[118] What de-fines "bookness" is in-finitude as well as inter-textuality, cosmic boundlessness and/inside boundedness. Underlying the latter is, fundamentally, otherness, the others and their books' presence in a particular book. This book, which *Nostalgia* emulates, does not only "put up" with a "parasitic" other to it within itself; the book simply cannot have a self, an identity, cannot be "original," in short, cannot be what it is without that "alien" presence inside it, without having its roots, its origin, somewhere else, in another text. It follows that the Aleph is not just unlimited and intertextual—and intertextual because unlimited, transgressive, liable to cross over to the other side time and time again—but also "alterial," a repository of alterity. It is being that *is* while also being what it is not, its other, much like the Aleph includes its "counterpart," the Zahir, and everything else between the A (Alpha) and Z (Omega) of existential, cultural, and political "alternatives."[119]

Borges's "Aleph" is not only the novel's primary intertextual ingredient but also the Kabbalistic-cosmological trope and cultural stratagem through which Cărtărescu reveals his cosmology as planetary cosm*allogy* and Bucharest as an Aleph, a site of astonishing otherness and size locked *inside* the nation-state's paranoically policed borders.[120] A carceral space, the Romanian capital is also "*une ville devenue monde*,"[121] a city made into world—"mondialized"—by the writer's planetary imaginary. Describing Los Angeles as the "epitomizing world-city" and utmost sample of postmodern urban geography, Soja notices that the metropolis is a cosmopolis because it "reproduc[es] *in situ* the customary colours and confrontations of a hundred different homelands." A microcosm of the illimitable and itself without limit, bursting with "fulsome" heterogeneity, Soja's L.A. is, in his own formulation, a Borgesian "LA-leph," at once "everywhere" and "the only place on earth where all places are." And they are there because, as the critic implies apropos, again, of Borges, the Aleph is a "radical[ly] open," "all-inclusive simultaneity" sheltering a whole panoply of otherness.[122] This makes the Californian Aleph so mind-bogglingly "global" that it preempts critical survey.[123] Instead, Cărtărescu's Aleph stimulates and entices, leading on and out of the all-too-limited. Not the Balkans' Paris any more, Bucharest has yet to become their L.A. The stakes of its planetary projections are different. If in Pynchon's *The Crying of Lot 49* Oedipa Maas follows real roads, signs, and maps to famously "project a world,"[124] in Cărtărescu the geoimaginary blueprint of Bucharest is jarringly at odds with the plans drawn by the city officials. De facto, the latter's cognitive world maps do not include the real Bucharest, and, truth be told, there are plenty of reasons to doubt both the cognitive and the worldly pertinence of those maps, if such maps exist at all to begin with. Not so in *Nostalgia*'s camera obscura. Here, a world picture slowly forms, one in which Bucharest registers.

More memorable still is the other image, which the writer develops "microscopically" from the city's negative: the planet's profile, the Face across and amid the faces, facets, and petals on Bucharest's wet, black bough. Make no mistake: this is not just the by now banal view from above; neither is it the "view from nowhere," as critics of "universalist" cosmopolitanism might quip. A view from within, inside, or underneath a temporally and spatially anchored locale, this is a "consideration" of place that takes in and honors this place as "situated" or *placed planetarity*, an effort to account for the world relationality intrinsic to place and subsequently to do away with the pseudo-disjunctions of place and planet, micro and macro, and so forth. For, as Tariq Jazeel echoes D. Massey, "[p]lace is not opposed to the planet. It is instead," the critic underscores, "an ongoing assemblage, constellation, and agonistic coming together of narratives and trajectories that are in themselves insufficiently conceptualized as either local or global." Thus, "[t]he spatialization of place, in this sense, provides the sphere of the possibility of existence of multiplicity. . . . The negotiation of difference in place is always a process of, and invitation to, reconstellate the 'we,' and place's geographical challenge thought this way is precisely that it is never closeable."[125]

To "reconstellate" this "we"—the spatialized communality of the polis—the planetary critic must look not only around and over the nation-state's fences, horizontally, but also over the horizon, up, where the constellations turn and where the earth itself turns into Earth by trading its topographical surfaciality for geopolitical voluminosity and its semiotic luminosity. A triangulation of place *in the micro mode* susceptible to withstanding parochial and clannish attempts at cordoning off cultural domains, the critical maneuver likely to redraw, à la Hollinger, the Theophrastian circle of "we"[126] for the twenty-first century actually depends on macro ("Apollonian") vistas and their "mondial" mental pictures. To be more exact, this dependence is an interdependence. For the macro itself collapses, Aleph-like, into the micro, but, upon geomethodological "decompression," it becomes readable in the cultural small print as much as the Stoics' innermost circles (selfhood and family) present themselves as ripple or butterfly effect—outer circles—of far-off and incongruous, themselves eccentric "we"-constellations.

§23. The Origami Face

> And if conscience became prescience, reflecting itself in itself, it would then become omniscience, rising above this telescoping memory to see the center of the rose with infinite petals, to see the enchanting spider that weaves illusion, modeling it quickly into universe, spaces and times, bodies and faces, with its infinite, articulating legs.
>
> —MIRCEA CĂRTĂRESCU, *Blinding: The Left Wing*

> Europe [i]s [s]haped like [m]y [b]rain[.]
>
> —MIRCEA CĂRTĂRESCU, *Pururi tînăr, înfăşurat în pixeli*

The thematization of the dialectic of micro and macro world pictures becomes more transparently political in Cărtărescu's later work, especially in

Orbitor (Blinding), a three-part narrative tour de force. Available in several languages and pivotal to an extensive *oeuvre* accumulated over more than thirty years, *Blinding* is one reason Cărtărescu has garnered coveted literary awards and most flattering accolades all over Europe and his name keeps coming up, year after year, among those with a shot at the Nobel Prize in literature. The 1,400-page meganovel took him more than a decade to complete. The first installment, *The Left Wing* (*Aripa stîngă*), was published in 1996 and was followed by a second volume, *The Body* (*Corpul*), in 2002, with the final one, *The Right Wing* (*Aripa dreaptă*), coming out in 2007.

The recently released English translation of *The Left Wing* has all the makings of a world literary event.[127] As I reminded the reader under §14, Goethe's *Weltliteratur* model sets great store by the original's broad dissemination and, subsequently, translation, for they test and eventually establish the work as they attempt to legitimate it elsewhere, for others, in the world arena and in the exigent embrace of remote idioms and cultural codes. In that, "great literature" involves and in certain cases ultimately boils down to an away kind of cultural game, played out in tongues not just foreign but, ideally, of planetary circulation. It goes without saying, this hardly means that *Blinding* does not amount to much in French, German, and Swedish, let alone in Romanian. Cărtărescu's strikes me, however, as the type of literature Sean Cotter's admirably competent rendition can further and perhaps decisively energize insofar as it affords *Blinding* not only a bigger stage but also a vehicle, an overall form subtly apposite to the novel's foundational fascination: the planet. Put differently, but in a way that essentially rehearses Walter Benjamin's mystic-creative view of translation, English, our time's main lingua franca and most "worlded" language, is what this world-hungry Romanian book has been calling for, as it were, so as to fully become the world-text, the Borgesian script its narrating protagonist and authorial alter ego, Mircea, sets out to write.

The planetary critic should resonate to this deeply constitutive, fundamentally worldly appetite of the book. For one is undoubtedly struck by *Blinding*'s intrinsic and insatiable yearning for the greater world, by its insistently affirmed desire to take this world's measure and bear witness to it, painful as it may be, from a place half a century of brutally isolationist politics purported to cut off from other geographies and their vaster repertoires of topography, affect, and material culture. Here again designated as "(the) *All*," this larger, geopolitical and cosmic-metaphysical world continues to be the novel's ontological provocation, challenging *Blinding* into existence by fueling and frustrating its writing at once.[128] While the Cold War allows

Mircea to experience, *in situ*, the *All* only "in part" (hence the Saint Paul epigraph to *The Left Wing*), this non-totalist totality becomes accessible through the imagination. More precisely, what is activated here is a feverish, hyperconnective, planetarily (w)holistic imaginary that, over and over again, telescopes out to plug the forlorn, the isolated, the ostracized, the incarcerated, and the trivial into the ecumenical and cosmic, and, vice versa, telescopes the last two into the rest. Thus, the subversively metonymical poetics of a whole cultural-aesthetic movement—Romania's programmatically postmodern "Generation of the 1980s"—reaches in Cărtărescu's prose a climactic moment as it successively juxtaposes and collapses the domestic microcosm and the world's macrocosm, laying them side by side and inside each other, showing how they intersect, dovetail, and communicate. Prosopopoeia, the art of face-making, and what gets this "facial" poetics going—the "provocation" mentioned earlier—are keynote here, for the wider beyond is both master theme and impetus, *primum movens*, which *Blinding* echoes by conjuring it up obsessively and mesmerizingly, page after page. This is how and why these pages come into being and tell their story, which turns out to be the story of the world's literal inscription into the crumbling stucco of Bucharest's buildings and into the sinewy sheets of Mircea's manuscript alike.

Mircea is a postcommunist Marcel of sorts. The paronomasia is both accidental and illuminating, for it helps place *Blinding* in the right context. While this excludes neither José Saramago's 1995 *Ensaio sobre a Cegueira* (translated as *Blindness*) nor Elias Canetti's 1935 *Die Blendung* ("The Blinding," known to the English-speaking public under the title *Auto-da-Fé*), think of *Blinding*'s non-stop memory spectacle, if you will, as a latter-day Proustianism, one filtered through Borges—and, not surprisingly, through Borges's Kafka as well. And think, in the same vein, of Cărtărescu as a postmodern Marcel Proust who has survived the Cold War on a diet of Pynchon novels and now shares with the befuddled world the absurdity and surrealism of things past—very real things albeit not entirely past, mind you.

But Mircea—the empirical and textual one—is also a Job. Atop his heap of memories in the Eastern bloc's cul-de-sac, he cries out to God and to his world as nobody else ever has, in a language that is both strange—the language of space wasted and time lost, personally and collectively—and familiar to that world. It is in this sense that *Blinding* simultaneously calls out to the world and calls for it and for an idiom in which the planetary world-as-world—now post-1989, post-blocs, post-nationalist—gives itself a greater chance of hearing itself. In this sense also, coming before this world and its American readers is a homecoming, but one that reaches far beyond the linguistic and is in turn likely to make English audiences, specifically the aficionados of American postmoderns from John Barth on, feel at home. Therefore, I hesitate to call *Blinding* "exotic." For it is not, or, if it looks so, its looks are deceiving. On the one hand, it does paint a starkly alien urbanscape—Bucharest's concrete inferno—at Europe's ever-convulsive periphery. On the other hand, Communist-era neorealism, magical realism, and postmodern, textual-political subversion of reality and realist representation blend in it memorably. Thus, the same readers will likely recognize shapes and sounds closer to home. These are, once more, Pynchon—*Gravity's Rainbow* is one of the author's favorite books—then Márquez, Julio Cortázar, Borges, Kafka (and Bruno Schulz), the German Romantics, and the biblical-Judaic tradition, which Cărtărescu interpellates alongside a host of national masters and styles from poet Mihai Eminescu, whose fantastic prose *Blinding* occasionally evokes, to playwright and short fiction author Ion Luca Caragiale (Ionesco's foremost precursor) to Caragiale's son and flamboyant man-about-town, Mateiu, to post–World War II Romanian surrealist and "oneirist" poets like Leonid Dimov. These two threads entwine in Cărtărescu and, more broadly, in his generation's postmodernism. This planetary *mestizaje* is as cultural-intertextual as it is political. The author dwells on it at length in his 1999 monograph *Postmodernismul Românesc* (Romanian Postmodernism), where he explains how the most vibrant direction in his country's post–World War II literature came about by turning to outside, principally North American sources as to its own inheritance and by the same token revisiting the tradition concept along the lines of the "lateral," non-territorialist, anti-nationalist, and worldly model described in §14 as "posttraditional."

To this model, *Blinding* gives a fictional body: one of a kind, larger than life, haunting. The originality of this supremely ambitious and cross-cultural comedy of literature stems to a notable degree from the dazzling (not to say "blinding") scope of Cărtărescu's talent. The bookishness of his work is conspicuous. A polymath who thinks like a poet, he composes his book like a novelist, though. Granted, what drives the spatio-temporal mobility of the novel is the unique, all-encompassing vision, which is in turn fueled by a descriptive fervor quintessentially poetic in nature. The novel's lavishly baroque surveys of the Communist concentric *bolgie*—the crummy family apartment on Ștefan cel Mare Road, the nondescript neighborhood, the panopticon-like city ravaged by the bulldozers of the Leader's pharaonic projects—bespeak the imagination of a poet like Dante trying his hand at an Allen Ginsberg pastiche. Such tableaux remind one of Cărtărescu's earlier poems, and so do the several poetry fragments actually inserted into *The Left Wing*. Nevertheless, *Blinding* is and must be read like a novel. It does have a narrative arc to it. This takes shape across volumes, which volumes, on this account, must be read together. The author tells a story as personal as Marcel's and occasionally as close to a memoir as Proust's, even though later in *The Right Wing* Mircea explicitly distinguishes his work in progress from the diary genre. His author has published, in fact, a multivolume *Diary*, but, again, although what pushes it forward is memory, *Blinding* remains a work of fiction.

Strictly speaking, Mircea's memory is neither involuntary nor limited to recollection, or to *personal* reminiscences for that matter. To remember is here also to fictionalize, perchance to dream, even to dream other people's dreams should Mircea's own remembrance sputter.[129] All Mircea feels left with in *The Left Wing* is the past (75), but that slice of time, the only dimension in which temporality can be said to have (ever had) any "reality" to it, is both ontologically unavailable and ethically implausible, "absurd and delusional" (319). In fact, it is not so much that Cărtărescu starts writing his book after the fall of Communism, but, given its forty odd years of documented horror and absurdity, the Communist past has become quasi unrepresentable, an impossibility both unlikely to have been and, to the extent that it *has* been, morally disconcerting. In that, *le temps perdu* of Communist autocracy mounts a serious challenge to memory, concomitantly setting it off and jamming its works, as well as to expression, to the notion of narrating and relaying all this. The basic question, then—equally faced by the survivors of the Nazi Holocaust and of the so-called Communist experiment—is not just how you might go about recalling this temporality of perdition, but also how you might talk about it, furthermore, how you might convey its monstrosity to somebody who has not lived through it to understand that which, in hindsight, defies understanding.

A striking phrase Mircea, the fictional writer, uses to relate what he sees when he climbs on top of the roof of a Bucharest building suggests a possible answer: "[a] nation of melancholy" (31). A psychoanalyst's bonanza, *Blinding* teems with Freudian moments. This one stands out because it provides an all-clarifying insight into the protagonist's psyche and the social unconscious dramatized by it. With the rise to power of the tyrannical regime in the aftermath of World War II and especially since the 1950s, when Mircea's story gets under way, melancholia becomes the nation's defining mood. Under a most brutal totalitarian system, this mass psychology becomes psychopathological and, as such, usurps the place of politics as civil society implodes and the "mood" translates, within a decade, into a full-fledged political mode prohibitive of any freedoms whatsoever—into an institutionalized "melancholic inhibition," as Freud calls it. Generalized and painstakingly enforced by a repressive apparatus that some of Mircea's acquaintances eagerly join, this disposition cancels out individual initiative and resistance. The society falls apart inside and outside families like Mircea's, and this leads to social "loneliness" and its political corollary, "impotence," which Hannah Arendt deems so typical of totalitarianism. "Melancholy" more than ever in their history, Romanians watch passively the silent movie of their own ruin in a country the Communist Party oligarchy, before long reduced to the quasi-illiterate Ceauşescu clan, runs virtually unchecked by implementing aberrant policies that all but turn Romania into an absurd and desolate land in the late 1980s. Collective self-destruction is thus the final upshot of Cold War melancholy, but neither the material devastation carried out in the name of pseudo-developmental fantasies nor the dark humor—the mass wistfulness—that made it possible abates following the regime's bloody collapse in December 1989. The past's protracted agony makes itself multiply felt in the panorama of urban abjection repeatedly rolled out by Mircea in the postcommunist present, which cannot part company with the involuntary surrealism of Communist realities and occurrences, such as the church on wheels, relocated to make room for Ceauşescu's new residence, The People's House.

The world-infamous behemoth is a symbolic presence in Cărtărescu's Bucharest and narrative. Demolition crews had uprooted urban life on many square miles to make room for this architectural aberration. Built against history, The People's House became, however, the Palace of the Parliament and, ironically enough, a historical landmark and major tourist attraction after the regime's downfall. Both a monument and a memento—the words are etymologically related—"the biggest building in the world" solidifies a mercilessly resilient time in the language of a Saturnine architecture. In the latter, Romanians contemplate their history and responsibility for it, their guilt, past and present helplessness, and the overall "worthlessness" derived, as Freud would point out, from the gazing subject's narcissistic identification with the abject object. This identification afflicts the community as well as the individual, including extraordinary individuals like Mircea and Herman, our main hero's alcoholic and visionary friend. Perfect illustration of what Freud also determines as the melancholic ego's "consent to its own destruction," Herman is Mircea's master up to a point.

Solitary, dejected, and wistful, the aspiring writer has his double, Victor, the twin brother, much as the butterfly, Cărtărescu's arch-symbol and fictional "mascot," has its mortal enemy, the spider. Separated from Victor as an infant, Mircea will reunite with him in the monstrous palace on *The Right Wing*'s climactic last page, making the infinitesimal and the infinite, good and evil, inside and outside fuse explosively.

Malefic as he appears, Victor is also the envoy of a much bigger and resplendent world. This world, however, has been lying inside Mircea all along. It is the twin world and face, the world's otherness as self-consciousness buried behind Mircea's face and "telescop[ed]" (77) within the world of memories and within those memories' world with which his brain is pregnant. That face is both an inside and an outside or environs. "That hyaline cartilage," Mircea tells us, "there on the shield where the three heraldic flowers meet—dream, memory, and emotion—that is my domain, my world, the world. There in the sparkling cylinder that descends through my mind" (88). The individual mind is a cosm*all*ogical assemblage because it harbors its other, its double, a cosmic hypostasis and fraction, and, conversely, the "neurological"—neur*all*ogical?—template for another, bigger and wiser brain through which "we will climb, unconscious and happy, onto a higher level of the fractal of eternal Being" (283). This Being is "made of cosmoses," we find out later (417), but these cosmoses are composted and refracted by the authorial brain into the downtown Bucharest "scenery" across which Mircea's parents, Maria and Costel, stroll "drowned in the whirls and fractals of history," and yet, *nota bene*, "without distinguishing themselves from their world, and without understanding that they lived on a grain of sand on a beach wider than the universe, spread out and sifted, melancholically, by a mind that chose the two of them and decided their destinies" (247). Where Herman only sketches out, rather abstractly, a vision of symmetries, analogies, antagonisms, *coincidentia oppositorum*, and cosmic connections, Mircea lives this vision out by trekking across a fractal universe in which the story of his family and his childhood meshes with the history of post–World War II and postcommunist Romania as well as with other temporalities and spaces of centuries past and faraway landscapes from Bucharest to Bulgaria and from Louisiana to the Netherlands.

The eventful late December 1989 is the euphoric-liberatory, post-authoritarian and planetary *kairós*—"right time" but also "right place" in Ancient Greek—when the macro and the micro finally fasten onto one another as if "you have pierced" the planet's "folded map with a needle, uniting incompatible and disparate places in an incomprehensible trajectory, perpendicular to the paper" (309). Now, the Face and the city's face gaze into each other because kairotic time, dislodged from its totalist-totalitarian chronology of repetitiveness, is one of suddenly accelerated, world-making worlding. At this point and *in* this point of the new world, Cărtărescu's telescopy reaches its apex, for, in fact, *kairós* is best understood as a paroxysm of planetarization, radical reorientation of mind, body, and place in and toward the world. At this moment, the planetary maze and Mircea's whereabouts in a "revolutionary" Bucharest (his "cobweb map of [his] place in the world" [309]), the world's macro cartography and that worldly portrait's scaled-down versions in "the filigree design of coffee cups" and snowflakes (309–310), the cosmic butterfly and the one resting in your palm, the world's geopolitical intrigues and the patterns of Maria's handmade rug in *The Body*[130] snap into place, into the same co-incident, synergetic spot of co-presence to withness—be with and bear witness to—each other alongside all the other, countless instantiations of the internal-external, small-large, inward/inworld-outward/outer-world planetary dynamic. At long last, the Face, with its previously illegible topography, barely visible on a world map either crumpled and rolled up into an ignominious ball to be discarded by a careless author/cartographer or folded up origami-like, becomes once again "legible."[131] Its "fractals, twisters, non-linear equations, folds . . . , Russian dolls crammed one inside another . . . Spaces pregnant with spaces pregnant with spaces" may now come out into the open and play.[132]

§24. Balzacian Reeducation

> [S]pellbound by the mystery of the outside world.
> —DAI SIJIE, *Balzac and the Little Chinese Seamstress*

Amplifying exponentially across the post–Cold War novel, the macro-micro telescopic rites take center stage in DeLillo (*Underworld, Cosmopolis, Falling Man*, and *Point Omega*), Chang-rae Lee (*Native Speaker, A Gesture Life, Aloft, The Surrendered*, and *On Such a Full Sea*), Cole (*Open City*), Gish Jen (*World and Town*), Jonathan Safran Foer (*Extremely Loud and Incredibly Close*), Nicole Krauss (*The History of Love*), Hemon (*Nowhere Man*), Gary Shteyngart (*The Russian Debutante's Handbook* and *Absurdistan*), Bharati Mukherjee (*The Holder of the World, Desirable Daughters*, and *Miss New India*), Jhumpa Lahiri (*The Namesake*), McCann (*Let the Great World Spin* and *TransAtlantic*), O'Neill (*Netherland, The Dog*), Ondaatje (*The English Patient*), Houellebecq (*Les particules élémentaires* [The Elementary Particles],

Plateforme [Platform], *La possibilité d'une île* [The Possibility of an Island], and *La carte et le territoire* [The Map and the Territory]), Alexandru Muşina (*Nepotul lui Dracula* [Dracula's Nephew]), Zadie Smith (*White Teeth, On Beauty, NW*), Ian McEwan (*Black Dogs, Saturday, Solar, The Children Act*), Dubravka Ugrešić (*The Ministry of Pain*), Christos Tsiolkas (*Dead Europe*), Brian Chickwava (*Harare North*), Michael Parker (*The Watery Part of the World*), David Mitchell (*Cloud Atlas*), Hari Kunzru (*Transmission*), Orhan Pamuk (*Kar* [Snow]), Sorj Chalandon (*Le quatrième mur* [The Fourth Wall]), and Dai Sijie (*Balzac et la petite tailleuse chinoise* [*Balzac and the Little Chinese Seamstress*]), to list only a few of Cărtărescu's kindred spirits.

Originally published as *Balzac et la petite tailleuse chinoise* in 2000 and translated into English the year after, Chinese-French writer and filmmaker Dai Sijie's international bestseller *Balzac and the Little Chinese Seamstress* is, despite its "minimalism," historically and politically to *Nostalgia* what Dai's 2003 novel, *Le complexe du Di*, is to *Blinding*.[133] Rendered into English as *Mr. Muo's Travelling Couch* in 2005, *Le complexe du Di* furnishes a critical glimpse into a global-age China where, as in *Blinding*, the officially forsworn totalitarian past lives on; *Balzac*, Dai's most widely acclaimed work so far, takes us back to the darkest years of pre-Tiananmen China. With a well-calibrated sense of tragic that dampens neither humor nor compassion, the novels set in train fictional telescopies of arresting literary, cultural, and political insight. Dai's may be, as some reviewers imply, literature that pays homage to literature, but this need not be the backhanded compliment it sometimes is. "True book lover's book[s],"[134] his novels are "bookish" if this means that he is working his way through other books as he is writing his own. However, they are not if "bookish" signifies "aestheticist." In point of fact, his bookishness, or intertextualism, rather, is not a generic, effete aestheticism but an astute and pointed *geoaestheticism*. The literature inside his is, as in Cărtărescu, of a particular kind, and, as such, it *does* something within and without his fictional universe. This literature is twice more than ("just") literature—it is *world* literature that lives up to the double condition to which *Reading for the Planet* attends. That is to say, not only is this literature of the world, but it also prompts the world's worlding, coming together across time, space, language barriers, out-of-bounds libraries, and barbed wire fences; not only is this literature of and in faraway tongues and languages, but its reading, a characteristic preoccupation of Dai's characters, works planetarily, "smuggling" those forbidden idioms and landscapes into China while reembedding Chinese places, people, and traditions back into the outside world.

This reembedding is, also like in Cărtărescu, purposeful, provocative, and overtly political. It wields the power of fiction to retrain the polity's geocultural imagination over and against the Cultural Revolution's brutish attempts at "reeducating" millions of Chinese in its *laojiao* ("reeducation through labor") detention sites in the early 1970s. Worth keeping in mind here is that, in spite of its declarations and of the reclassifications of the country's incarceration facilities, the Chinese government has never dismantled the *laojiao* network, as it has not done away with the *laogai* prison labor system either. Also known as the Chinese Gulag, the sinister *laogai* was geared, especially during Mao's rule, more deliberately toward torture, starvation, and other forms of physical extermination *en masse*. If the differences between the two subsets of the Chinese penal apparatus widen over time, in 1971, however, when seventeen-year-old Dai himself was sent, like *Balzac*'s teenagers, to be reeducated in a Sichuan village, the *laojiao* had all the makings of a death factory. The book's narrating protagonist and his friend Luo realize, in effect, that the odds they face of ever rejoining their families are indeed "terrible" ("three in a thousand") due to their putative social background:[135] even though neither has graduated from high school, they were considered "intellectuals."

Reflecting Mao's "hatred of intellectuals," the "revolutionary" method of fostering a "new generation"[136] and a wholly new human type with it—an ideal pursued by Nazi and Communist regimes alike—is, as Dai's storyteller comments, distinctively anti-intellectual. It seeks actually to weed out the whole intellectual class, which is too "cosmopolitan" not to be vulnerable to noxious "outside" influences. *Balzac*'s author stresses from the outset that "foreignness" is a priori suspicious (3), and so are intellectuals, who are more likely than other social categories to catch its disease because, living mostly in cities, they have presumably more contacts with "aliens." The intellectual cosmopolite, then, is or is also assumed to be an urbanite. On that ground, reeducation is not only an anti-cosmopolitan but also an anti-urban campaign in remote and isolated rural settings, with millions of "young intellectuals" and high school students like Dai's heroes cast out into backcountry exile and its mix of hard labor, interrogation, summary executions, and deprivation of all sorts, especially cultural deprivation.

The latter is key to reeducation's cardinal objective, indoctrination. Of course, one cannot indoctrinate thoroughly if one does not brainwash, and one cannot brainwash—one cannot wipe the human slate clean—if one does not keep out external "cultural influences." In general, culture and its "contagious" effects are what reeducation pushes against. Culturally speaking, the *laojiao* "labor farm" is a sanitary cordon around the inmate. To be sure, as far as indoctrination goes, exile and internment would be toothless without censorship and the banning of any potential "competition" to the doctrine and its bible, in this case, Mao's *Little Red Book*. Remarkably isomorphic, these spatial and cultural deterritorializations work hand in glove. In the repressive topo-economy of reeducation, confining somebody to a certain place is pointless unless the site is culturally "decontaminated." That site becomes a true reeducation venue once it has been closed off not only carcerally but also culturally, that is, once its outside has been blocked out by roping off the culture pregnant with it. Particularly targeted by cultural censors in the more extreme forms of twentieth-century imagined and existing dystopias (Orwellian, Stalinist, Maoist, Albanian, North Korean) is therefore outside culture and, more broadly, the outside world altogether. A paranoid isolationism—a fallaciously solipsistic ontology—totalitarianism revels in a perpetual quarantine that scrambles to shut out the world. If it bans huge swaths of world literature, if it confiscates and burns foreign books in public, as Dai's Red Guards do during the Cultural Revolution (51), this is because these books are cosmoses, brew possibilities, and bear withness, because they comprise or blaze paths to other worlds even in western China villages like the Phoenix of the Sky, where no European has set foot since the 1940s and where the main storyteller and Luo undergo reeducation by hauling buckets of human waste up the mountain.

But reeducation fails. And, if it does, this is largely because reading deprivation does not work either. As it happens, our heroes come upon a treasure trove: a suitcase full of banned Western classics from Victor Hugo and Stendhal to Honoré de Balzac, Gustave Flaubert, Romain Rolland, Alexandre Dumas *père*, Charles Dickens, Emily Brontë, and Nikolai Gogol. Not only does the "elegant" valise "g[ive] off a whiff of civilization" (49); it is civilization itself, vestige of another culture now distant and forbidden yet capable of playing the role of the carpenter's case Robinson Crusoe manages to salvage. Cut off from the nurturing presence of others, the incarcerated self still possesses their tools, the blueprints of autopoiesis,[137] and with them self-reconstruction—rather than Maoist reeducation—can begin. With a nicely aimed irony, Dai's narrator calls this self-reconstruction "Balzacian re-education" (180). Where Mao's reeducation fetters and disables the self, Balzac's enables it, encouraging its growth, its morphing into the desired image of itself. This "metamorphosis" is, Luo acknowledges, reading's "ultimate pay-off" (180), and reading to his girlfriend from Balzac does pay off because she is magically "transformed" (100), no longer a "simple mountain girl" (100). *Père Goriot—Old Go*, in Chinese translation—"seduce[s]," "overwhelm[s]," and "spellb[inds]" as it "reveals" to its readers the "mystery of the outside world, especially the world of women, love and sex" (109).

But the outside leads inside and, indeed, contaminates, spawns inner growth. As it reveals itself, the other prompts self-revelation, helps the self rediscover himself and his world. By no means the most realistic piece of *La Comédie humaine, Ursule Mirouët* de-realizes the dire environs. The "truth" of the 1841 novel gives the lie not only to official rhetoric but also to the hollow reality government parlance is trying to couch. "Picture, if you will," Luo invites us,

> a boy of nineteen, still slumbering in the limbo of adolescence, having heard nothing but revolutionary bladder about patriotism, Communism, ideology and propaganda all his life, falling headlong into a story of awakening desire, passion, impulsive action, love, of all the subjects that had, until then, been hidden from me.
>
> In spite of my complete ignorance of that distant land called France (I had heard Napoleon mentioned by my father a few times, that was all), Ursule's story rang as true as if it had been about my neighbors. The messy affair over inheritance and money that befell her made the story all the more convincing, thereby enhancing the power of the words. By the end of the day I was feeling quite at home in Nemours, imagining myself posted by the smoking hearth of her parlour in the company of doctors and curates. . . . Even the part about magnetism and somnambulism struck me as credible and riveting. (57)

"Wrapped up" like the Little Seamstress in Balzac's "story of miracles" (57), the narrator is entranced by this fiction truer than life and cannot help notice that the "credible" fantasy debunks a whole world that claimed to be "scientific." Balzac manages to "reeducate" where Mao does not because the Balzacian text carries its reader in the right direction. Balzac "educates" in the etymological sense of the Latin *edūcere* (to "lead forth"). He leads not away from the self, nor does he take away the self from the learning subject in the process. Quite the opposite: Balzac is the good teacher who teaches the ways of the self; the other's "story of awakening" prompts the narrator's awakening into selfhood. This happens because the narrator's perusal of *Ursule Mirouët* "naturalizes" the novel. In other words, the text does remain "distant" and "different," but at the same time it throws a bridge across worlds, instituting a fictional continuum between the reader's world and his reading's worlds. Distinct as these worlds remain, they nonetheless become compatible and overlap in the reader's mind, so much so that Dai's hero feels that Ursule's story could have been about his "neighborhood" as much as he would have felt "at home" in her home and thus his own "story" could have taken place in the world of hers. Remapping Balzac's Nemours onto Szechuan's Chengdu, telescoping fictional France into Mao's China, Dai builds Ursule a home away from home in his hero's reading, and in turn Balzac gives his Chinese reader a home away from the one he had to leave behind. Canceling out the squalor of the narrator's living quarters, this imaginary shelter can make the imagining self at home, accommodate and boost the individual, his desires and dreams.

Translating Balzac's language into the idiom of specifically Chinese situations, these projections and "revelations" (110) are "salutary" (110), the narrator understands, precisely because what they unveil is the dignity of the individual. Similarly, Romain Rolland's Jean-Christophe, we learn,

> with his fierce individualism utterly untainted by malice, was a salutary revelation. Without him I would have never understood the splendour of taking free and independent action as an individual. Up until this stolen encounter with Romain Rolland's hero, my poor educated and re-educated brains had been incapable of grasping the notion of one man standing up against the whole world. The flirtation turned into a grand passion. Even the excessively emphatic style occasionally indulged in by the author did not detract from the beauty of this astonishing work of art. I was carried away, swept along by the mighty stream of words pouring from the hundreds of pages. To me it was the ultimate book: once you had read it, neither your own life nor the world you lived in would ever look the same. (110–111)

Dai's protagonist is "naturally drawn" to *Jean-Christophe* (110). Not only is he a musician, like Rolland's hero; they also have the same kind of enemies and face comparable obstacles. Critics have pointed out that Jean-Christophe is based on Beethoven, whose biography Rolland wrote too, but also on Wagner's and Mozart's lives—incidentally, Dai's narrator calls the Mozart violin piece he plays before the stunned villagers when he arrives at the Phoenix of the Sky "Mozart is Thinking of Chairman Mao." But Rolland also put a lot of his own life into his character's, whose trajectory speaks to the author's exile of body and mind, to his antinationalist pathos. A self-declared "internationalist at heart" and "citizen of the world,"[138] Rolland writes the "ultimate book" because, as Dai's hero reads the novel, the novel in turn "reads" its reader, its other, as it were, sees through his misfortunes and helps him see himself and his place with new eyes. This very personal and very political exchange between people so unlike in so many respects reeducates Dai's passionate reader in the very best sense, teaching him the "notion of standing up against the whole world" and thus for himself. And so does Dumas's *Count of Monte Cristo*, in whose hero he has even more reasons to see himself, what with his friend Four-Eyes completing his own reeducation but leaving behind a treasure of books, with which the narrator and his friend will indeed change their own lives and others'.

More importantly perhaps, both Jean-Christophe and the Count are Romantic idealists of a bygone era. Nor is Dai unaware of the marked contrast between such stories and the world of Chinese labor camps. At first blush, the disconnect between Dai's realistically limned China and Dumas's "pseudohistorical" France, as it has been called, is absolute. But the anachronistic insertion, the "mistranslation" of Balzac, Flaubert, Herman Melville, let alone of Rolland and Dumas into the "Cultural Revolution" serves a rhetorical as well as a political purpose. The more Romantic, extraordinary, and "incredible" the heroes of the banned books, the more they behave like individuals, affirm their freedom, and proclaim a value in painfully short supply in the reader's world, and so the more credible they become and speak to this world, showing what Dai's heroes are not allowed to be, what dreams they are not allowed to dream. Somnambulism, dreams, oneiromancy (like in *Ursule Mirouët*) or psychoanalytically pursued *Traumdeutung* (like in Dai's second novel), "cloak-and-dagger" fantasies, Romanticism—all these are in fact more palpable and make a greater impact than any nitty-gritty realism exactly because of their "excessive," "extravagant" psychologism, because of a display of individualism that declines to acknowledge a limit, a system of conventions, be those the conventions of verisimilitude. In Gogol and Flaubert no less than in Dumas and Rolland, Dai is looking for a psychological model—for an encoding of the individual—as far away as possible from conventionality, in particular from the psychological conventions ossifying inner life in Stalin's and Mao's infamous "soul engineering."

Two verisimilitude concepts clash here. "Realistic" as it may claim to be, one covers a narrow range of psychological "types" in turn pegged as either "progressive" or "reactionary" politically. This scheme renders the fictional and cinematic varieties of socialist realism Dai's heroes are treated with—Chinese, North Korean, and Albanian, with Enver Hoxha's "complete works" an amusing stand-in for "Western Literature" (51)—ham-fisted as far as inner life goes. While not necessarily nonrealistic—after all, Balzac, Gogol, and Flaubert founded European realism—the other kind of verisimilitude does not rule out Romantic, sentimental display of feelings, and derives its credibility from psychological representation unhampered by ideological predetermination. This does not mean that there is no ideology in Balzac or Flaubert, but that this ideology does not set out to contain in advance psychological expression. Further, it means that, given the political and ideological backdrop over and against which Dai's heroes peruse Balzac, Dumas, and Rolland, the writers' unconventional, high-flown, "outlandish" reports of inner life convey a sense of individuality, freedom, and openness, of something different and bigger than the here and now, putting forth exactly what the "Cultural Revolution" purports to quash. This makes their books "sacred objects" (62) and subversively so in a regime quite reluctant, like all apparatuses of this sort, to share its cult status with anybody and anything else. One more time, *Lost Illusions* and *The Count of Monte Cristo* may not be political a priori, but this kind of reading ends up "politicizing" them.

Undoubtedly, in a different world, Miguel de Cervantes, Dumas, Fyodor Dostoevsky, and James Joyce would have taught Dai's characters different things. But, in the People's Republic and its iron bubble of cultural and political "collective" solipsism, what they teach their readers first and foremost is the ways of the self, more exactly, the way of the world *as* a way to the self and its unique life. Most remarkably, Dai's individualism is not autarchic but worldly. Stepping into other worlds and, vice versa, telescoping those worlds into self-isolating China by reading the other's forbidden writing become, together, a compensatory exercise in selfhood, a stage where the self can go on by performing the vital routines of soul and mind, empathizing and sympathizing, suffering, rejoicing, and ultimately growing an identity in response to the passions, crises, and similar displays of inner life in the other's mesmerizing fiction. After reading to the Little Seamstress from *Ursule Mirouët*'s "scene of private life," an awestruck Luo tells his friend that "[t]his fellow Balzac is a wizard. . . . He touched the head of this mountain girl with an invisible finger, and she was transformed, carried away in a dream. It took a while for her to come down to earth. She ended up putting your wretched coat on. . . . She said having Balzac's words next to her skin made her feel good, and also more intelligent."[139]

The girl wears Balzac, literally. She wraps herself up symbolically in the text of *Ursule Mirouët*, or at least in the fragments Luo's friend was able to reproduce on the inside of a sheepskin coat. "I copied out," the friend reveals, "the chapter where Ursule somnambulates. I longed to be like her: to be able, while I lay asleep in my bed, to see what my mother was doing in our apartment five hundred kilometers away, to watch my parents having supper, to observe their gestures, the dishes on the table, the color of the crockery, to sniff the aroma of their food, to hear their conversation. . . . Better still, like Ursule, I would visit, in my dreams, places I had never set eyes on before" (58–59).

"Longing" here unfolds as cross-cultural identity mimesis at equal distance, on one side, from René Girard's "I covet what the other covets" paradigm of confrontational desire first sketched out in *Mensonge romantique et vérité romanesque* and, on the other side, from Lacan's "I desire *as* the Other" substitutive scenario. In the former, the other is what the self aspires to become, but also a competitor. In the latter, the self is a detour "in the trajectory of the desire of the Other."[140] Therefore, neither model fully applies. In Dai, the scintillating "out there" and the dreary "in here" do not compete but cooperate at a distance on the self's project, with the elsewhere and the other a necessary sponsor and cultural creditor, an *other* route and an aesthetic apprenticeship the self must complete to come into its own. This apprenticeship is also an education of desire; in Dai, one craves the world's literature and for the world in this literature so as to grasp and live out craving, yearning, and other forms of desire. Notably, Dai's narrator does not want *what* the other does. Instead, he learns, or relearns to want *as* the other wants, to long, dream, and imagine as Ursule does in Balzac's short story. Make no mistake: he does not want to be Ursule; not unlike the Little Seamstress, he does not wish to give up *his* self. Quite the contrary: it is in order to be himself that he wants to be *like* Ursule, to have a self as she does and to go through the same calisthenics of selfhood transaction: dreaming, daydreaming, imagining, in brief, desire. Via Balzacian desire, Dai's nameless narrator desires; across an other's images, he imagines himself elsewhere, neither in Ursule's town nor in the shabby room he shares with Luo above the pigsty, but back with his family (57).

A profound and complex transformation occurs, no doubt, and it refashions selves and places, bodies and cultural practices, habits and maps. Predicated as it may be on the rekindling of desire and on the reeducation of the imagination, this transformation and the worlding of the *laojiao*, and of mainland China with it, are nevertheless more than a figure of speech. If Balzac changes how Luo and his buddy feel about women (151), Balzac also "transforms" (100) the Little Seamstress, who decides to become a "city girl" (178) and lead the urbanite life denied to her friends. As for Flaubert, he is not only a great writer but apparently also an underrated haute couture designer, for *Madame Bovary* inspires her to make herself a brassiere and, more brazenly still, to turn a Mao jacket into the kind of "smart" garb that "would only be worn by a woman in the city" (179). Along the same lines, Dumas's Marseille may be "on the other side of the world" (124), as the narrator tells her father, but the Count's adventures cast such a spell on the village tailor—a transparent reincarnation of Cibot from Balzac's *Le Cousin Pons*—that "some of the details he picked up from the French story started to have a discreet influence on the clothes he was making for the villagers. Dumas would have been most surprised to see the mountain men sporting sailor tops with square collars that flapped in the breeze. *You could almost smell the briny Mediterranean air*" (127; emphasis added). Thus, the fictional world of Balzac, Dumas, and Rolland begins to bleed into the peasants' everyday. Discrepant ontologies, cultures, and politics collapse into each other. And this is precisely what the bonfire in *Balzac*'s last pages suggests: if the Red Guards would set books on fire to destroy them, to make them disappear, Luo and the storyteller burn them so as to hint that, since they have read the texts, learned them by heart, and can retell them so creatively—so *self*-creatively—they have been reeducated, and the books have done their job. They are now worlds of this world, embodied visions, lifestyles, ways of seeing and doing things, of dreaming, and of hoping against hope.

§25. Freudian Reeducation: Mao, Muo, and "Geopsychoanalysis"

> [T]his foreign tongue to unite us . . .
> —DAI SIJIE, *Mr. Muo's Travelling Couch*

Set in twenty-first-century China, *Mr. Muo's Travelling Couch* speaks to another context. The difference is by no means dramatic, though. A Chinese expatriate living in Paris since the early 1990s, Dai's Muo returns to his native country only to discover that censorship of readings and persecution of readers are still alive and well. Alongside other forms of authority, they have become both sloppier and more focused. Recycling *Balzac*'s Dumasian treasure chest theme, the city of Kunming's "Department of Clandestine Anti-publications" has amassed a whole "treasure house" of "forbidden books." This features two main categories of texts (196). The first includes the memoirs of Mao's personal physician, books on the 1989 Tiananmen Square student uprising, the power struggle within the Chinese Communist Party, the "reeducation camps" of the "Cultural Revolution," and the bizarre "cases of revolutionary cannibalism" (197). These dwell on China's recent past and tell stories the current regime does not want told because they are incriminating chapters in its own biography. In sum, they expose the authoritarian heritage—one might say the political unconscious—of "free-market" China. This explains the Department's interest in a second class of publications, which comprise "erotic novels," "licentious writings by libertine monks," the Marquis de Sade, ancient pornography, the Chinese Kama Sutra, "Taoist treatises on ejaculation," Freud, and psychoanalysis generally.

What we are dealing with, then, is, on the one hand, unorthodox accounts of the Chinese collective self and its troubled history; on the other, a no less provocative understanding—a disturbing *reading*—of the private self, Freudianism. Both worry a regime that has historically shaped the former by systematically repressing the latter. In *Balzac*, Dai throws light on the "reeducation" version of this repression. A psychoanalyst apprentice of Freudian and Lacanian persuasion, Muo reads Mao and Maoist legacy, the "new" China, through his masters' lenses, and what he discerns from the vantage point of radical otherness provided by Freud and Lacan is the "revenant" past, the uncanny survival of the world limned in *Balzac*. Through the analysis he does, in the "observations" he cannot help making, Muo's return—a psychoanalyst's—bears out yet another, of the repressed, of old pains and wrongs whose public acknowledgment the Department is dead set to preempt. As it becomes clear, Freudianism and authoritarianism are at loggerheads, as much as Balzacianism and Maoism were in the Little Seamstress's village. Not only do their distinct ontologies collide, though. In Dai's worlded imaginary, they also communicate and dovetail. Moreover, one also seeps into the other to query it and erode its setup. The former's "truth," Muo warns, "no one can escape, . . . not even an official representative of law and order" (123). Etched in dreams, fantasies, slips of tongue, and the like, the psychoanalytic truth invariably unsettles the official truths, either complicates or renders them partial, more or less than whatever they claim.

Tearing down this pseudo-rational discourse, psychoanalysis had been banished or treated with suspicion throughout the Communist world. After 1989, this status has changed radically in Central and Eastern Europe; in China, less so. While otherwise advertising itself as globalization-friendly, the regime keeps the country outside what Derrida describes as psychoanalysis' "becoming-a-world," its "ongoing *worldification*."[141] In "liberalized," "cosmopolitan" China, Freud's teaching remains an "ostracized foreign body" because it promotes a definition of the self *other* than abovementioned discourse's crude determinism, because it acknowledges this self, its uniqueness, and needs, and thus, most significantly, situates its genesis and welfare in the world while bringing the world into its universe. Muo's self model is indeed "worldified," as Derrida might say; as both a genealogy *and* recourse of the self, psychoanalysis is, with another Derridean term, "geopsychoanalysis."[142]

It is noteworthy, in this light, that recent Freudians have not hesitated to look into Chinese politics and especially Mao's legacy and scan the system's self-styled progressive rationalism for symbolic, phallocratic-autocratic drives carrying on under new codes, languages, and institutions (210). Not unlike Balzac and Flaubert, Freud and Lacan warrant in Dai feelings and emotions—algorithms of private life and ultimately of privacy, of an individual's most intimate rights. Their psychoanalysis thus provides a psychological and political—no less than cultural—other to the regime, an other whose texts Muo inscribes between himself and this regime's rhetoric to institute a "methodological" distance, a *discerning* interval. Via Freud, Muo sees how much of the "Cultural Revolution" still lingers in the public or private unconscious. As in *Balzac*, the other helps the self make out his self-alienation, the asymmetry between self-representation and the actuality of the self's circumstances. Balzac and Freud afford this revelation by inserting themselves between Dai's characters and the context in which they read *Ursule Mirouët* and *Beyond the Pleasure Principle*. Self-awareness arises in the resulting fertile rift as an effect of a reading that distances the readers from an evening-up, serializing environment. But as they secure this protective and clarifying distance, Luo, his friend, the Little Seamstress, and even her father come to share a passion, learn a secret language, and bind together.

Notably, "Western literature" opens a gap at the same time that it closes those keeping apart the readers drawn to taboo texts, as well as the vaster gap between these texts' authors and their Chinese audience. The other brings them together as they pull him into their midst, a dynamic the 2003 novel spells out perceptively. In a letter to his beloved Volcano of the Old Moon, now in a Chinese prison, Muo ponders his reasons for writing to her in French, a language "of which the dearly addressed understands scarcely a word" (215):

> It is a small enigma, resonant with the sweet sound of happiness. . . . From now on, my dear Old Moon, my splendid Volcano, we can look to

> this foreign tongue to unite us, reunite us, bind us together in a magical knot that blossoms into the wings of an exotic butterfly—an alphabetic language from the other side of the world, whose orthography, complete with apostrophes and diacriticals, lends it the heady, impenetrable air of esotericism. Your fellow prisoners, I can well imagine, will envy you your passing the time poring over love letters, to extract even the slightest triumphant particle of meaning from them. Do you remember those wonderful times we sat together listening to our favorite poets: Eliot, Frost, Pound, Borges? Their voices, each with its own personality and sonorous beauty, enveloped us, uplifted us, and made us dream, even though neither of us understood much English, much less Spanish. Those accents, those incomprehensible phrases, remain for me, even today, the loveliest music in the world. Music for the elect few, filled with the spirit of romance and melancholy. Our music. (215–216)

If he could, Muo confesses, he would learn not only English and Spanish but also Vietnamese, Catalan, Tibetan, Mongolian, Latin, Greek, Hebrew, and Sanskrit, then the language of Egyptian hieroglyphs—the less "common" the tongue, the more "recherché" (216) and unyielding, the better. These are highly "complicated" idioms of prayer and scholarly pursuit, not unlike "the Tumchooq language" in which, with a self-referential wink at *Balzac*, a "sacred Buddhist text [was] copied word for word onto the inside of the sheepskin jerkin [Paul d'Ampère] wore day in and day out, summer and winter" in a *laogai* camp in the late 1950s in Dai's third novel, *Par une nuit où la lune ne s'est pas levée* (Once on a Moonless Night [2007]).[143]

Like Ampère's friend Hu Feng, himself imprisoned for a "thought crime," like Four-Eyes, Luo, and *Balzac*'s storyteller, Muo too yearns for all these languages and venerates their scripts. As we saw, in *Balzac* this fascination is neither abstract nor artificial. It is palpable. The worlds it projects are real, material, almost plushy in their texture. In *Once on a Moonless Night*, Hu Feng "touche[s] those words written on sheepskin with [his] hands[,] and they [are] warm as living things."[144] What they are and do has ontological density to it, and so the window they open for Muo onto sacred and secular truths while shielding those truths by creating a sodality of study and worship and protecting this circle from intruders is real. Muo suspects that these languages' "inner sanctum" can be "penetrated," moreover, that he can "pray" for his beloved and himself in those languages on the altars of their unyielding grammars. Thus, in Muo's imagination the alien and exotic idiom suddenly becomes exoteric. One more time, the outside moves inside, gives birth to an inside, to a private world. It opens up to embrace the studious linguist-lover and his beloved, to become a tenor and vehicle of withness, available to them yet still impenetrable to this other language's others. Remarkably, it is the very "esotericism" and foreignness of French or any *other* language for that matter that "unite" and "bind," which means that the otherness ensconced in the other's "incomprehensible" tongue is never absolutely exclusive. This linguistic and cultural restrictiveness cannot be done away with completely either. But Muo draws exactly from the *other* tongue's reserve of secrecy to develop a language of privacy, an idiolect in which he and his former girlfriend can be together as long as the likes of Judge Di cannot "translate" it. The words of the other draw their own world maps, mark off a space, "translate" or take the lovers to a place where they can "talk" to each other, can "communicate" and understand each other in a language ultimately "incomprehensible" because only this language allows for both self-expression and privacy. As Muo relives a Dantesque, Francesca da Rimini-like episode, the music of T. S. Eliot's poetry—the *other*'s music—becomes *their* music, again. In appropriating it once more, they appropriate themselves, and, in so doing, they take, as Luo's friend would insist, the ultimate "action" an individual can take. The "mesmerizing, voluptuous overtones" of the "foreign word" (157) from "the other side of the world" (215) conjure up an intimate "here and now" in which Muo and his girlfriend, separated by time and space as they are, can nonetheless be "reunited" and bask in each other's company.

The unknown, the unheard, and the unfamiliar bewitch. Little Sister Wang, another female acquaintance, finds Muo's impenetrable rote recitations from Victor Hugo, Charles Baudelaire, and Paul Verlaine entrancing, mysteriously erotic (213). Not even the wild Lolos can resist the magic of the "foreign word." The tribesmen are so intrigued by Muo's francophone skills (239) and overall show of "Frenchness" that they feel prompted to show off their own "chivalrous" ways (240). Muo discovers with surprise that the Lolos are not so uncouth as they seem, for they appear capable of sensing in his deportment a defining French value: the "spirit of chivalry" (193). Ironically enough, the "savages" prove sophisticated—and "empathic," one could say—in recognizing the "essence" of Muo's French virtues and accepting it as a part of who he is, as well as a part of themselves, whereas the local authorities take a similar cultural display (peppered with quotes from Freud, Lacan, Foucault, and Derrida) as symptoms of mental illness and commit him to the Chengdu Psychiatric Institute (66–67). Not too far away from *Balzac*'s *laojiao* both in space and method, they diagnose Muo's French "foreignness" as pathological. To the supposedly uncultured, isolated mountain villages, however, Muo's strangeness is a matter of course. Identity, they suspect, *presupposes* it, and so does communication between different identities. Muo and his attackers understand each other, come *closer* as soon as he starts performing the foreignness setting him *apart* from the Lolos, that is, as soon as he acts out his Frenchness by speaking French, producing his Carte Orange, and lecturing (in Chinese) his audience on the unlikely topic of the Parisian metro. His linguistic and cultural "out-of-placeness" bridges a seemingly unbridgeable gap between separate places, worlds, and norms by helping the psychoanalyst and the Lolos see each other as culturally structured entities, not as "aberrations" or "anomalies."

In Dai's translational imaginary, the strange—the other as strange—does not estrange. On the contrary, it works as an intercessor. It mediates a mutual recognition, a rapprochement between Muo and the natives, who acknowledge and accept his French and Chinese identity simultaneously. Or, we saw above, it "reunites" Muo and his former and current women acquaintances, brings the Volcano of the Old Moon magically into being despite—or perhaps precisely due to—its "foreign tongue." In turn, this presence is best seized as planetary co-presence, intimate aggregate of selves—Muo's and the Volcano's—both alike and unlike at same time, brought together by what they know and are no less than by what they do not know and are not yet prove able to imagine. Imagining other worlds, fantasizing about the meanings of the other's language and books, the self both leaps into a markedly different world and links up to other selves inside its own.

Notably, the former world is a prerequisite to the latter. We connect to our kin and kind, Dai implies, and we relate "authentically" to our relatives and our familiar universe insofar as the unfamiliar and the offbeat are already written into the formula of our being and as such shape our worldview. Our proximal, direct bonds abbreviate and dissimulate intervals, distances, and zigzags. Unlikely as it may seem, our cultural identity and, with it, our community belonging rest on these discontinuities and "impurities," and this debt must be owned up to—by planetary critics in the first place given that, as I have said, planetarity is a world structure of mutual indebtedness. It does not matter that this recognition is imperfect, that we cannot always "recognize" French or Tibetan. Nor is the self required to be an expert on otherness, to be fully conversant with its strange language, for example, or to "figure out" its culture through and through, provided such an expertise exists in the first place. In fact, the other's idiom, style, or text need not be completely "comprehensible," or, more exactly, this comprehension or proficiency does not have to be philological. Dai does not argue for this sort of competency and for the comprehension derived from it but for a more elementary recognition, for an intuition of, or "feel" for, what the other means in the petri dish of selfhood. To feel this way—to honor the original debt—all the self must do is reach the level of a certain empathy, of a certain propinquity or rapport between itself and other, a relation on which it can then build its own fantasies and play its own games. Stemming from these games, Dai suggests one more time, the individual is always a worldly composite: interlocutional and interlocational, intertextual and intercultural. Ever "derived" and "second-order," profoundly unoriginal at its very origin, it springs from a matrix of otherness.

§26. Taking Shelter

> We know this is our house, because it feels ours.
> —E. M. FORSTER, *Howards End*

"There is such shelter in each other," Carlene tells her friend Kiki in Zadie Smith's 2005 novel *On Beauty*.[145] The sentence, critics have been quick to point out, can be traced to *Howards End*'s famous epigraph and chapter 22 passage: "Only connect! . . . Only connect the prose and the passion, and both will be exalted, and human love will be seen at its highest. Live in fragments no longer. Only connect, and the beast and the monk, robbed of the isolation that is life to either, will die."[146] Smith herself has acknowledged that, "from the first line, . . . [*On Beauty*] is a novel inspired by a love for E. M. Forster, to whom my all fiction is indebted, one way or the other." "This time," she goes on, "I wanted to repay the debt with *hommage*."[147]

On Beauty can be read as a tribute to Forster on several levels. An exquisite response to *Howards End*, the novel repays Smith's debt with cultural interest by retelling Forster's story for the new millennium's globalizing world, with the politically conservative, religious-minded Caribbean-British Kippses and the racially mixed, more liberal American Belseys playing in today's Boston the parts the British writer assigns the Wilcoxes and the Schlegels, respectively, in *Howards End*'s early twentieth-century London. What is more, Smith's intertextual tour-de-force has a precise focus. Her novel's "Forster connection" vividly foregrounds connectedness itself. It is this very concept and the whole array of cosmopolitan cultural-emotional experiences associated with it that, through Forster, *On Beauty* carries into our time and retrofits planetarily.[148]

For Smith's world is world-saturated, markedly nethospherical. This is true at the macro level, and, as her 2012 novel *NW* assures us, at the micro level as well, for instance in Northwest London, a sort of urban strainer of the modern world's biocultural nutrients, with the symbolic "fat worm" in the "lump of London clay . . . passing the world through itself."[149] To live, we metabolize the world. We live fully, Smith suggests, to the extent that we take the world in, make connections, and relate to one another, because to be is to be in the world, and to be in the world is to be with others. In her 2000 debut novel, this defining togetherness is profoundly engrained in minds and bodies alike, in people's notions and complexions, in their thoughts and words, in their digestive systems and teeth, in linguistic roots and tooth roots. Deep as these roots may be, in *White Teeth* they are intertwined with other roots and thus make selfhood impossible to isolate as an ontologically and culturally discrete unit. The harder one digs—the deeper Smith's narrative "root canals"—the more the vertical cut through a self's biography proves to be a cross-section through other individual and collective destinies, and the political and ethical bearings of this netospherical revelation cannot be underestimated. *White Teeth* explicitly cautions us that, considering the heteroclite architecture of who we are, literal self-engendering—"autogamy," Smith calls it—is philosophically dubious, a repression of or cover for a process the author seizes as "cross-pollinating."[150] Of course, *White Teeth* itself is a fictional cross-pollination in its own right, what with its Salman Rushdie and Hanif Kureishi textual implants; so is Smith's next novel too, *The Autograph Man,* where one of the main heroes, Alex, is a "philograph," a collector and trader of autographs—others' quintessential writings, as it were—but also a writer, of late at work on a book of sorts listing in two separate (yet inevitably overlapping) columns all things "typically" Jewish and gentile;[151] and no less cross-pollinating is, we shall see in detail, *On Beauty.*

What draws Smith to Forster, in particular to the 1910 classic, is her precursor's relational imagination and, behind it, his uniquely cosmopolitan mind-set. The connection passage is just one among many setting forth the strong emphasis Forster lays on disinterested ties, friendship and affective bonds, human affiliations, and generally on the other and his or her world's nurturing proximity to the self no matter how far apart the two may be by location, ethno-racial background, or politics. Significantly, in Forster the modernist esthete of the Edwardian age, the closeted homosexual and sometimes critic of the British Empire, and the lover of Italian and Indian culture, the Jamaican-British writer finds a generous model of worldedness, of world sociality that she extends critically yet optimistically to a place and time where such values seem in short supply. We shall observe, the dearth of connectedness and of those others without whom neither connection nor self can develop is in Smith a matter of ethics as much as aesthetics. Also typical of her planetarily upgraded cosmopolitanism is a quintessentially and multiply connective—existential, historical, intertextual—approach to connectedness. For she tackles the latter with help from others and the books in which they broach it: Elaine Scarry's 1999 *On Beauty and Being Just*—from which Smith's *On Beauty* borrows more than just the title—and, first and foremost, *Howards End*.[152]

While Smith does not use Forster's title too, one of her lead characters is Howard Belsey, and the novel does *end* with him lecturing, assisted by "Smith," his graduate student, on Rembrandt before colleagues at Wellington College. Although *On Beauty* has Howard admit that he "can't stand Forster" (298), the ending is just another Forsterian clue, one more time decoding Smith's text as a narrative digestion of *Howards End*. This "metabolization" of the precursor gets under way from the outset, with the e-mail Howard receives from his son, Jerome. Critics like Gérard Genette would probably advise against ignoring the real "threshold"—and code breaker—of Smith's fictional world, namely, the H. J. Blackham motto to the novel, "We refuse to be each other." No doubt, the line can be read in more than one way, but, like Dai, Smith prompts us, via Forster, to take it as an invitation not to be *like* each other, interchangeable, but to imagine ourselves in the other's place so as to be there *for* one another and so, at last, be ourselves to the fullest.

Place, more exactly residential place, holds in *Howards End* a truly pivotal role, which in turn is part and parcel of a gender drama. Unquestionably more than an address, the place identified in the title of Forster's novel is a withness stage. It unfolds a bonding space, a domain of female "comradeship" (Forster's own word) and cradle of an evolving, worldly, cross-cultural, and cross-topological women's tradition. Serving to Ruth Wilcox as the one-time companion and "spiritual heir" Kiki Belsey is to Carlene Kipps, Margaret Schlegel is hardly committed to feminism yet vows that "if men came into Howards End it should be over her body" (98, 248). She does not dislike all men—including men like Henry Wilcox, whom she marries following Ruth's death—but the narrow-minded authoritarians Henry and his son Charles prove they can be. Their authority expresses itself in a blend of male chauvinism, jingoism, and self-centered, materialist, and individualist parochialism whose explicit target is, time and over again, early twentieth-century philosophies and practices of cosmopolitanism.

If Margaret's slogan is "connect," "My motto," Henry promptly replies, "is Concentrate." He makes no apologies either: "I've no intention of frittering away my strength with that sort of thing" (168). "It's no frittering away the strength," Margaret protests his dismissal of "connections," but "enlarging the space in which you may be strong" (168). Yet strength, Henry implies, comes from inside. It issues from within the individual and *his* culture, from the only concentrated space in which people can apply themselves, concentrate, and succeed even though they eventually wind up taking over other spaces for political and economic benefit, like Henry himself. They act with a markedly masculine authority and assert it topologically as they monopolize space, excluding from it undesirable presences such as women and aliens. In this regard (theirs), Howards End makes for a political synecdoche of the United Kingdom, an autarchically authoritarian and patriarchal *mise-en-abyme* of British society. Like the latter, the place is not to be opened or "left" to an "outsider, who'd never appreciate" it anyway, according to Henry and his son—on this account, in "conveying" Howards End to Margaret, they decide, "Mrs. Wilcox had been treacherous to the family, to the laws of property, to her own written word" (99). In Henry's view, a self coalesces as it fills out and lays exclusive claim to a determinate place. Intellectual and cultural self-possession and ownership of the place are coextensive; both are absolute and absolutely "allergic"—we noted apropos of Cărtărescu, and it is worth remembering here, that "allergy," as its etymon teaches us, is adverse reaction to "others," *álloi*. This is not Margaret's reaction, though. Instead, she believes we truly come into our own provided we open up ourselves and our homes to others or seek them out at their places. There are surely dangers we need to be aware of such as conquest, subjugation of others and their lands, and the like. After all, Margaret is weary of what cosmopolitanism itself might become, and oftentimes did become, at the hands of empire—a source, like the latter, of worldly "grayness" (276), a "caricature of infinity" not unlike the modern metropolis of London (242).

In this London, in Edwardian England generally, and in Forster's novel alike, socialism, equitable distribution of wealth, women's rights, and cosmopolitanism are hotly debated topics. Tibby, Margaret's brother, proclaims himself a cosmopolitan (146), and Helen, his sister, acts like one pointedly. Margaret, however, suspects that the cosmopolites of the time live cut off from "earth" (227)—the place *par excellence*—and, all "dust, and a stink, and cosmopolitan chatter" (190), they could not care less about other people. The "English," she thinks, is a "better vein than the cosmopolitan" (145), which, however, does not prevent Charles from pegging her as a "cosmopolitan," and a "German cosmopolitan" to boot, exactly the kind of type he "cannot stand" (100).

Charles's apprehension is worth pondering. In a sense, he is right. The Schlegels, Margaret included, represent an interesting "type" of cosmopolite. To Mrs. Munt, they are "English to the backbone" (25) and thereby distinct from the Germans, whom Margaret herself deems "too thorough." The "thorough" is the cosmopolitan's flipside in that it tends to leave little room for ambiguity, experiment, and adventure, for the alternatives and the outsiders who usually try them out first. Thoroughness evokes completion of an itinerary, a spatial voluntarism that implies carrying through a certain project as well as projection into and over space, henceforth adjudicated (mine) through and through, completely and for that reason exclusively, and marked as such geopolitically and culturally. The thorough kind invariably completes its actions, follows and is eventually "through" because it concentrates in Henry's sense, that is, because it acts with limited purview and within limited space and is if not hostile at least indifferent to others and their worlds. Thoroughness and self-centeredness are thus equivalent and, also in this context, provincialism's other names.

They are also what Margaret's father had sought to leave behind when he moved from Germany to England, but, oddly enough, imperial and acquisitive England is now turning into the Germany he had fled. This goes to show that neither country embodies "true" cosmopolitanism, nor is either its antithesis. In Forster, the cosmopolitan can be, in principle at least, nowhere and everywhere but not in an "uprooted," disembodied, and free-floating way. It lies in-between, much like the Schlegel sisters' type, which falls somewhere between the "English to the backbone" and the "Germans of the dreadful sort" (41). Indeed, cosmopolitanism is not confined to a place as long as it eludes the logic of thoroughness and imperial (German or British) adjudication. It goes without saying, it cannot be *of* a place, cannot be *one* place's monopoly no matter how "concentrated" human presence and its culture may be in that point in space. For, its own logic, its *other* logic, does not develop discretely or punctually, in or at unconnected points but in aggregate structures that world the separate dots together. At odds with self-absorbed "concentration" and its "fragmentary" *Weltanschauung*, cosmopolitan culture largely comes "after" fragments. It is exactly this notion of worlded culture that Margaret has in mind when she urges Henry not to live "in fragments" any more. On the other hand, whether spatial or cultural, imperial cosmopolitanism is not one of those loose world aggregates. As I have shown in part I (§10) and elsewhere, both private and collective, colonial-era and even classical models of cosmopolitanism often postulate, condone, and overall participate in ominous geocultural totalities insofar as such cosmopolitan philosophies, aesthetics, and lifestyles threaten to concentrate, centralize, level out, and equalize, thus marking the global onset of "gray" at the expense of the offbeat, the atypical, the incomplete, the less-than-thorough, and the well-composed emotionally and otherwise.[153] Smith's cosmopolitan parable, to which Forsterian intertextuality is so instrumental, reacts subtly against this threat. She is looking to Forster and, more specifically, to Forster's own "homage" to the great Romantics August Wilhelm and Friedrich Schlegel in an attempt to reimagine German Romanticism's cosmopolitanism and its relational philosophy for the planetary moment.

§27. "Greetings from Other Worlds"

Is, then, planetarism a neoromanticism? Given the growing number of Romantic references in *Reading for the Planet*, the question is not ill-placed. Admittedly, Romanticism and planetarism do share a sense of worldedness. They are both fascinated with those worldly convergences that will become "correspondences" in Baudelaire and in symbolism generally. With the Romantics, this supremely integrative drive of the imagination leads or at least aspires, very broadly, to absolute oneness, to the aesthetic of the absolute, and to the transcendental sublime. A postromanticism rather than a neoromanticism, planetarism is the immanent and shifty underbelly of such metaphysical-spiritualist categories. The rise of the netosphere has only sped up the piecing together of our multicentric, disjointed, and conflicted world. Therefore, as far as I am concerned, planetarism is not a new Romanticism. I would point, however, to Romanticism and, in it, especially to some less metaphysically leaning and less synthesis-tempted definitions of cosmopolitanism and world letters as important harbingers of twentieth-century ontologies of worldedness and, of late, planetarity.

So does Smith, actually, in Margaret's exhortation. Cosmopolitan despite its anti-cosmopolitan rhetoric, this is an indirect paean to her father and, through him, a salute to the other Schlegels often mentioned apropos of Margaret, Helen, and Tibby. However, few have noticed that not only does Forster "borro[w] Margaret and Helen's patronymic from the Romantic philosopher Friedrich Schlegel," but that the German thinker's "early thought [also] becomes the (unelaborated) touchstone for their beliefs" as the novel "elevates his value for personal relationships and love to such heights that they just might overcome world-historical problems such as the fate of [the British] Empire" at the dawn of the last century.[154] The English Schlegels' *pater* refers the reader quite transparently to his German patrons. He was a "distant relation of the great critic [Friedrich] Schlegel," as we learn from an earlier version of the novel,[155] and also a cultural relay in a cross-national tradition of relatedness, living proof of a more generous, "worlded" model of kinship, of the notion of a family of spirits and ideals in which intellectual and emotional ties may outreach those grounded, and oftentimes locked, in a common birthplace, mother tongue, or ethnicity. "He was not," *Howards End* assures us, "the aggressive German, so dear to the English journalist, nor the domestic German, so dear to the English wit. If one classed him at all it would be as the countryman of Hegel and Kant, as the idealist, inclined to be dreamy, whose Imperialism was the Imperialism of the air" (41). Dismayed by "bigness," "Pan-Germanism," and the utilitarian "thoroughness" of the "vulgar mind" deprived of the "imagination" (42), the quasi-"unclassifiable" German is of a sort "that was more prominent in Germany fifty years ago than now" (41).

August Wilhelm died in 1845 and Friedrich sixteen year before, but in mid-nineteenth-century German culture this category was undeniably influential. Alongside Friedrich Hölderlin, Jean Paul, Novalis, Friedrich Schelling, and others, the Schlegels themselves illustrated the so-called Herder effect in the Germany and Europe of the time.[156] Accordingly, they formulated after Johann Gottfried Herder a two-pronged Romantic aesthetics that sought, on the one hand, to identify an independent, distinct profile for German literature and rising national literatures across Europe, to "nationalize" and define in specific terms the continent's "young" cultures, and on the other, to deal with modern literature comparatively—*weltliterarisch*, after Goethe—in international and historical contexts of codependence by "connecting" recent and ancient, European and Asian traditions philologically. The duality of the project lived on beyond Herder's time and got increasingly troublesome as German nationalism escalated and the imperialism abhorred by Margaret's father took off. But, overall, Forster is quite right to stress the supranational, "synthetic" element. Friedrich Schlegel theorized Romanticism itself as a new if incomplete and fluctuant synthesis, a rhetoric of worldedness capable of taking on but not necessarily of "overcoming" the fragmentation of modern life. On this topic he composed his own *Fragmente*, among other works published in the journals *Lyceum* and *Athenäeum* in the late 1790s and the first years of the next century.

In an essay on the Schlegelian aesthetic of the fragment, J. Hillis Miller offers that "[i]f [Schlegel's] fragments are really fragments, they cannot be joined together in a chain, garland, or system. However they are assembled, they still remain a contiguous set of incompatibles. It would be a dangerous mistake, for example, to try to use a chain of fragments to anchor a boat. They just cannot be connected to one another in a way that will hold. A chain of fragments is a chain that does not enchain or concatenate." Neither part of a whole nor a whole unto itself, a "true fragment" is in Schlegel, Miller proposes, a "catachresic allegory," a figure of the "wholly other," or what the German idealist calls "chaos."[157] The point is, of course, to "sublate," to abolish while also somewhat preserving this chaos so as to convert it into a positive value, a structure likely to capture some of its swarming heterogeneity and irreducible meaning.

Following his conversion to Catholicism later in life, Schlegel himself tried to rewrite his own fragmentary thoughts into a clarifying synthesis. But the attempt met with scant success. More consequential for Forster and his characters was Schlegel's early wrestling with a chaotic concept that presents itself as an ontological given as well as a moral and aesthetic dilemma. The fragment dares us to acknowledge the incomplete, unconnected, isolated, and "sheltered" mode of existence as a reality of life and at the same time to aim beyond fragmentariness, isolation, and parochialism by opening our own selves and places to others. Margaret's "Live in fragments no longer" injunction recognizes the fragment with all that it implies and thus gestures toward a form of sociality—rather than a firm social totality—in which fragments, individuals, and cultural models link up and shore up one another *mindful of each other's incompleteness and distinctiveness*. For, sheltering an other, if authentic, entails sheltering the other's otherness itself and thereby stops short of taking the other in "thoroughly," assimilating it into the host. The metabolization of the world obtains ethically if, as in Dai, both the self and the world are still distinct at the end of the autopoietic process. Assimilation, the fall into non-distinction, and the reduction of the world to the structure of selfsameness are high on the agenda of the imperial cosmopolitanism Margaret casts aside. Uniformity-inducing, this is a cosmopolitanism of economic, cultural, and interpersonal ties that takes us into a "gray" world and, insists *Howards End*, eventually "outside humanity altogether" (287) because humanness quintessentially inheres in variety, nuances, and dissimilarities. Without them, it loses its aura, its "glow." Still, "[a] place, as well as a person, may catch the glow," she tells Helen, and "this all leads to comfort in the end." "It is," she discloses, "part of the battle against sameness. Differences—eternal differences planted by God in a single family, so that there may always be colour; sorrow perhaps, but colour in the daily gray" (287). Following her father and his philosophical mentors, Margaret recommends nurturing those connections that lead up to a chromatic, mosaic-like world where people connect because they rescue their differences, where they feel for each other because they "feel" these very distinctions. Difference, they suspect, provides a *common* language, is the bond, the ethical as well as the aesthetical glue of a world of "beauty and adventure" (281); we talk to one another and are with each other not over but through or across our differences.

While acknowledging in the *Howards End* chapter of *Others* that Forster names his characters after the illustrious Romantics, Miller opines that readers will have to figure out for themselves what to make of this, for "the book will not clearly decide."[158] The critic does make his decision, however, when he contends that in *Howards End* "the otherness of race, nationality, class, and gender can in one way or another, by tolerance and sympathy, be reduced to the same." "This is true," he explains, "in spite of Forster's celebration of difference. The nation-, class-, and gender-grounded other can be comprehended and so incorporated, at least in principle, into an ideal society such as Margaret and Helen Schlegel imagine as their utopian goal."[159] But it seems to me that the *Howards End* passages reproduced above, which Miller also discusses, lend themselves to an "other" sort of reading, and let me point out too that they are hardly isolated in the novel's Friedrich Schlegel–derived economy of otherness. Further, it is this economy itself that tips the balance in favor of en ethical "decision" that the novel, I would also maintain, does make. This decision, Miller himself recognizes, gives pride of place to the "unseen" and the "obscure," the "unknown" and the "invisible," in brief to a "wholly other" whose features fit almost perfectly the description of Schlegel's "chaos" and thus of the fragmentary.[160] Margaret contradicts herself more than once much as her philosophical ancestor did (to Hegel's despair), but she does not advocate sameness, nor does the novel overall push "assimilation." What they both promote, by and large, is the world and its places and human associations—homes, families, communities—as domains and regimens of connections among entities who are held together emotionally by their fundamental humanness, to wit, by that which in each of us affords our individuality, makes us different from one another, and thus ultimately if paradoxically sets us apart.

It is this visionary, "differential" cosmopolitanism that draws Forster to the Schlegels and Smith to Forster, the culture of linkages that boost life's colorfulness and make the world concurrently more hospitable and more beautiful. Worlding as world-shrinking, as netospherical becoming, but, by the same token, worlding as sheltering, hosting, beckoning, and taking in: Carlene, Kiki, and at last Howard himself are not immune to this *geoaesthetic* of planetarity. They respond to the inviting radiance of this worlding world, to the heartwarming aura that renders the different, the unassimilated, the un-conceptualized, and the mysterious out of the reach of the instinctively rationalizing self yet no less approachable for that matter, worth caring for and sheltering. As in Forster, the moral and the beautiful are the two faces of the same coin, share the same space, and ultimately make space itself a space of sharing. In a larger sense, the world itself becomes a geography of sharing where the topological, the ethical, and the aesthetical coincide. Smith's planetarism no longer treats world space as a conquest zone or as surface, "acreage," or real estate, but as an affective commons, a cultural-affective field of feelings and circuitry of bonds. The world is worlding but it does not induce identicalness; in the highly complex spatial, ethical, and aesthetic dynamic of planetary sheltering, the nethospherical provides the necessary correction of the netospherical: sheltering's price—not that there should be one—is not the co-optation of the guest into the host. Blackham's "We refuse to be each other" ventriloquizes Margaret's apprehension of sameness—this refusal is, after all, a rejection of equivalence quite literally—while deploring separation, "discreteness," and disinterest in the other's welfare. For, indeed, "[t]here is such a shelter in each other," or there should be, regardless of what Monty Kipps, Smith's version of Henry Wilcox, means when he quotes Jean-Paul Sartre's *Huis clos* infamous "L'enfer, c'est les autres" ("Hell is others").[161]

These seem to be the two ethical poles of Smith's novel. I say "seem" because the contrast is far from absolute, based as it is on a misreading of the famous dictum, which, as the French writer himself complained, had been "misunderstood." What he meant was not that our "relations with others are tainted," troublesome, and "infernal" by definition but that *if* these relations are "twisted, vitiated, then the other can be to us nothing else than hell." That is "because in reality the others are the most important thing within ourselves that we can draw from to know who we are." "When we think about ourselves, when we try to find out who we are," Sartre clarifies his paradox, "we actually use the knowledge others already have of us. We form an opinion of ourselves by means of tools others have given us. Whatever I say about myself, an other's judgment is always contained in it. This means that if my relations with an other are bad, I am completely dependent on this other. And then I am truly in hell."[162] Forster and Smith after him refute this sort of subjection of the self to the other and of the other to the self. It is not hierarchical "dependence" they argue but co-dependence, ethical relation, which is precisely what Sartre intended to underscore. In this light, we do not have a choice: our selves have always absorbed others and their views, which we have used to view and represent ourselves, to stake claims to our identities. We develop a proprietary sense of our being and place as we borrow from others, as we let them into our lives and thoughts. We give them sanctuary, for a night or forever, but they also lend us the shelter of their minds so we can make up our own and thus come to grips with the secret of our beings. This is a process of inclusion intellectually and affectively, pertaining as it does to politics, psychology, morals, as well as aesthetics. Throughout his career, Howard has endeavored, as Smith writes in *On Beauty*, to "recast Aesthetics as a rarefied language of exclusion" (155), with beauty as elusive and forbidding as the unfathomable shadows of a Rembrandt painting. Opposed to this understanding of art is Carlene and Kiki's passion for the Hyppolite painting, which the older woman leaves the younger one with a transparent nod to the testamentary nexus between Ruth and Margaret in *Howards End*.

This intertextual ploy is among many others suggesting that Smith's reading of Forster's own reading of the Schlegels reworks *Howards End*'s cosmopolitan discourse of connectedness into a more ethically worlded vision. Anticipating Smith's planetary remapping of the circumatlantic world so as to collocate London and Boston and the Caribbean and New England, Margaret's struggle to associate disparate and often conflicting values such as practicality and aesthetic sensibility, "prose" and "poetry," "England" and "Germany," and thus expand the latticework of people, ideas, and feelings across the barriers of class, ethnicity, geography, and culture, is undercut by the webs of exploitation, inequality, and pain into which the British and German Empires themselves were turning at the time. Margaret's endeavor testifies to the "good," difference- and distinction-grounded cosmopolitanism; the imperial networks, to the "bad" sort, which is, as far as Margaret is concerned, the one that unfortunately carries the day. If, generally speaking, her attempts fall short, in her family and outside it, that is not only because her project and its historical context are at odds but also because this project remains too "Schlegelian," too idealistic. As a result, the sodalities and solidarities she aims at across and against both absolute distinctiveness and complete sameness do not strike roots as she has hoped. Responding to this failure, or quasi failure, of Forster's cosmopolitan designs, Smith employs the Haitian painting—an actual artwork, she specifies[163]—as a more productive "bonding" device.

Paul Gilroy has warned about the shortcomings of those bonds and alliances predicated on, and thus limited by, a "raciological" understanding of communal interaction and political effectiveness. "The spaces in which 'races' come to life," he maintains, "are a field from which political interaction has been banished. It is usually replaced by enthusiasm for the cheapest pseudo-solidarities: forms of connection that are imagined to arise effortlessly from shared phenotypes, culture, and bio-nationalities." The "glamour of sameness" stemming from the latter is certainly deceiving.[164] Controversial as this position has been, it helps us come to grips with what happens between Carlene, a Caribbean-British woman, and Kiki, her African American friend, and more broadly with what occurs intertextually "between" *Howards End* and *On Beauty*. Simply put, what the Haitian canvas offers the two black women is a more tangible, affective-aesthetic space in which, and in response to which, they connect across their all-too-conspicuous differences. Nor does this connectedness arena annul race. But this bond lends race an emotional substance that proves more palpable, more immediate than anything else two women of African background might have in common. That is to say, what Smith is after is a more nuanced form of sharing. This form does not preexist. It is not a priori rooted in putative racialist-genomic sameness but implies a project, a state of being with an other that self and other work toward rather than take for granted. Carlene has developed her own relation to the painting while Kiki has hardly one at the beginning of their relationship, but, following her son's "liberating" the painting from Monty's Wellington office, she begins to respond to the art object and through it to its previous owner, which response in turn interpellates her estranged husband's own aesthetic dealings and thus might just mark a fresh start in their own relationship.

As Milan Kundera notes in a commentary on Kafka, beauty is "perpetual astonishment"; it shocks us because it is essentially the "beauty of strangeness."[165] In this sense, on which Smith, Cărtărescu, Dai, McEwan, and other planetary writers are so keen, Howard Belsey is not off the mark: in beautiful paintings and books, we are intrigued by the unfamiliar and the non-familial, by what differs from us and our kin, from what we normally do, know, and surround ourselves with. We tend to like that which surprises us. And so even though one should not charge the sheltered for shelter, he or she offers something in exchange anyway: beauty itself. Lying, one more time, where the ethical and the aesthetic intersect, the beautiful is *intrinsic* to an other's strangeness and to otherness generally, thus reinforcing the affective-aesthetic thrust of geoaesthetics. No doubt, this other, this different, may be forbidding, hard to figure out, to put together conceptually. That is, it may be, like the Schlegelian chaos and fragment, wholly different from what we expect and are used to. As such, it may keep us off. But the different *qua* different in the object we gaze at, daunting as its difference may be, is also that which draws us. In that, any aesthetics, or, as Kundera calls it, any "poetics," is or can become cosmopolitan.

What I find truly remarkable, though, is that, as Elaine Scarry contends in the book that made such a powerful impact on Smith, we react to this object mimetically regardless of how bizarre and strange it appears to us. "[B]eautiful things," Scarry contends, "always carry greetings from other worlds with them."[166] However, our impulse is often to try and replicate their beauty, to "follow" them no matter how otherworldly their call. This is a befitting reaction aesthetically as well as ethically. For, the internal equilibrium, the formal achievement we appreciate in the beautiful and the fair outshine "loveliness of aspect." They spill over the boundaries of the admired object, flood the extra-aesthetical, the social, and the interpersonal, and hint at ways of making sociality itself beautiful by suggesting that art's "fairness" and balance of proportions must convert into a "symmetry of everyone's relation to one another" outside it. Art's inside and outside become then hard to delimitate, and with them, one more time, the ethical and the aesthetical too, which overlap once art has issued its unique "invitation to ethical fairness."[167] Beauty is thus poised to hold sway both within and without beautiful things, with ethics and politics "field-specific" applications of aesthetic criteria. The latter's jurisdiction stretches out beyond museums and libraries into the sociocultural sphere, which can now be judged on its "sheltering" effectiveness, in terms of how "symmetrically"—how "aesthetically"—it is occupied by "me" and "you," "my" kind and "yours." Thus underpinned by an aesthetic, "differential" cosmopolitanism, space—social, national, planetary—at long last becomes, suggests Smith, a domain where self and other come together by virtue rather than at the expense of their individualizing traits.

To reiterate: planetarism does not merely "aestheticize" the world. Writers like Cărtărescu, Dai, and Smith do not cut artworks off from the "real world," nor do they make the world into an aesthetic object showcased outside the purview of the ethical and the political. If any aestheticism is in play here at all, its Prevailing Operating System is, indeed, geoaesthetic. And, to reemphasize this aspect of planetarism, geoaesthetics does not limit itself to taking the measure of the world's beautiful things. As a branch of geoculture, it also positions things in the world; it "finds" them present in the world rather then "putting" them in there. At the same time, as I have argued throughout, being present in the world, being present *tout court*, is an offshoot of worldly co-presence because being-with comes before—and comes to afford and sustain—being to the point that *it renders ontological and aesthetic well-being a function of ethical with-being*. This is, in fact, a planetary principle, a (or perhaps *the)* planetary *nomos*. Planetarily speaking, things and places—whatever pleases, expresses, and locates us—*are* because they are worlded, located in the world themselves, and so, from the standpoint of the planetary artist and, by the same token, of the planetary critic, to fancy all these things, to weigh them, and otherwise to imagine them require first and foremost imagining them in the world, *enabling the imagination to world its object*. In that, planetarism works as a geolocating system; planetary criticism's job—the reverse engineering described earlier under §17—is to take the system apart, to show how it works, and evaluate what its workings yield.

Ethical, ontological, topological, political, and economic simultaneously, the planetary *nomos* regulates a number of interrelated world-positioning operations: it renders the insular vicinal; it sets up location as collocation, putting "me" (up) at "your place" and putting me and "my place" in "yours," and the other way around; and it affords the hosting aptitude of the guest and the other reciprocities and amphibologies of hosting/guesting, in the great line of thought linking Ancient Greek *xeniā* and Roman *hospitium* with the French *hôte* (both "guest" and "host"), Levinas, Derrida, J. Hillis Miller, and other recent philosophers and theorists.[168] These protocols trace a certain progression of planetarization—of planetarization viewed as contiguous or shared space, location, and dwelling—depending on the intensities and extensities with which the writers' imagination translates the planet's collocational principle into fictional space. This gradation of planetarity runs the whole gamut of co-spatiality from vicinity (adjacency of habitation) to contractual (a posteriori) mutuality of hosting to ethical (postulated) sheltering that makes hosting both a duty and free of charge because one has already been hosted and sheltered in the planetary commons before one hosts and gives shelter or sanctuary to an other. What we have in this withness spectrum is, at one pole, "softer" forms of planetary situatedness clustered around topological juxtapositions in which self and other may border on one another while remaining territorially separate, and, at the opposite pole, "stronger" varieties of shared space in which self and other crisscross each other's zones or, also to varying degrees, coincide geographically. Accordingly, one can adjoin an other's space or home, living side by side with it; one can cohabitate, that is, share the same territory or abode; one can live in it, alongside or among others; or your space or home can overlap with his or hers.

§28. Snowflakes: The Imagination as Geopositioning Technology

Planetary co-spatiality and the geopositioning system behind it are signature themes of post–Cold War fiction. Roughly put, they originate with postcolonial literature. However, authors like Kureishi, Smith, Lahiri, Foer, Krauss, Houellebecq, Muşina, Hemon, Shteyngart, Ugrešić, Iva Pekárkova (*Gimme the Money*), Olga Tokarczuk (*House of Day, House of Night*), Saša Stanišić (*How the Soldier Repairs the Gramophone*), Yelena Akhtiorskaya (*Panic in a Suitcase*), and Hamid (*The Reluctant Fundamentalist* and *How to Get Filthy Rich in Rising Asia*) rewire the system's spatial capabilities. The new, planetary Prevailing Operating System functions as a literary GPS that registers preponderantly those geolocational or, more exactly, geocollocational phenomena that I have called "telescopies." "Strong" as these co-spatial arrangements and apportionments of polity, language, religion, race, and ethnicity may be, they rarely result in utopias of harmoniously multicultural cohabitation.

Take, for example, Pamuk's 2002 novel *Snow*. In the book, contemporary Istanbul, a mere three hundred miles south of Cărtărescu's Bucharest, then, farther away, the eastern Anatolia town of Kars, and with them Turkey claim "accessions" to wider geopolitical aggregates such as the European Union and are concurrently reclaimed by multiple forces of religious, regional, and separatist entrenchment dead set on rescinding Mustafa Kemal Atatürk's secularist legacy. Historically between a rock and a hard place, Pamuk's country finds itself trapped between ill-assorted geopolitical models and choices. One is the greater world of NATO (since 1951) and Europe (an increasingly contradictory aspiration), for which the Young Turks' modernity-bent reformism had paved the way. Pulling in the opposite direction are Iran-backed Islamists and, yet in another, radical Kurdish autonomists (the Kurdistan Workers' Party, or PKK), of late also fighting ISIS (Islamic State of Iraq and Syria). Turkey's predicament, Pamuk hints, lies in what might be called the extraneous fallacy: the assumption that, first, such options, positions, affiliations, and the cultural-religious models derived from or attributed to them are indomitably unworlded, external to each other, following as they allegedly do separate—rather than intersecting—trajectories in space and time; and second, that they are mutually, and self-evidently, exclusive.

Nowhere is this antinomic worldview more ingeniously refuted than in the telescoping episode where Ka, the protagonist, talks about "All Humanity and the Stars," the "constellating" poem he composes in reaction to his companion's comment that "the history of the small city [of Kars] has become as one with the history of the world."[169] "In the notes he made afterward," Ka "described [the poem's] subject"

> as the sadness of a city forgotten by the outside world and banished from history; the first lines followed a sequence recalling the opening scenes of the Hollywood films he had so loved as a child. As the titles rolled past, there was a faraway image of the earth turning slowly; as the camera came in closer and closer, the sphere grew and grew, until suddenly all you could see was one country, and of course—just as in the imaginary films Ka had been watching in his head since childhood—this country was Turkey; now the blue waters of the Sea of Marmara and the Bosphorus and the Black Sea and the Nişantaş of Ka's childhood, with the traffic policeman on Teşvikiye Avenue, the street of Niğar [*sic*] the Poetess, and trees and rooftops (how lovely they looked from above!); then came a slow pan across the laundry hanging on the line, the billboard advertising Tamek canned goods, the rusty gutters and the pitch-covered sidewalks, before the pause at Ka's bedroom window. Then a long tracking shot through the window of rooms packed with books, dusty furniture, and carpets, to Ka at a desk facing the other window; panning over his shoulder, the camera revealed a piece of paper on the desk and, following the fountain pen, came finally to rest on the last letters of the message he was writing, thus inviting us to read:
>
> ADDRESS ON THE DAY OF MY ENTRANCE
> INTO THE HISTORY OF POETRY: POET KA,
> 16/8 NIGÂR THE POETESS STREET,
> NI[Ș]ANTA[Ș,] ISTANBUL, TURKEY

As the narrator adds in a reference to the snowflake-shaped cosmic diagram he comes across in one of Ka's notebooks, "discerning readers will already have guessed" that Ka's address "is located on the Reason axis but positioned to suggest the power of the imagination."[170] Intersecting Reason and Memory,[171] the Imagination re- or geo(-)positions Ka(r)—the artist, the place, and Turkey with them—planetarily, as it does, we have noticed, with Cărtărescu's Bucharest, with Dai's Szechuan village, and with Smith's London neighborhood and buildings. An intercontinental quilting point, Turkey is remapped by Pamuk's planetarism interstitially, "between continents," as we say forgetting that this is geographically impossible and that the interstice is as much a cleft or crevice as it is a contact zone, a test *and* a provision for a continuum. Turkey thus lies across worlds, religions, rationalities, and individual-collective memories; it brings them all together, as it has since the fifteenth century, and probes their togetherness, their capacity and willingness to be together as much as its own. The most "Caribbean" among Eurasian political entities, its making is a historical dramatization of the *poétique de la relation* Edouard Glissant formulated in *Le Discours antillais* and Spivak, Ramazani, and others lean on in their treatment of planetary poetics. By a mix of zoom-in and zoom-out scenes, Pamuk and his authorial alter ego both locate their places in the outside worlds and make out these worlds in the Turkish quotidian, lying inside one another like so many Chinese boxes, overlapping, or traversing each other to weave the Alephic fractality—the "snowflake"—of planetarity.

Like Cărtărescu's Mircea, who, we have seen, also screens snowflakes for cosmic geometries and elaborated, translucent worlds, Ka does not have to invent the "little things" his compatriots live and die for. These things are already there, in the Universal Studios picture of the turning planet. But he needs to turn to the picture a director's eye trained for this kind of planetary "detail." The magnifying-glass workings of the microanalysis also enable the macroanalytic flipside, which helps him detect the world's multitudinous footprints in snowy Kars. It is, arguably, all a matter of scale, of a revisionary scalarity no longer keyed to national-linguistic territoriality but willing to take the risk of another direction performatively and geoculturally, of other understandings, dramatizations, and mappings. Both imaginary and real, so vivid in Kars's Turkish-Kurdish-Iranian-Armenian-Russian-West European urban potpourri and so subtly reinforced by Pamuk's Brechtian-Pirandellian theatrical and intertextual games, this is a complex cartography in which place, affect, faith, gender, ethnicity, and governance crystallize snowflake-like into aggregates of culture inside, outside, and astride statal and sectarian turfs.

Staged in Kars's back alleys and teahouses as well as in the local theater during the botched anti-Islamist military takeover is a world drama at once thespian and geopolitical, imagined and unfictitious, literal and metaphorical, private and collective, Turkish and transnational, historical and contemporary, Ottoman and post-Atatürk, past and unfolding. The copula, the "and" linking up such assumed antinomies, sets up too the reciprocities, mutual inclusions, co-spatialities, and co-temporalities fostered by "as," "in," "or," "alongside," "with," "while," and "at the same time." We can think of these connectors as narrative-imaginary and geosyntactic operators that reposition Kars in the world at the same time that they co-position Kars *and* the world by variously enforcing and qualifying their conjunctive pathos. Such qualifications do not simply bring out the multifarious and self-conflicted worldliness lying inside or astride Kars; they also point to the reciprocal encroaching of these worlds and of their ontologies.

This is where the Brechtian play produced, directed, and watched by Kars's residents at the aptly named "National Theater" comes in (155). Only, the jarring *Verfremdungseffekt* of the lethal shots fired by the soldier actors into the auditorium does not "distance" the audience from the world on stage properly speaking. Or, if it does, it does so insofar as it de-fictionalizes what goes on behind the imaginary "fourth wall" through which modern drama theory and, after it, common parlance ordinarily separate the stage and its fictional realm from the first rows and the "real people" in them. Obviously, *Snow*'s spectators recognize themselves (how could they not?) in the dramatis personae. True, in a way, the play's world is a dramatic production, and, further, according to Bertolt Brecht's *epische Theater*, in order for the spectators to remain detached from the plot and maintain contact with their own world so as to rediscover it anew, perhaps critically, the theatrical artifact has to be flaunted as such, as an illusion-spawning mechanism. In another way, though, that world is no make-believe but a clip of the everyday footage, complete with Kars's urban grimness, religious strife, power grabs, women's plight, the Kurds' struggle for autonomy, and, again, recognizable figures. To that extent, that world *is* ontologically on stage in the National Theater, where the Turkish drama plays out as a world show and, on another level, as a show of worldedness, as well as a show-and-tell of sorts, a display of experience. The "distancing" effect thus does not inhere so much in an intervening distance as in one that has more complex intellectual properties, a distance that "estranges" and defamiliarizes (*fremd* means "strange," "foreign," and "alien" in German) while pulling the public into the play's fictional fold. For the estrangement and defamiliarization are not achieved as the gap between the world-as-play and the attendees' world widens but, to the contrary, as it closes, as the aesthetic violence of community theater and the political violence scripting the theater of Kars's communality ooze into one another and ultimately suspend the ontological interval—the "fourth wall"—between illusion and war, metareality and reality.

§29. The Beirut Wall

> Returning to Lebanon was taking me on a world tour.
> —SORJ CHALANDON, *Le quatrième mur*

The fourth wall is both the central theme and the title of French journalist and fiction author Sorj Chalandon's internationally acclaimed 2013 novel *Le quatrième mur*. The parallels between Chalandon's work and Pamuk's are geoculturally, politically, religiously, narratively, and aesthetically unmistakable, so much so that *Le quatrième mur* reads at times as a replay of *Snow*'s situations, issues, and tensions on a larger scale and in a more acutely tragic tonality. Thus, in Chalandon, Beirut and Lebanon overall provide a similarly convulsive and geopolitically "intersectional" backdrop to a civil war and an ethno-religious factionalism that greatly escalate the social unrest and Turkish-Kurdish skirmishes of Kars and its surroundings; the Palestinian tragedy reprises the Kurds' ordeal with a vengeance; Ka, whose liberal leanings got him in trouble earlier in his career and had to leave his native Turkey, has been living in exile in Frankfurt, Germany, while Chalandon's narrating protagonist, far-left activist Georges, hails from Paris, but they travel to same area, the Near-Middle East (the Levant), where they are both treated as Westerners; in Beirut—the "Paris of the Middle East"—Georges too involves himself in a turmoil whose roots are entwined with various episodes of Turkish, French, British, and Russian imperialism, and, of late, with the American presence in the region.

Both heroes act as intermediaries also. They go back and forth between various feuding parties and even attempt to bring them together. Drawn to Kars by a flurry of female suicides, on which he has been commissioned to do an article for a European newspaper, Ka meets and interviews the local political players, including Islamic militants who have taken up armed resistance. The poet is wearing a reporter's hat surely not his size. He insists on giving everybody a fair hearing, even though his own convictions are a matter of public record and, as we gather, will eventually cost him his life back in Germany. His goal is to bear witness rather than to take sides. Equally out of his depth, Georges does, one might say, just the opposite. An outsider too, he eventually chooses the path of action, of violent retribution, and survives. Unlike Ka, the Frenchman is not a foreign correspondent bound by the laws of objectivity. But, in principle at least, he cannot be an actor politically either because he is supposed to be a director, namely, to direct a play whose cast is representative, as in *Snow,* of virtually all political, ethnic, and religious factions. While his pro-Palestinian position is a secret neither to the reader nor to most people he comes across in war-ravaged Lebanon, it must take a back seat to his impossible task and to the quasi neutrality this task presumably calls for.

Not a stage director by training, Georges becomes one reluctantly, at the bequest of his friend Samuel. A Jewish-Greek theater director well known for mounting his plays in war zones and sites of social conflict, Sam lies terminally ill in a Paris hospital bed, and Georges agrees to complete Sam's project and fly to Beirut to see through the production of Jean Anouilh's *Antigone* forty years after its writing and thirty-eight years after its 1944 premiere in Nazi-occupied Paris. The Beirut performance is set for October 1, 1982, with a string of rehearsals during the previous months. But Kataeb leader and president-elect of Lebanon Bashir Gemayel is assassinated on September 14, and the massacres in the Palestinian refugee camps of Sabra and Shatila follow suit on the sixteenth and eighteenth. Imane, the Palestinian woman playing Antigone, is raped and murdered in Shatila. Charbel, the Maronite Christian picked for Creon's part although, unlike his brother, he is not a Phalangist (an important distinction, as we shall see), and the rest of the cast—Nakad, a Druze assigned Haemon's role, Yevkinée, the Armenian Ismene, the Shia Euridice, and the others—are either dead, back to the daily business of killing and being killed, or have fled. Sam's dream is shattered.

Or so it seems. On a closer look, things prove more complicated. One could argue, in fact, that Chalandon pulls it off as a novelist—as the director of the novel, if you will—where the director-in-the-novel fails, or, more accurately, that the former builds on the latter's work, picking up where Georges, his alter ego, left off. That is, if Georges does not actually keep the promise he made Sam, Chalandon, who, like his hero, also witnessed Shatila's atrocities, does, through the novel itself. As a whole, *Le quatrième mur* performs the *Antigone* whose performance Georges rehearsed, practices what the rehearsals practiced for. For, indeed, the book can be read as *Snow*'s National Theater episode writ large, with Pamuk's Brechtian play-in-the-novel episode scaled up to become Chalandon's novel-as-play and by the same movement taking over the entire book. This is how the multiple walls between the aborted tragedy and the play's tragic staging as *Le quatrième mur* tumble down; this is how the divide separating, on one side, the protagonist and his own universe and ideals and, on the other side, the author, his commitments, and his world disappears but only to echo and reinforce the wiping away of cognate fault lines inside and outside the novel, as well as of the very inside-outside distinction: between the (fictional) tragedy, the *Antigone* that never happened (was never produced), and the (actual) tragedy of Sabra and Shatila (and Damour and Karantina before them), even though the war's horrors are recorded fictionally, in and by Chalandon's novel; more broadly, between imagined tragedy and historical tragedy; further, between tragedy as performance, as enactment, and tragedy as pure act, as factual occurrence; between the actors' and actresses' own private existence and the imaginary destinies they conjure up *as* actors and actresses; finally, and perhaps more starkly, between the raw ontology of eventfulness sanctioning the "real lives" of the spectators in their seats and the aesthetic ontology framing the cast's imaginary exploits on stage.

Summing up the rest, the last divide is encapsulated by the novel's title. As Chalandon tells an interviewer, "[t]he fourth wall is, of course, a fairly well-known drama term referring to the 'wall' that demarcates the universe of the play from the real universe, and an actor shatters this wall to pieces when, during a representation, he addresses the public directly." But, he adds, the title is also a pun. Accordingly,

> this fourth wall is the one imprisoning Georges, the wall closing up his prison and making his return impossible. It is the wall dividing the living from the dead. Georges is the one who builds this wall; he walls himself alive into his madness and into the war. The choice for this title was also a way of designating the impossibility of producing the play amidst Lebanon's raging war and with actors from all camps involved. As a writer, I wanted this to work out, that is, I wanted the representation to take place, but I realized that this was not possible. The novelist himself had to face up to the unfeasibility of this foolish project.[172]

This recognition notwithstanding, the novel is not all doom and gloom. It does not give up all hope that the war will end. "Let us say," the author allows, "that a war is over when the monuments honoring the dead have been built. There is a monument for the dead in each French village. But where are the monuments for those killed in the Lebanese war, for the Druze, for the Christians, for the Palestinians? Where will one go to collect one's thoughts and pay one's respects? We need to make sure," Chalandon insists, "that the memory of the dead stays alive, that we preserve it, that the war's traces remain visible. The monuments erected for the dead are war's collective graves." "War," he goes on, "is an infernal machine that blows to pieces everything within its reach. And, when we are not talking about a war in which two countries face off but about battles moving from one street to the next, battles in which neighbors, friends, or even members of the families fight each other, what we are talking about is a war that cannot be won, which is something I find very unsettling." If this is not the kind of "message" some might expect a novel such as *Le quatrième mur* to convey, that is because, Chalandon declares, his literature has no message to deliver. Instead, what he wants his fiction to accomplish is to "confront [his] characters with huge problems, which they must handle the best they can, whether these problems involve a betrayal, a promise, or a sham. . . . Here, Sam and Georges have run into something too big for them, something that will crush them. I feel for them, but I also do for Creon, as much as I do for Antigone."[173]

The novel may not carry a straightforward "message," or a single message for that matter, but this makes it neither meaningless nor defeatist. What bears underscoring, rather, is the remarkable complexity of a message striving to capture the "bigness" of the world scenario into which the two directors set out to work *Antigone*'s representation: the mutually contested, parallel, dovetailing, or overlapping geohistorical narratives, the co-territorialities and reciprocal land claims following from them, the entangled jurisdictions, rights, and responsibilities, the shiftiness of Lebanon's victim-victimizer dialectic, and, more broadly, the sheer quagmire of Lebanese politics itself, all of which are only magnified by the post–Cold War, regional and international angle from which *Le quatrième mur* surveys the war theater of the Lebanese early 1980s.

But the reality on the ground, whose intricacies the writer understandably declines to explain away, is only one source of this almost disconcerting richness of meaning. The other two are largely performative. They have to do with tragedy and its aesthetic and civic attributes across the ages. The first is primarily space, viz., tragedy as aesthetic and communal spatiality produced literally, materially, alongside dramatic production itself, specifically through stagecraft and theater design solutions to the "fourth wall" problem; I might add, I write "solutions" advisedly, for, as we have noticed in the interview excerpt, the plural is warranted given that the book features not one but several approaches to this multifaceted issue. The second source is tragedy as text, specifically, the intertextual liberties Chalandon takes with *Antigone* in its various forms as he reads, revisits, and "localizes" not only Anouilh but also Sophocles and Brecht.

Of course, the French playwright remains the novelist's self-acknowledged, main inspiration. But Chalandon also went back to the original *Antigone,* as he must have turned to Brecht as well. The Brechtian version is particularly relevant because, before intersecting in *Le quatrième mur*, the two filiations described here already met in Brecht's *"Antigone" des Sophokles*. Indeed, four years after Anouilh, Brecht retrofitted Sophocles's masterpiece ("adapted" from Friedrich Hölderlin's German translation) with a prologue that broke down the imaginary wall to insert, also like in the French playwright's work, *Antigone* into the greater tragedy of World War II and the Nazi nightmare. Most interestingly, the twin tracks of textual tragedy and of tragedy as event connecting with and impacting on world events over classical aesthetics' gulf between representation and reality cross again in the *Antigone* put on "by young Palestinians at the Jenin Refugee Camp in the northern West Bank, years after the Israeli invasion of 2002 and around the time when the Museum of Tolerance was being constructed."[174]

In all likelihood, Chalandon was not aware of the Palestinian production. And, as his personal politics, journalism, and interviews given following *Le quatrième mur*'s appearance go to show, Anouilh appealed to him more than Sophocles and Brecht. In his reading, the Greek Antigone's opposition to Creon and to the law he symbolizes evinces, more than political commitment to people and ideals in the world of the living, transcendent duty—to the dead, their underworld, and the laws set by the gods, including the customs and obligations of burial, mourning, piety, "recollection," and related "cleansing" rites Creon's decree denies to Polynices. "In Anouilh," the novelist points out, Antigone "rises up against the King, against modern authority."[175] Besides, unlike the pacifism advocated upfront by Brecht's Antigone in response to Creon's warmongering, peace obtains in Anouilh through secular political practice, representing as it does the bonus of concrete resistance to a no less palpable "order"—Creon's state and/as Nazi power—and this stance requires getting your hands dirty in what Anouilh's Theban ruler calls the "kitchen of politics."[176] The same Creon claims that he was forced to step in and become the chef-in-chief, but, whether we buy it or not, Antigone accepts the metaphor herself.[177] This corroborates Judith Butler's rebuttal of famous Sophoclean commentaries by Hegel (*Phenomenology of Spirit*) and Lacan (*Seminar VII*), a critique revolving around the point that Antigone and her uncle are alike, a similarity neither Brecht nor Anouilh seem unaware of. Brecht, for example, has Creon lecture Antigone on the state's "divine order,"[178] a speech that collapses the oppositions between the world of the dead and the world of mortals and between the laws of gods and human laws, respectively, while, in Anouilh, Creon tells his son Haemon that "[he, Creon, is] master [of Thebes, but] under the law. Not above the law,"[179] which, in turn, makes the case against Creon's "tyranny" more difficult (and probably placated Anouilh's German censors as well). Furthermore, as Butler maintains, a careful reading of Sophocles himself suggests that

> [o]pposing Antigone to Creon as the encounter between the forces of kinship and those of state power fails to take into account the ways in which Antigone has already departed from kinship, herself the daughter of an incestuous bond, herself devoted to an impossible and death-bent incestuous love for her brother, how her actions compel others to regard her as "manly" and thus cast doubt on the way that kinship might underwrite gender, how her language, paradoxically, most closely approximates Creon's, the language of sovereign authority and action, and how Creon himself assumes his sovereignty only by virtue of the kinship line that enables that succession, how he becomes, as it were, unmanned by Antigone's defiance, and finally by his own actions, at once abrogating the norms that secure his place in kinship and in sovereignty.[180]

In short, the critic concludes, "Sophocles' text makes clear that the two are metaphorically implicated in one another in ways that suggest that there is, in fact, no simple opposition between the two." In essence, says Butler, Antigone and Creon are "chiasmically related."[181]

§30. Chiasmic Spatiality, Planetarity, and the "Monumental" Novel

The observation is pertinent but incomplete and also potentially misleading insofar as it restricts the chiasmus of relatedness to the territory controlled by the sovereign, namely, to the state or, with a word used by Sophocles's Creon, to the "fatherland."[182] In Butler, as well as in previous interpretations of Sophocles, be they more traditional, such as George Steiner's, or psychoanalytic, such as Žižek's, the polis circumscribes the space of relation and of the law derived from it.[183] State-saturated, its play reined in by the Theban walls, relation becomes synonymous with consanguinity and its crisis another episode in the Labdacids' family saga.

But this not what Chalandon takes away from Sophocles and, more significantly still, from Anouilh's rereading of Sophocles. In an important way, *Le quatrième mur* throws Thebes's seven gates open to let in not the Argive army but the world. Or, with a metaphor more apposite to this discussion, he knocks down the city walls to widen the dynamic of relation beyond relatives, polis, and the living. Thus, in a polyethnic and plurireligious Beirut that, "cut off from the world"[184] as it may be at times, also brings together Georges's Paris and Sam's Thessaloniki,[185] the chiasmus-like kinship Chalandon sets up bridges distances that are geographic as they are ethnocultural, political, and ontological, shrinking down to the Lebanese capital's size and moment histories, traditions, differences, and antagonisms stretching across whole continents, ethnicities, and faiths. As Anouilh puts it, the "civil war" makes everybody "dirty" no matter who and where they are, with equalizing guilt—for nobody can in the end claim innocence any more—a prelude to the equivalence, to the *bond* of indistinctiveness and tragic likeness death bestows, notes Creon himself, on Eteocles and Polynices, on former adversaries, and on natives and strangers.[186] As Chalandon too implies, in literary tragedy and in the tragedies of history alike people bond not only in life but also in death. In fact, the latter's bond may be stronger because it is irreversible, binding us together "chiasmically," over the chasm of our ethno-religious asymmetries, rivalries, and violence. Oedipus's sons ford the tragic gulf of fratricide to rebecome brothers in death. And, when Brecht's Creon proclaims that "[t]he enemy, even when dead, does not become a friend," Antigone retorts promptly: "Of course he does. I don't live to hate, but to love."[187]

Since this kind of love is possible, as Creon replies, only "down there," in the kingdom of death, this is where Antigone is headed by taking her own life: not to "hell" as such, where Creon curtly and literally dispatches her,[188] but to the netherworld. The distinction is important. In Sophocles, Anouilh, and Chalandon, the world below is quite worldly because this is where Antigone reunites with her brothers and where foes and friends, aliens and citizens, Polynices's allies (the "seven foreign princes")[189] and Eteocles's comrades, and the ecumene and the polis embrace each other. Neither entirely *intra muros*, inside the walls of the city-state and of the ethnocentrically relational model enforced by it, nor completely "out there," "in the middle of nowhere," Antigone's sepulcher lies just outside the walls, *inside the city's outside*: not fully separated from Thebes but not wholly Theban, totally territorialized, spatially, legally, culturally, and politically contained by the city either. So, neither is her "act . . . territorially circumscribed to a singular polity," as in Butler and other critics,[190] nor does this act make her a total "stranger," a word preferred in some translations and insistently attended to by some critics;[191] although her parents' hubris and all the tragic events flowing from it deny her the home more law-abiding Thebans enjoy, Thebes remains the "city of / [her] fathers and her land."[192] A tragic co-spatialization of the fatherland, Antigone's standing up to Creon makes her own wall, her resolution to be walled in, and her suicide ultimately both an enclosure, an enclave within the polis and its reach, *and* an opening, a "No!" and a "Yes!" at the same time, a contestation of the ingrown world of patriarchal rule's parochial-territorialist politics but also a reaffirmation, a re- or, better yet, trans-territorialization of politics. These permutations of territory, kin, and polity world or reorient ethically ethnically oriented political activity, bring the world into it by extending funereal rights—and thus a post-mortem citizenship of sorts—to all war casualties. A withnessing monument, one that honors the dead regardless of their polis and politics, Antigone's grave is a place where the former combatants finally take a break from hostilities to rest in a peace beyond the shaky ontology of any conflagration and negotiated truce and where, by the same token, war itself may rest or, as the novelist hints, perhaps even end.

To this effect, to jam the war machine in the war's own commemoration, in a monument understood and erected as war *and* world testimonial, the novel must perform—must imagine—the monumentality both forfeited and rehearsed by the aborted performance of Anouilh's *Antigone*. That is, *Le quatrième mur* must enact narratively the co-spatial remapping of Beirut Georges did not see premiered in the ruins of a former cinema in the Christian zone of the Lebanese capital; the Antigonean, world-communal reimagination of the city *by* the novel has to succeed where the theater of communality *in* the novel—*Antigone* as stage production as well as staging of a certain Lebanese community and shared space—remained an unfinished project. To achieve all this, Chalandon also confesses, he must assume his own "luminous contradictions,"[193] which largely coincide with those embedded in Antigone's double bind as someone bound at once by the laws of the state and the world, by the customs of the living and of the underworld. In other words, much as Antigone's "No!" does not place her entirely outside the polis, politics, and war, neither the author nor Georges—who both identify with Antigone and act on her behalf[194]—can bypass war and death. Writing for *Libération* is to Chalandon what directing *Antigone* is for Georges: politics, fighting, taking sides by other means.[195]

Not so much an incongruity in either Sophocles or Anouilh, Chalandon's "luminous" inconsistency is surely consistent with the Brechtian performative-political tactic of pulling down the walls between acting and action, between directing scenes and directing (affecting) events, between the fiction and reality of "neutrality," between life and death, and so forth. This is another way of looking, of course, at Georges's wall quandary: Does the author build a wall around Georges, dragging him too into the war as the character kills the "real" Creon, the Phalangist Joseph-Boutros, brother of the actor playing Anouilh's Creon, or, more likely, does Chalandon, by the same movement, do away with the pretense of an impartiality that has never been there to begin with? Does he demolish the wall of a hollow convention? Either way, and more notably still, it is not just the director who ends up taking sides, but also the imaginary Creon: in fact, not only does Charbel take sides, but he also *crosses over to the other side* by turning his brother in for his involvement in the Shatila atrocities. Georges may be forced to shoot somebody presumably sharing his Christian faith and thus commit another killing in the family to save his own life—after all, like Oedipus, the director has been literally, if temporarily, blinded—but Charbel acquiesces to the putting to death of his brother. A radical departure from all versions of the tragedy, the punishment of the Greek/Phalangist Creon by its Lebanese twin—or Creon's turning into an avenging, parricidal Haemon and thus against himself—paints a mirror image of Antigone's brotherly piety: where she steps outside her polis, into the cosmopolitical, interstitial space in which she can honor Polynices and bring him back into the fold of the community and thus transform, "world," and bring peace to Thebes itself, Charbel takes on the same task as Antigone and de facto revenges her murder by aiding in Joseph-Boutros's ambush.

With this specular chiasmus, we have reached a crucial point in *Le quatrième mur.* A new type of communal space can now be envisaged. With it, a new kind of community and another form of monumentality, themselves chiasmic, differential in nature, cobbling together contrasts and discontinuities instead of similitudes and continuities, can now arise. They are forward looking rather than merely commemorative. They have been made possible by the executioner's execution by Georges, which presupposed Charbel's assent, which had been "rehearsed" through *Antigone*'s actual rehearsals in the bombed-out Beirut theater building with a fourth wall allegorically missing[196] but also all over the city, as the actors, actresses, and the director himself had been trekking back and forth across all sorts of front lines, ethnic neighborhoods, and "zones" controlled by various militias. The boundaries and frontiers drawn by the civil war are annulled or challenged by this brave and resilient movement, whose "communitarian symbolism" (Georges's phrase) is as striking as Anouilh's play itself.[197] On- and offstage, the cast produce and reproduce Lebanese space planetarily, if *in situ*, like Cărtărescu, by following a mental map at odds with the ever-contested demarcations of territory, belonging, allegiance, and community in war-torn Lebanon. Not only does Georges seek out his artists all over the country, scouting camp after camp and neighborhood after neighborhood for his performers and managing to extricate them from the theater of war to cast them in another performance and another time, a time out or *répit* ("respite") from fighting, but this performance, along with its preparations, drills, reading, and logistics, also makes up a topo-political dramatization of Lebanese community in its fundamental plurality.[198] As Dr. Cohen tells Georges, the representation project "associate[s the country's] communities in an identical dream of peace."[199] The dream does not come true in the opening night, in the representation proper, but is represented, if in another medium, in the premiere's poster that Georges had printed in Paris. The *affiche* features all the actors and actresses' names, Sam's, Georges's, and "the official insignia of the Beirut consular services and of the cultural associations [that have sponsored the project. The flyer is] white, red, green, and beautiful, with a cedar as a genealogical tree grouping together [all these war] enemies [represented here on the poster], branch after branch, all of the limbs leading toward a tree trunk springing from the same, common soil."[200]

Charbel's "ethical" betrayal, then, does not come out of the blue but indexes an emerging, Antigonean worlding of consciousness, the rising awareness of a relatedness and attendant obligations transgressing the turfs of faith, ethnos, kin, and family, and their "closed-circuit" reproductions.[201] Such breaches of demeanor, language, custom, dress, and even gender codes soften and query identities, make people rethink who they are. Obviously, Antigone's transgression provides the role model here, but, broadly speaking, *all* the roles in Anouilh, *insofar as they have to be prepared*, train the Lebanese cast for identity roles insufficiently, marginally, or inadequately represented in available community scripts. *Antigone*'s collective rehearsal itself, the actors and actresses' inevitable, dramatically fostered being-together and teamwork on and around the stage transform, quasi imperceptibly, the play, its *répétitions*, and the interactions around them into a theater of planetary communality. They perform—"repeat" into being—a new sociality. They sow the seeds for a togetherness that, in turn, lays the groundwork for hope-giving, less orthodox, and less partisan kinds of identity performance. As Georges points out to his cast, "We are wearing the masks of tragedy. They allow us to be together. As soon as we drop them, we are putting our military armbands back on, and this is war."[202]

§31. "Where the Print Is Finest"

> Cricket is first and foremost a dramatic spectacle. It belongs with the theatre, ballet, opera and the dance.
>
> —C. L. R. JAMES, *Beyond a Boundary*

> Thinking small is not enough; agency is not to be had so predictably. The unit of coherence where transformative energies have the best chance of seizing hold is not predictable in advance; it might well be larger, not smaller.
>
> —BRUCE ROBBINS, "Comparative Cosmopolitanisms"

In O'Neill's 2009 PEN/Faulkner Award-winning *Netherland*, sports—cricket, more exactly—hold the communal role Chalandon assigns to theater.[203] For cricket, the Turkish-Irish-American author teaches us through his Dutch protagonist Hans van der Broeck and especially Hans's West Indian friend, Chuck Ramkissoon, is more than a pastime. It is not in the past either. Its time has not passed. Or, if it has, so has the exceptionalist-autonomist temporality in which American communality has traditionally pictured itself. As a community, Chuck believes, the United States still has to pass the geopolitical and cultural-demographic test of the planetary present. Popular with Americans since the early eighteenth century but gradually elbowed aside by baseball's modern "hegemony," the game of cricket is thus more than a trope or fictional ploy. It is a concrete, athletically embodied modality of presentifying or updating an America that, in the September 11, 2001 aftermath, must reconstellate itself *qua* community so as to work through the meanings of not only the World Trade Center tragedy but also of the planetarization without which the traumatic event would remain meaningless. A community driven to the limit by the violently worlding world, the United States cannot afford *not* to use its new, liminal position in the world to think through its communal cultural-ethical limits and spatio-political limitations. As Faruk Patel, one of the rumored financial backers of Chuck's New York Cricket Club project and adept of a "one with the cosmos" life philosophy, implies, cricket uniquely brings together liminality, Americanness, and understanding, or, less redundantly, simply *brings together*.[204]

Beck is right to lay bare the global economics behind the "cosmopolitanization" of big-city sports clubs (soccer is his example). These clubs, along with their "cosmopolitan" players and fans, attest to world cosmopolitan culture as much as they do to the "global cities" our metropolitan centers have become.[205] Chuck's idea is different, however, even though he needs some serious financing to get it off the ground. His cricket club purports to be not only a platform for global business, Internet broadcast rights, and so forth, but also for a planetary community project. He wants to build a team, a field and its facilities, and socialize with teammates, opponents, fans, and the cricketers' families, in a nutshell, to deploy cricket as a twenty-first-century ritual of American togetherness. There may be, as Faruk opines, "a limit to what Americans understand," and that "limit" may well be, as he goes on, "cricket" itself. But if that is true, then the game ceases to be trivial in an axiological sense ("rubbish," "insignificant"), and becomes trivial, and thus highly significant, in an etymological-dromological sense that articulates the communal the way theater does in Chalandon.

Indeed, playing Anouilh and playing cricket entail the same planetary orchestration of identity, space, and belonging. That is not just because, as O'Neill glosses on C. L. R. James's *Beyond a Boundary* only months before *Netherland* came out, the sport constitutes "an art on a par with theater, ballet, opera, and dance";[206] James demonstrates in his 1963 extraordinary "cricket memoir" that this indeed is the case.[207] Like performance, cricket also takes, both in James and in O'Neill's 2007 novel, on a spectacularly sociological and political "consequentiality" beyond the putatively inconsequential ludic. There is a *sociologically* spectacular "practical" part to it, James argues.[208] More exactly, cricket is a sociality practice. What Gilroy determines as cricket's "imperial logics" and what James himself pinpoints as "the clash of race, caste[,] class," and more largely "the injustice in the sphere of sport" testify to the broader inequalities, rifts, and conflicts of society.[209] But, like Greek drama, the Trinidadian critic suggests—and this suggestion is crucial for an adequate reading of *Netherland*—that cricket provides an exercise in democracy[210] to the extent that, as James also notes repeatedly, athletics, what occurs in the field and around it, puts, like in Chalandon, all kinds of pressure on the ways players and those near them interact ordinarily in a world of "racial partisanships,"[211] isolationist-chauvinist predispositions, and so on. As O'Neill comments on *Mariners, Renegades, and Castaways*, James's 1953 Melville book is a "pioneering effort to reject the insular, exceptionalist narratives by which America explains itself," and, most notably, this early "postnationalist"[212] critique's anti-autonomist tenets further underpin the symbolically named memoir-cum-scholarly study. "Using cricket to blur the boundaries between white and black, colonized and colonizer, ancient and modern, political and social,"[213] *Beyond a Boundary* supplies, not unlike *Le quatrième mur*, the agonal venue where people might recontest the meanings of being in the world. It is in this sense that, to quote the title of *Beyond the Boundary*'s first chapter, cricket is a "window to the world." Rephrasing James's question, "What do they know of cricket who only cricket know?"[214] as "What do they know of America who only America know?"[215] *Netherland* cracks America's window with planetary impatience. Americans, O'Neill echoes James, cannot afford "insular" self-perceptions and narrow identity classifications any more, nor can they limit themselves to purely theoretical de- and re-limitations of territory, society, culture, ethnicity, race, and subjectivity overall inside somewhat less rigid boundaries and categories, to mere re-conceptualizations of what it means to be in the world. They must also, and fully, "experiment" with worldliness, that is, with being-in-the world as a *community-fostering* modality of being.

Hans and others are aware of the "laboratory experiment" under way.[216] But the laboratory, Chuck maintains, is not restricted to the grassy ground because the latter's liminal condition necessarily marks and unmarks this terrain as an enclosure, limit, or terminus. Thus, the pitch and its surroundings set themselves up as an American microcosm. Or, with another metaphor activated by my geomethodological model of reading, the laboratory is also a photo lab—better yet, a socio-photo lab. In it, not only "developers" like Chuck but also Americans at large, players, crowds, and the whole body of *socii* give themselves another chance to learn or relearn how to develop, from the ludic negative of the cricket community, a new picture of the United States and of the world inside and outside the country.

"The bigger you think, the crappier it looks," Theo avers in McEwan's 2005 novel *Saturday*. As in *The Children Act* (2014), where the British author's Fiona cannot go through her workday without feeling the weight of the "planet's lot" on her shoulders,[217] the world's "big things" are bearing down on Theo's private world and concerns, and "So," he announces, "this is going to be my motto—think small."[218] "My motto is, Think fantastic," Chuck lets Hans know instead, with one of the novel's frequent nods at *The Great Gatsby*.[219] As logicians might jump in, this is a one-way contradiction because Chuck's plan is not to import, from the outside, worldly "bigness" into cricket-reconstellated American smallness. He just does not envision worldliness as an outside, or solely as such; no optional, flavor-enhancing additive to the American melting pot, the world is neither external nor supplemental to the United States. His goals are, first, to flesh out the big tightly already packed within the small, the history burrowed inside our seemingly ahistorical contemporaneity, the potential future with which the flat present is thus interleaved, the macro within the micro; and second, to help Americans *visualize* this multilayered structure, picture their home as, with, and of the world and the world as and deep inside it, in brief, turn to the planet by turning meaningfully, self-analytically and ethically, to each other, their country, and its renewed hospitality to the world inside and outside the national territory. As he tells Hans, if "[y]ou ask people to agree to complicated rules and regulations," the sport might just be the answer because, in spite of its colonial dissemination, it has served and can serve again as a "crash course in democracy. Plus—and this is key—the game forced [players from the warring tribes of Papua New Guinea] to share a field for days with their enemies, forced them to provide hospitality and places to sleep." "Hans," he carries on, "that kind of closeness changes the way you think about somebody. No other sport makes this happen."[220] When Hans wonders if his friend thinks of Americans as "savages," Chuck rejects the implication by bolstering not only his "fantastic" vision's import as a world-communal picture but also the planetary relationality over whose filigree, specifically and deliberately, the world picture is laid palimpsest-like. "'I'm saying,'" he elaborates, "that people, all people, Americans, whoever, are at their most civilized when they're playing cricket. What's the first thing that happens when Pakistan and India make peace? They play a cricket match. Cricket is instructive, Hans. It has a moral angle. I really believe this. Everybody who plays the game benefits from it. So I say, why not Americans?" The question is timely because the 9/11 attacks triggered a crisis of the planetary optics on whose prosopopoeial working condition a community's welfare depends. Chuck's diagnosis is right on target: "Americans cannot really see the world. They think they can, but they can't. I don't need to tell you that. Look at the problems we're having. It's a mess, and it's going to get worse. I say, we want to have something in common with Hindus and Muslims? Chuck Ramkissoon is going to make it happen. With the New York Cricket Club, we could start a whole new chapter in U.S. history. Why not? Why not say so if it's true? Why hold back? I'm going to open our eyes."[221]

Critics who have wondered if Chuck has read his fellow Trinidadian James have here an answer.[222] Both James's and Chuck's project, "opening our American eyes" in order to see and "get" the world picture, is to "fulfill [our true] destiny,"[223] in other words, to rebecome the hospitable community for which cricket can offer a model morally urgent, plausible (still in Westphal's sense), and, once again, practical. The only "white man [he] saw on the cricket fields of New York," Hans is surrounded by "teammates" who "variously originated from Trinidad, Guyana, Jamaica, India, Pakistan and Sri Lanka," with "Hindus, Christians, a Sikh, and four Muslims" drawing together "into a circle for prayer" before the match.[224] In the finite circle of "we," a new communality becomes readable at long last. "I've heard," Hans confesses,

> that social scientists like to explain such a scene—a patch of America sprinkled with the foreign-born strangely in play—in terms of the immigrant quest for subcommunities. How true this is: we're all far away from Tipperary, and clubbing together mitigates this unfair fact. But surely everyone can also testify to another, less reckonable kind of homesickness, one having to do with unsettlements that cannot be located in spaces of geography or history, and accordingly it's my belief that the communal, contractual phenomenon of New York cricket is underwritten, there *where the print is finest*, by the same agglomeration of unspeakable individual longings that underwrites cricket played anywhere—longings concerned with horizons and potentials sighted or hallucinated and in any event lost long ago, tantalisms that touch on the undoing of losses too private and reprehensible to be acknowledged to oneself, let alone to others. I cannot be the first to wonder if what we see, when we see men in white take to a cricket field, is men imagining *an environment of justice*. (italics added)[225]

The passage draws the fine distinction between immigrant "*sub*communities" and communities that could be called planetary or in which planetarization can be "experienced" and witnessed socially, but also experienced with, observed as if under a microscope. Let me clarify.

Typical of earlier, postcolonial diasporas, "subcommunities" cohere around ethnos, more specifically, around effectively or imaginarily separate and competing *ēthne*. Here, "competition" tends to be disjunctive and topoculturally exclusionary, further prying the competing bodies apart and spacing them out literally or figuratively across intervals of territory, affect, faith, belonging, and cultural practice. What matters is ethnos-as-*gamesmanship*. The communality game is played on a field athletically and socially finite, limited as to what the players might do and mean together.

Gathering around one trans-ethnic ethos—the ethos of cricket—the second group category, "community," is de facto cross- or supra-communal, integrative. In its finitude of time, space, skill, and membership, an infinite, because infinitely definable, communality awaits.[226] Its *ludus* is multiply ethical, in fact: it relies on cricket's civic behavior injunction and play-by-the-rules principle; it works as a language conveying "others," playfully, quasi-ineffable emotional states ("tantalisms") that, by the same movement, can be either sublated or "mined" for bonding purposes; and, since it is inclusive of winners and losers, hosts and guests, Americans and "foreigners," main actors and family extras alike, it is also, if not already just, then a template for justice. At premium in this playful zone is an agonally *ethicized* ethnos, ethics-as-*sportsmanship*; the contest is not primarily a face-off but a face-to-face preamble to a planetary prosopopoeia, to a glance at the Face. While the tiny relational community of cricket is not and cannot substitute itself for the world, this world's face is legible in Chuck's contractual vision, where the contract's "print is finest"—where, in making sense of the Van Cortland Park cricket photo Hans and his wife look at ("it looks like a Brueghel," exclaims Rachel), one makes sense of the planet.[227]

EPILOGUE 🌐 CRITICISM AS PLANETARY STEWARDSHIP

In Ersilia, to establish the relationships that sustain the city's life, the inhabitants stretch strings from the corners of the houses, white or black or gray or black-and-white according to whether they mark a relationship of blood, of trade, authority, agency. When the strings become so numerous that you can no longer pass among them, then inhabitants leave: the houses are dismantled; only the strings and their supports remain.

From a mountainside, camping with their household goods, Ersilia's refugees look at the labyrinth of taut strings and poles that rise in the plain. That is the city of Ersilia still, and they are nothing.

They rebuild Ersilia elsewhere. They weave a similar pattern of strings which they would like to be more complex and at the same time more regular than the other. Then they abandon it and take themselves and their houses still farther away.

Thus, when traveling in the territory of Ersilia, you come upon the ruins of the abandoned cities, without the walls which do not last, without the bones of the dead which the wind rolls away: spiderwebs of intricate relationships seeking a form.

—ITALO CALVINO, *Invisible Cities* (75)

§32. Strings of Life

Face the worlding world's face: if not in so many words, this is what O'Neill and other planetary writers urge on us. Popping up among the cricket players' faces, the Face shows itself in all its confoundingly Archimboldian hodgepodge, unflagging shiftiness, and self-contradictory mien in Cărtărescu's Bucharest, Ugrešić's Amsterdam, Foer's and Beigbeder's New York, Houellebecq's Paris, and McEwan's London, as well as in Mușina's Brașov, Pamuk's Kars, Chalandon's Beirut, Hamid's Lahore, and Mukherjee's Gauripur—in the world, its cities, its less glamorous towns, and everywhere else in between them; indeed, this face has become a "world and town" staple, as Jen suggests in her 2010 Chinese-Cambodian-New Englander Riverlake saga.

Ubiquitous as this enigmatic profile may be, it is a fragile one, though: anguished, unstable, unfinished, ever precariously in balance. O'Neill makes no illusions about it. His take on things, American and otherwise, is hardly Pollyannish. As we seek and perhaps recognize this face, we should remember that, with another extreme twist on the Gatsby story, Chuck's handcuffed body gets dumped in the Gowanus Canal. The inevitable question, then, is whether his vision ends up in the same place. My answer is that, although Hans leaves New York to join his family in the United Kingdom, the reunion with his son Jake, his estranged British wife, her parents and his former colleagues, Londoners, strangers, and even with his own past and long-passed mother, farther and farther away spatially, temporally, and empathically from the inner circle of "we," enacts what Chuck describes as cricket's "lesson in civility."[1]

This lesson is important. But no less important is this: as in Cărtărescu, whose characters keep climbing up on the roofs of their destitute apartment complexes to hug the world, or in Jen, whose small town has its own observation ("twin") towers, or in Lee's *vol d'oiseau* surveys from *Aloft*, the lesson is not learned, or is only half-learned, from afar. The at-distance, macro pedagogy of aerial-theoretical planetary togetherness and empathy can only do so much. But what it does do, the ontoscopic opening that it marks, matters a great deal. Planetary optics is, to stress it again, an ethoscopy whose distant self-positioning sows dialectically the perspectival "micro" seeds of nearness, closeness, intimacy, and being-with: we shoot up and above in space to draw near and see our place anew as a place of places and the face of the earth as a Face of faces; we pull back to come back, enlightened; we extend our life-sustaining "strings" and ties so we can strengthen them; with Cole, McCann, and the later Pynchon (*Against the Day*), we uncover the world, rise to bask in the planet's aura above cities, above the horizon, so we can recover our humanness on the ground and in ways that may also reground us; with DeLillo's earlier "Human Moments in World War III" story, we ascend to our "orbital" stations to reconceptualize the big things, to un- and re-think them so we can "talk about small things, routine things"[2]; with Lee's Hector (*The Surrendered*), we screen, from such intellectual altitudes, "tumultuous world history" for also small but intensely private moments;[3] we temporarily, tactically decouple so we can recouple, rejoin, regroup and "reunite," relate and endure in our relations. True, with McCann, we get reports that the "ontological glue" is thin up there. But this is why that is where we must walk first, alone on our individual tightropes as DeLillo's and McCann's acrobats, in our Skylabs, in our space suits, or, with Joseph McElroy's cyborg hero Imp Plus (*Plus*), in our high-tech space bodies: so we can fight the gravity-like pull of inherited notions and navel-gazing whims and walk the earth with others again, "feel" what it truly takes to be a couple, with the loved ones and family, but also with those who are not relatives, not from "around here" and yet related to us.[4] Hans's residential limbo, New York City's Chelsea Hotel, and his bizarre affaire with Danielle in it measure spatially, communally, and affectively an "interlude of togetherness," a "time-out" from, but also a retraining for, being together with family and the world, again.[5] Like Chuck's Cadillac, through which "[a]n intercontinental cast of characters pas[s],"[6] the hotel is a world transit, a halfway house for an incredibly diverse population that, "furtive" and "ornamental" as it may be, nonetheless feels the hotel is the place where it can be itself even it that means—or because it means—wearing angel wings.[7]

As Houellebecq jokes in *The Map and the Territory*, the "satellite image" may not be God's viewpoint. To be sure, the reasons to doubt the picture's divine provenance are legion.[8] Think only about how the world's spatial technology-enhanced visual availability has led to increased vulnerability to surveillance, control, space weaponization, and military "targeting."[9] Authors like O'Neill, DeLillo, Kunzru, Hamid, Pynchon, and Richard Powers do want us to think about the world panopticon. But, at the same time, these writers push us to envisage a world *demotikón*. They prompt us to follow the dialectical ontology of the macro and micro all the way to its ethical end, where the planet's face turns—and turns us as well—to the faces of those around us and to the problematic of care "in" or, better still, across "territory," to a responsibility idea and practice notionally and nationally reterritorialized, extended conceptually and physically to other spaces and people. This is where the geomethodology dramatized by planetary fiction should take us: to the point at which reading with the planet turns itself into reading for the planet and criticism into a "moral" enterprise, into planetary stewardship. "Decompressed" along these generous lines, *Netherland*'s final chapter declines to work like Deleuze and Guattari's uniformity-inducing, picture-"ruining," "bad"-infinity-keyed telescopy.[10] If they telescope the world, those pages do so in the term's opulent, fundamental amphibology: they simultaneously condense and enlarge a world, bring it closer and spread it out so we can contemplate the planet's dazzling gallery of faces.

§33. Mastering the Mystery

Let us remain masters of the mystery that the earth breathes.
—EMMANUEL LEVINAS, *Difficult Freedom*

The Romantic sublime of at-distance contemplation bounced the aloof gaze back to itself. This is what happens to Caspar David Friedrich's solitary hero in the 1818 canvas *Chalk Cliffs on Rügen*, and this is what Nietzsche fancies we see as we stare into the famous abyss of *Beyond Good and Evil*: the depths reflecting our look straight back to ourselves.[11] Instead, the planetary sublime is refractive rather than sterilely reflective. If the planetary gaze—the one that has "the physical planet in [Hans's] sight[12]—comes back to its origin, it does so ethically, not by reinforcing the selfsame's epistemological cocoon through a scopically self-centered, repetitive pantomime, but by a withnessing detour. The "alternative" route is just that: an alternate trajectory optically and ethically, an itinerary across alterity that acknowledges others and their faces. It may start out in a telescopically distancing mode, as does one of the several "Google scenes" in O'Neill's book, with the "satellite image" of the earth's a-semiotic crust, on which "a human movement is a barely intelligible thing . . . no signs of nations, no sense of the work of man."[13] Or it may begin, also in a classically telescopic fashion, up in a gondola of the aptly named London Eye, where Hans, Jake, Rachel, and their German and Lithuanian companions—the world's bona fide ambassadors to Hans's private moment—climb higher and higher to the zenith so that once again the city and the world of humans with it "becom[e] . . . less recognizable." But the episode belongs to an act that comprises a second scene, which the novel's ending both directs (shapes theatrically) and directs *us* to it, "denudes" and places under the microscope for us.

Thematically and structurally, the stage for this scene is laid by another "telescopy," that of the human dramas stratified in the season's geo-meteorological texture. "The English summer," writes O'Neill on the previous page, "is actually a Russian dolls of summers, the largest of which is the summer of unambiguous disaster in Iraq, which immediately contains the destruction of Lebanon, which itself holds a series of ever-smaller summers that led to the summer of Monty Panesar and, smallest perhaps, the summer of Wayne Rooney's foot."[14] And so, inside the Ferris wheel ride lies, in other time and space, another (Staten Island) ferry ride, which Hans took with his mother one September evening years before. On the deck, after admiring the "world lighting up" in front of them as the Manhattan sunset was "concentrating" that "world" in the "lilac acres of two amazing high towers going up above all others," Hans and his mother instinctively turned their smiling faces to each other. Back on the Ferris wheel following this quick flashback and after his capsule "reach[es] the very top of our celestial circuit . . . to a point where [we] can see horizons previously unseen, and the old earth reveals itself newly," Hans "come[s] to face his family with the same smile" while "Lithuanian ladies" ask about London landmarks and Jake "befriends a six-year-old boy who speaks not a word of English."[15] "You only had to look at our faces," Hans comments on a scene that otherwise can do without any commentary.[16]

This instant is, as Deleuze and Guattari would probably call it, aesthetic in that it ultimately "create[s] the finite," the little situation, the tiniest "Russian doll" of human life, or the infinitesimal that "rediscovers," "restores," and shows off the "infinite."[17] Within this aesthetic dynamic, neither the infinite nor the infinitesimal is anterior/posterior or superior/inferior to the other. "The town," the philosophers stress, "does not come after the house, nor does the cosmos after the territory. The universe does not come after the figure, and the figure is an aptitude of the universe."[18] They are telescoped inside each other, available—reluctantly perhaps—to our geomethodological microscopy. The figure figures a universe because there is a universe—a planetary universe, the one in Hans's "sight"—to be figured and figured out, and that universe, the planet itself, is a figure, a representation and a face of many faces, all alongside one another and oftentimes all in one or in one place.

Let us be mindful of this, because it sums up geomethodology's basic tenet, from which the decompressing technology of reading follows. It is the kind of distancing-cum-de-distancing technique some critics have hinted at. "Whereas the localist poem," Ramazani argues in echoing Glissant, "requires one kind of critical attention to tease out its cross-culturalism in borrowed verse forms, sea-traversing allusions, or subterranean influences that establish unexpected lines of cross-cultural relationality . . . , the planetary poem, viewing the Earth from the extraterrestrial perspective of Heaney's astronaut, Auden's orbiting dog, or Walcott's traveler, requires another kind of critical pressure, to specify its local, regional, and national bearings." The labor of his "transnational and translocal poetics" takes places "[i]n-between these poles." Attending to this genetic space, the planetary reader may learn that "even Heaney's brief imaginative glimpse of his planetary origins from a spaceship window quickly pivots to a recognition of his more immediate, if unhomely origins."[19] But this also means, one more time, that the issue, or the solution, here is not vague in-betweenness, and the dubious compromise it might underwrite, but another, telescoped topology of culture in which a particular place and event are already creased and cleft, fraught with, and in all actuality afforded by, the in-between. By virtue of this topology, "our gardens," in Candide's sense, and the world garden are set up, somewhat like Semiramis's "hanging" gardens, in an overlaid structure, one on top and inside another, as it were, with one garden's flowers, trees, and the trees' branches, roots, and seeds reaching over, deep into other gardens, growing, grafting themselves onto other plants, and bearing fruit there. It is only now, as they subscribe to this fully horizontal (horti)cultural model—a model of culture as rhizomatically luxuriant, wild rather than "disciplined," geometrically organized, and conceptually "pruned" *cultura*—that the "figure of the astronaut" and of the "air-borne traveller," the van der Broeks up in the London Eye, and all the "distant eyes" with them no longer renew the universalist-distant claims made, as Ramazani aptly notes, by an "older model of cosmopolitanism."[20]

Levinas is even more explicit, and more optimistic also, about the geomethodological resourcefulness of such a figure, which he welcomed in his "Heidegger, Gagarin, and Us" essay against Heidegger's apprehensions about the fast-growing human capabilities of "measuring and executing, for the purpose of gaining mastery over that which is as a whole."[21] As Michael Lang explains in a 2003 essay on Heidegger's "planetary discourse," for the German thinker the new, de-distancing technologies wind up supplanting human relationships. The only relationships left are technological or, in the more extreme, Pynchonian formulation from *Gravity's Rainbow*, *téchne*'s relation to itself. In the Heidegger–David Harvey line of thought, Lang demonstrates, this de-distantiaton is tantamount to circumventing the human and its undergirding relatedness. Eventually, this leads to a "compression," congealing, and preordaining of everything in this world, including the material texture and the meanings of the post-Enlightenment West and of the whole globe with it, now seized mechanically and "totalistically" as a passive reflection ("globalization") of the Western model.[22] Not only does Heideggerian technology de-spatialize, but its topological intervention is unethical.[23] The resulting *Weltbild* globalizes the planet and its understandings.

What Levinas admires in the astronaut's "feat" is a completely different technology. This technology is not a technocracy or a disempowering rationality any more because it *spatializes*—more precisely, spaces out—ethically. Distance is here retained. In fact, it is reinvented and valued because, in spreading things and people out, it opens up the world to responsibility and care for others and hence to a new place ethos. Thus, distance and its technology hold out the promise of an ethicization of terraqueous space. The feat's basic gist or feature inheres in the features themselves, in the face whose gaze the technological feat brings to bear on us all and on our planet and which helps us rediscover the latter as commons, "hospitality" that "precedes private property," as Derrida puts it in his *Adieu to Emmanuel Levinas*.[24] But, most notably, for the astronaut and then for those below on whom his eyes fell, this commonality arises as a site of multiple and multiply positive displacement, subject to certain transactions imposed on place and life concurrently in the name of an *ethic beyond the ethnic*: an ethic that neither erases nor dismisses ethnic background and all backgrounds, grounds, and *Gründe*, but, to the contrary, one that acknowledges and honors them by working with, through, and over their contested geography, their territorially and ethno-culturally demarcated spaces, turfs, and discourses.

Going squarely against "nationalist place-based ideologies of dwelling"[25] and other exclusionary-autochthonist and chauvinist topo-monopolies, Levinasian ethic "redistricts" place planet-wide to help both the comfortably placed and the displaced to relate and come together. Less "dangerous than the spirits [*génies*] of the *Place*" that, throughout history, have placed to include, shelter, and nourish, but also to exclude, control, and enslave by "splitting . . . humanity into native and strangers," this is a distancing technology liable to make stronger the "strings" between us, between our places, and between mankind and place overall, to renew the earth as common home. In this vein, Yuri Gagarin's is a technologically discriminating perception of place that, in a way than reminds this reader of Michael Parker's *The Watery Part of the World* and its drifting Yaupon Island, sets the place in motion and unlocks its gates so that the world may flood it and soak it in its lifeblood. For Levinas, Gagarin, the first human in outer space, comes to instigate a certain positive mind and body restlessness technologically. He can do so because he arrives from a distance at once distancing and de-distancing: distancing insofar as it separates us from the place and thus does away with the distinction native-stranger; and de-distancing because a new togetherness, a world structure of withnessing, and a "kindship" above any kinship become possible once said distinction no longer operates. "[W]hat counts most of all, Levinas says, is that [Gagarin] left the Place," the Earth as Place. In Levinas's assessment, the Soviet cosmonaut rose "beyond any horizon" but only to open up new places, horizons and understandings, within which the planet's mystery, its many facets, faces, and the relations in which they are all necessarily enmeshed in the world at large and in this world's Karses and Riverlakes are reaffirmed and cared for rather than fatuously mastered.[26]

Or, perhaps a mastery of sorts is in play here, after all. In its ethical facing of the world's otherness, this mystery mastery would be, deep down, rather modest and unassuming, an understood duty actually. For here, facing the world and its others would not efface their faces. So what we are talking about is not control over other people, their worlds, and the world as a whole, but responsibility and care. We must commit to these not only as citizens but also as critics and humanists, through a reading that does not disfigure the figures in which mystery is offered to our descriptions. To the contrary, this reading should honor and enhance the secrets our planet exhales. Thus, reading with the planet would reveal itself as a reading for the planet, a critic's plea on behalf of the earth. By the same token, criticism would become a form of planetary stewardship.[27]

It is, indeed, a more subdued mastery of the mystery that fleetingly brushes our faces when we turn to the planet's face and to the countless faces glued together, mosaic-like, in neighborhoods, cantinas, and playgrounds, at Bar Mitzvahs, in Ferris wheel cabins, and in other little places. Going down the trail blazed by this technological breakthrough, a really viable geomethodology is going to be a balancing act between, on one side, the understandable euphoria (perhaps cockiness too) of leaning on such a deparochializing "world picture" and, with it, as Appadurai says, on such a critically enriching "research imagination," and, on the other side, the exploratory attitude, healthy skepticism, caution, resistance to the grandiose, and, most importantly, undissimulated humility before what may well evade inquiry.[28] The planetary critic must allow that this mystery, the enigma of the planet's others, may—and in effect must—persists as such, in plain sight and undefaced, protected by the very "nudity" of the face in which it comes forth. As Levinas never tires of reminding us, we are with those others in the world so that we ourselves can be. This is the core precept of his ethics-before-ontology argument and also the reason reading with the planet is or ought to be not only an analytic scenario but also a model of exemplary sociality. For, if we turn to the planet's face right, if we see it, as Levinas recommends, in its "nudity," as "*is* by itself and not by reference to a system" that precludes seeing and understanding, "with" will also turn into "for."[29]

NOTES

PROLOGUE

1. This is an excerpt from the *Salon* blurb reproduced on the 2004 Hyperion edition of Frédéric Beigbeder's *Windows on the World.*

2. Frédéric Beigbeder, *Windows on the World*, trans. Frank Wayne (New York: Hyperion, 2004), 255.

3. Beigbeder, *Windows on the World*, trans. Frank Wayne, 255.

4. Beigbeder, *Windows on the World*, trans. Frank Wayne, 252.

5. Frédéric Beigbeder, *Windows on the World* (Paris: Gallimard, 2005), 312.

6. See Mary Ann Caws, "The Poetics of the Manifesto: Nowness and Newness," in *Manifesto: A Century of Isms*, ed. Mary Ann Caws, xix–xxxi (Lincoln: University of Nebraska Press, 2000).

7. The "essay-manifesto" is only one of the many subcategories of a genre that keeps expanding and renewing itself throughout its history. See Caws, "Poetics of the Manifesto," xxix.

8. David Damrosch refers to "planiterati" as "literary globalists" in "World Literature as Figure and as Ground," American Comparative Literature Association, the 2014–2015 Report on the State of the Discipline of Comparative Literature website—Paradigms. http://stateofthediscipline.acla.-org/entry/world-literature-figure-and-ground-0.

9. David Harvey, *Cosmopolitanism and the Geographies of Freedom* (New York: Columbia University Press, 2009), 259.

10. Harvey, *Cosmopolitanism and the Geographies of Freedom*, esp. 177–182.

11. Christian Moraru, *Memorious Discourse: Reprise and Representation in Postmodernism* (Madison. NJ: Fairleigh Dickinson University Press, 2005), 224–234.

12. *The Planetary Turn: Relationality and Geoaesthetics in the Twenty-First Century*, ed. Amy J. Elias and Christian Moraru (Evanston, IL: Northwestern University Press, 2015).

13. Here, I refer the reader only to my article "Thirteen Ways of Passing Postmodernism: Introduction to Focus," *American Book Review* 34, no. 4 (May–June 2013): 3–4, and to the chapter "Postmodernism, Cosmodernism, Planetarism" that I have contributed to *The Cambridge History of Postmodernism,* edited by Brian McHale and Len Platt and forthcoming from Cambridge University Press.

14. Marjorie Perloff, *Unoriginal Genius: Poetry by Other Means in the New Century* (Chicago: University of Chicago Press, 2010), 136, 141–142.

15. Don DeLillo, *White Noise*, Text and Criticism, ed. Mark Osteen (New York: Penguin, 1998), 24.

16. Joseph O'Neill, *Netherland* (New York: Vintage, 2009), 15.

17. Wai Chee Dimock, *Through Other Continents: American Literature across Deep Time* (Princeton, NJ: Princeton University Press, 2008), 143.

18. In *Cosmodernism: American Narrative, Late Globalization, and the New Cultural Imaginary* (Ann Arbor: University of Michigan Press, 2011), I offer similar specifications on the "radically distinct cultural other" (23).

19. On Henry Sussman's "Prevailing Operating System" and its place in the author's larger project, see my review-essay, "Invisible, Ink.: Classics, Programmers, and the Reprogramming of Cultural History in the Aftermath of the 'Book Crisis,'" *Canadian Review of Comparative Literature* 39, no. 4 (December 2012): 415–426.

20. Gayatri Chakravorty Spivak, "World Systems and the Creole," *Narrative* 14, no. 1 (January 2006): 108.

21. Henry Sussman, *Around the Book: Systems and Literacy* (New York: Fordham University Press, 2011), 12.

22. Jean Baudrillard, *Telemorphosis Preceded by Dust Breeding*, trans. Drew S. Burk (Minneapolis: Univocal, 2011), 48.

23. On globalization's production though critical discourse, see, among other places, Sarika Chandra's *Dislocalism: The Crisis of Globalization and the Remobilizing of Americanism* (Columbus: Ohio State University Press, 2011), 3.

24. Gayatri Chakravorty Spivak, *Death of a Discipline* (New York: Columbia University Press, 2003); Eric Hayot, *On Literary Worlds* (New York: Oxford, 2012), mainly 23–102; Emily Apter, *Against World Literature: On the Politics of Untranslatability* (London: Verso, 2013), 217. Apter is one of the editors of the English translation of the *Vocabulaire européen des philosophies: Dictionnaire des intraduisibles*, ed. Barbara Cassin (Paris: Seuil, 2004).

25. On "emotional maps" and their geopolitics, see Dominique Moïsi, *The Geopolitics of Emotion: How Cultures of Fear, Humiliation, and Hope Are Reshaping the World* (New York: Doubleday, 2009). On "mental maps" and spatial aesthetics, see Nikos Papastergiadis, "Spatial Aesthetics: Rethinking the Contemporary," in *Antinomies of Art and Culture: Modernity, Postmodernity, Contemporaneity*, ed. Terry Smith, Okwui Enwezor, and Nancy Condee, 363–381, esp. 370 (Durham, NC: Duke University Press, 2008).

26. Bharati Mukherjee, *The Tree Bride* (New York: Hyperion, 2004), 236, 10.

27. Jacques Rancière, *Dissensus: On Politics and Aesthetics*, ed. and trans. Steven Corcoran (London: Continuum, 2010), 189.

28. On the digital world's *mise ensemble* logic and on the new "social contract" and "socia(bi)lity" overall derived from this logic, see Milad Doueihi's lucid book *Pour un humanisme numérique* (Paris: Seuil, 2011), 119, 65, 39.

29. On planetary "conviviality," see Paul Gilroy, *Postcolonial Melancholia* (New York: Columbia University Press, 2005), iv and the entire final chapter, 121–151. I have proposed a similar concept, "collegiality," in *Cosmodernism*, esp. 57–59.

PART 1

1. John Crowe Ransom, "The Planetary Poet," *Kenyon Review* 26, no. 1 (Winter 1964): 264.

2. Wallace Stevens, *The Collected Poems of Wallace Stevens* (New York: Vintage, 1990), 532.

3. Lauren Berlant, *Cruel Optimism* (Durham, NC: Duke University Press, 2011), 69.

4. Philip Roth, *Letting Go* (New York: Random House, 1961), 429.

5. See Moïsi, *Geopolitics of Emotion*, 4.

6. Ian McEwan, *Sweet Tooth* (New York: Random House, 2012), 191.

7. Fredric Jameson, *A Singular Modernity: Essay on the Ontology of the Present* (London: Verso, 2002), 165.

8. Jacques Derrida, *On Touching—Jean-Luc Nancy*, trans. Christine Irizarry (Stanford, CA: Stanford University Press, 2005).

9. For a "one-world" argument on globalization and its ethics, see Peter Singer's *One World: The Ethics of Globalization* (New Haven, CT: Yale University Press, 2002), 11–13.

10. See, more recently, Derek C. Maus, *Unvarnishing Reality: Subversive Russian and American Cold War Satire* (Columbia: University of South Carolina Press, 2011), and Daniel Grausam, *On Endings: American Postmodern Fiction and the Cold War* (Charlottesville: University of Virginia Press, 2011).

11. "Hombre Planetario," in Jorge Carrera Andrade, *Selected Poems of Jorge Carrera Andrade,* trans. and introduction H. R. Hays (Albany: State University of New York Press, 1972), 139–161.

12. Jahan Ramazani, "Poetry, Modernity, and Globalization," in *The Oxford Handbook of Global Modernisms*, ed. Mark Wollaeger with Matt Eatough (New York: Oxford University Press, 2012), 300. An older version of the Ramazani essay came out as chapter 1 in his book *A Transnational Poetics* (Chicago: University of Chicago Press, 2009).

13. David Held advances the "strong globalization thesis" in the "Afterword" to his anthology *A Globalizing World? Culture, Economics, Politics*, 171 (London: Routledge in association with The Open University, 2000). Christopher J. Kollmeyer takes up Held's weak/strong globalization distinction in "Globalization, Class Compromise, and American Exceptionalism: Political Change in 16 Advanced Capitalist Countries," *Critical Sociology* 29, no. 3 (October 2003): 369–391. On "late globalization" and its cultural relevance in the world and the United States, see, among other places, my book *Cosmodernism*, 33–37.

14. Ramazani, "Poetry, Modernity, and Globalization," in Wollaeger with Eatough, *Oxford Handbook of Global Modernisms*, 301.

15. Timothy Brennan, "From Development to Globalization: Postcolonial Studies and Globalization Theory," in *Global Literary Theory: An Anthology*, ed. Richard J. Lane (London: Routledge, 2013), 880.

16. See, for example, Ramazani, "Poetry, Modernity, and Globalization," in Wollaeger with Eatough, *Oxford Handbook of Global Modernisms*, 292–297.

17. Ken Jowitt, *New World Disorder: The Leninist Extinction* (Berkeley: University of California Press, 1992). Zygmunt Bauman refers to Jowitt's book in *Globalization: The Human Consequences* (New York: Columbia University Press, 1998), 59. For Tzvetan Todorov, see *Le Nouveau Désordre Mondial: Réflexions d'un Européen*, preface by Stanley Hoffmann (Paris: Robert Laffont, 2003). On the "chaos" of the contemporary world, also see Amin Maalouf's recent book *Le dérèglement du monde* (Paris: Grasset & Fasquelle, 2009) and Immanuel Wallerstein's article "New Revolts against the System," *New Left Review*, 2nd ser., 18 (November–December 2002): 37.

18. Christian Moraru, "The Global Turn in Critical Theory," *symploke* 9, nos. 1–2 (2001): 80–92.

19. One such instrument is Andrew Jones's *Dictionary of Globalization* (London: Polity, 2006).

20. In *Dislocalism* (4), Chandra talks about the lexical perfection of "the 'global,'" but, logically, her conclusion applies to "globe" before it does to any of the relatives of "globe."

21. Apter, *Against World Literature*, 78.

22. On the "abstract geometry of the global" as opposed, in Spivak, to "the lived history of the planetary," see Ramazani, "Poetry, Modernity, and Globalization," in Wollaeger with Eatough, *Oxford Handbook of Global Modernisms*, 301.

23. See Chandra's definition of the term in the introduction to *Dislocalism* (6).

24. Ulrich Beck, *What Is Globalization?*, trans. Patrick Camiller (Cambridge: Polity Press, 2000), 9–10.

25. Marshall Brown, "Globalism or Globalization?" in *Modern Language Quarterly* 68, no. 2 (June 2007): 143.

26. Brown, "Globalism or Globalization?" 137.

27. Roland Robertson, "Social Theory, Cultural Relativity and the Problem of Globality," in *Culture, Globalization and the World-System: Contemporary Conditions for the Representation of Identity*, ed. Anthony D. King, 73 (Minneapolis: University of Minnesota Press, 2000).

28. Allan Cochrane and Kathy Pain refer to Paul Q. Hirst and Grahame Thompson's 1996 book *Globalization in Question: The International Economy and the Possibility of Governance* (2nd ed., Cambridge: Polity Press, 1999).

29. Allan Cochrane and Kathy Pain, "A Globalizing Society?," in Held, *A Globalizing World?*

30. Bo Stråth, "World History and Cosmopolitanism," in *Routledge Handbook of Cosmopolitan Studies*, ed. Gerard Delanty (Abingdon, UK: Routledge, 2012), 73–75.

31. Immanuel Wallerstein, *Geopolitics and Geoculture: Essays on the Changing World-System* (Cambridge: Cambridge University Press; Paris: Maison des Sciences de l'Homme, 1991), 140.

32. David Held, *Global Transformations: Politics, Economics, and Culture* (Stanford, CA: Stanford University Press, 1999), 429. On Martin Albrow's "global age," see his book *The Global Age: State and Society beyond Modernity* (Stanford, CA: Stanford University Press, 1997).

33. Michel Foucault, *Language, Counter-Memory, Practice: Selected Essays and Interviews*, ed. Donald F. Bouchard, trans. Donald F. Bouchard and Sherry Simon (Ithaca, NY: Cornell University Press, 1977), 178.

34. Jean-Pierre Warnier, *La mondialisation de la culture*, 3rd ed. (Paris: La Découverte, 2004), 32.

35. On Pierre Chaunu's *univers cloisonné*, see his book, *Histoire, science sociale: La durée, l'espace et l'homme à l'époque moderne* (Paris: Société d'édition d'enseignement supérieur, 1974). On the contemporary world as network and the "network society," see Manuel Castells, *The Information Age: Economy, Society, and Culture*, vol. 1, *The Rise of the Network Society*, 2nd ed. (Oxford: Blackwell, 2000).

36. Slavoj Žižek, "20 Years of Collapse," *New York Times*, November 9, 2009, http: //www.nytimes.com/2009/11/09/opinion/09zizek.html?pagewanted=all&r=0.

37. Jameson, *Singular Modernity*, 215.

38. On Heideggerian *Miteinandersein*, see Martin Heidegger, *Being and Time: A*

Translation of Sein und Zeit, trans. Joan Stambaugh (Albany: State University of New York Press, 1996), 111–112.

39. Nicolas Bourriaud's "relational sphere," which also involves the notion of "proximity," is an aesthetic concept that emphasizes artist-public interaction. See his *Relational Aesthetics* (Dijon, France: Les Presses du réel; New York: Idea Books, 2002), 43.

40. See Pierre Teilhard de Chardin, *Le Phénomène humain* (Paris: Seuil, 1955), translated into English as *The Human Phenomenon,* a new ed. and trans. of *Le phénomène humain* by Sarah Appleton-Weber, with a foreword by Brian Swimme (Brighton, UK: Sussex Academic Press, 1999).

41. On Teilhard de Chardin and planetarization/globalization, see Bernard Sesé's article "Pierre Teilhard de Chardin, prophète de la mondialisation?" in *Etudes* 3964 (April 2002): 483–494.

42. On "the emergence of a global public sphere," see the chapter by the same title in Robert J. Holton's *Global Networks* (New York: Palgrave Macmillan, 2008), 152–161.

43. Mukherjee, *The Tree Bride*, 231.

44. Pico Iyer, *Video Night in Kathmandu and Other Reports from the Not-So-Far-East* (New York: Knopf, 1988); "The Nowhere Man," *Prospect* 30, no. 3 (February 1997): 30–33; *The Global Soul: Jet Lag, Shopping Malls, and the Search for Home* (New York: Random House, 2000); *Sun after Dark: Flights into the Foreign* (New York: Random House, 2004). For Thomas L. Friedman, see especially his highly popular *The Lexus and the Olive Tree: Understanding Globalization* (1999; New York: Picador, 2012); *Longitudes and Attitudes: Exploring the World after September 11* (New York: Farrar, Straus and Giroux, 2002); and *The World Is Flat 3.0: A Brief History of the Twentieth-First Century,* further updated and expanded (New York: Farrar, Straus and Giroux, 2006).

45. See, for example, Moraru, *Cosmodernism,* 35–44, 235–237.

46. For the concept of *potenza*, see Antonio Negri, *Art and Multitude: Nine Letters on Art, Followed by Metamorphoses: Art and Immaterial Labor*, trans. Ed Emery (London: Polity, 2011), 30.

47. Basarab Nicolescu, *La transdisciplinarité: Manifeste* (Paris: Éditions du Rocher, 1996). The American reader can consult *Manifesto of Transdisciplinarity*, trans. Karen-Claire Voss (Albany: State University of New York Press, 2002). Also see Nicolescu, *Théorèmes poétiques*, preface by Michel Camus (Paris: Rocher, 1994); Nicolescu, "The Challenge of Transdisciplinarity: From Postmodernity to Cosmodernity," paper abstract, Centre of Transdisciplinarity, Cognitive and State-System Sciences—Indexicals. http://indexicals.ac.at/abstractvienna05bnicolescu.html (accessed December 31, 2006); Basarab Nicolescu, Corin Braga, Ruxandra Cesereanu, Sanda Cordoş, Anca Haţiegan, Marius Jucan, Doru Pop, Vlad Roman, Nicolae Ţurcan, and Mihaela Ursa, "Ce este cosmodernitatea?" (What Is Cosmodernity?), Center for the Research of the Imaginary, Cluj, Romania, http://phantasma.ro/dezbateri/masa-/masa14.html (accessed September 23, 2007). On the "new vision of the world," the reader can turn to the *Manifesto*'s seventh chapter, 39–47.

48. See Jean D'Argoun, *La mutation planétaire* (Paris: Véga, 2005).

49. On planetary futurology and "terrapolitanism," see Bron Taylor, *Dark Green*

Religion: Nature, Spirituality, and the Planetary Future (Berkeley: University of California Press, 2010), esp. chaps. 8 and 9, 180–222.

50. Wallerstein refers to "globalization" in *World-Systems Analysis: An Introduction* (Durham, NC: Duke University Press, 2004) only in passing (86) and dismissively rather than engaging with the "rhetoric" the term is part of. The treatment of the global vocabulary and the overall "rhetoric of globalization" is typically perfunctory in world-systems theory. See, in this regard, Richard E. Lee, "The Modern World-System: Its Structures, Its Geoculture, Its Crisis and Transformation," in *Immanuel Wallerstein and the Problem of the World: System, Scale, Culture*, ed. David Palumbo-Liu, Bruce Robbins, and Nirvana Tanoukhi (Durham, NC: Duke University Press, 2011), 35.

51. Immanuel Wallerstein, *The Modern World-System*, vol. 1 (New York: Academic Press, 1974), 7–8.

52. Immanuel Wallerstein, *Geopolitics and Geoculture*, 198–199. See too Wallerstein's *Utopistics, or Historical Choices of the Twenty-First Century* (New York: New Press, 1998).

53. Yi-Fu Tuan, *Cosmos and Hearth: A Cosmopolite's Viewpoint* (Minneapolis: University of Minnesota Press, 1996), 187–188; Gérard Raulet, *Critical Cosmology: On Nations and Globalization—A Philosophical Essay* (Lanham, MD: Lexington Books, 2005), esp. 65–80; Félix Guattari, *Chaosmose* (Paris: Galilée, 1992); Anne Phillips, *Multiculturalism without Culture* (Princeton, NJ: Princeton University Press, 2007), 42–72. For an unsubstantiated reference to the "end of cosmology," see Fredric Jameson's *The Geopolitical Aesthetic: Cinema and Space in the World System* (Bloomington: Indiana University Press; London: BFI Publishing, 1995), 10.

54. On "cosmos" and cosmopolitanism versus "globe" and globalization, see the excellent essay by David Inglis and Roland Robertson, "From Cosmos to Globe: Relating Cosmopolitanism, Globalization and Globality," in *The Ashgate Research Companion to Cosmopolitanism*, ed. Maria Rovisco and Magdalena Nowicka (Farnham, UK: Ashgate, 2011), 295–311. On the cosmological and scalarity in Nicolescu's work, see his book *From Modernity to Cosmodernity: Science, Culture, and Spirituality* (Albany: State University of New York Press, 2014), 111.

55. Amy J. Elias, "The Dialogical Avant-Garde: Relational Aesthetics and Time Ecologies in *Only Revolutions* and *TOC*," *Contemporary Literature* 53, no. 4 (Winter 2012): 749–750.

56. The distinction is indeed a rough one. If done competently, the history of cosmopolitanism is likely to reveal forms and moments of a school of thought that, argue David Inglis and Roland Robertson, has been more "rooted in emerging world-conditions" and less metaphysically "speculative" than many anti- (and even pro-)cosmopolitan voices today might lead one to believe ("From Cosmos to Globe: Relating Cosmopolitanism, Globalization and Globality," in Rovisco and Nowicka, *Ashgate Research Companion to Cosmopolitanism*, 299).

57. Robert Fine, *Cosmopolitanism* (London: Routledge, 2007), 21. Fine's is also one of the best overviews of "new cosmopolitanism" in sociology, political science, and international law.

58. For a post-cosmological "world[-]system," see Jameson's *Geopolitical Aesthetic*, 10.

59. Neil Turnbull, "The Ontological Consequences of Copernicus: Global Being in the Planetary World," *Theory, Culture & Society* 23, no. 1 (2006): 133.

60. Turnbull, "Ontological Consequences of Copernicus," 137.

61. Masao Miyoshi, "Turn to the Planet: Literature, Diversity, and Totality," *Comparative Literature* 53, no. 4 (Fall 2001): 295.

62. Miyoshi, "Turn to the Planet," 295–296.

63. Miyoshi, "Turn to the Planet," 296.

64. Gayatri Chakravorty Spivak, "Imperative to Re-imagine the Planet," chap. 16 in her book *An Aesthetic Education in the Era of Globalization* (Cambridge, MA: Harvard University Press, 2011), 348.

65. Spivak, "Imperative to Re-imagine the Planet," 349.

66. Miyoshi, "Turn to the Planet," 296.

67. Bruce Clarke, "Autopoiesis and the Planet," in *Impasses of the Post-Global: Theory in the Era of Climate Change*, vol. 2, ed. Henry Sussman (Ann Arbor: Open Humanities Press/Michigan Publishing, 2012). http://quod.lib.umich.edu-/o/ohp/10803281.0001.-001/1:4/—impasses-of-the-post-global-theory-in-the-era-of-climate?rgn=div1;view-=fulltext.

68. Sonja A. J. Neef, *Der babylonische Planet: Kultur, Übersetzung, Dekonstruktion under den Bedingungen der Globalisierung* (Heidelberg, Germany: Universitätsverlag Winter, 2013), 25–27, esp. 26. Also see 153–155.

69. See also Joni Adamson, "American Literature and Film from a Planetary Perspective: Teaching Space, Time, and Scale," *Transformations* 21, no. 1 (Spring–Summer 2010): 23–41; Wai Chee Dimock's series of articles: "Literature for the Planet," *PMLA* 116, no. 1 (January 2001): 173–188; "Scales of Aggregation: Prenational, Subnational, Transnational," *American Literary History* 18, no. 2 (Summer 2006): 219–228; and "Planetary Time and Global Translation: 'Context' in Literary Studies," *Common Knowledge* 9, no. 3 (Fall 2003): 488–507. The reader might want to consult too her groundbreaking book, *Through Other Continents: American Literature across Deep Time*. Also see Amy J. Elias, "Interactive Cosmopolitanism and Collaborative Technologies: New Foundations for Global Literary History," *New Literary History* 39, no. 3 (Summer 2008): 705–725; Frances Ferguson, "Planetary Literary History: The Place of the Text," *New Literary History* 39, no. 3 (Summer 2008): 657–684; Susan Stanford Friedman, "Planetarity: Musing Modernist Studies," *Modernism/Modernity* 17, no. 3 (September 2010): 471–499; Ursula K. Heise's by now classic title, *Sense of Place and Sense of Planet: The Environmental Imagination of the Global* (New York: Oxford University Press, 2008), to be followed by another pioneering work in new ecological studies, her *Nach der Natur: Das Artensterben und die Moderne Kultur* (Berlin: Suhrkamp, 2010); Moraru, *Cosmodernism*; Caren Irr, "Toward the World Novel: Genre Shifts in Twentieth-First-Century Expatriate Fiction," *American Literary History* 23, no. 3 (Fall 2011): 660–679; Leerom Medovoi, "'Terminal Crisis?' From the Worlding of American Literature to World-System Literature," *American Literary History* 23, no. 3 (Fall 2011): 643–659; Mark Poster, "Global Media and Culture," *New Literary History* 39, no. 3 (Summer 2008): 685–703; Mary Louise Pratt, "Planetary Longings: Sitting in the Light of the Great Solar TV," in *World Writing: Poetics, Ethics, Globalization*, edited by Mary Gallagher, 207–223 (Toronto: University of Toronto Press, 2008); Min Hyoung Song, "Becoming Planetary," *American Literary History* 23, no. 3 (Fall 2011): 555–573; Robert T. Tally Jr., *Spatiality* (London: Routledge, 2013), *Utopia in the Age of Globalization: Space, Representation, and the World System* (New York: Palgrave Macmillan, 2013), and his edited collection

Geocritical Explorations: Space, Place, and Mapping in Literary and Cultural Studies (New York: Palgrave Macmillan, 2011).

70. See Elias and Moraru, *Planetary Turn*.

71. Spivak, *Death of a Discipline*, 72–73.

72. Moraru, *Cosmodernism*, 48–49.

73. Spivak, *Death of a Discipline*, 73.

74. Already upon us, the planetary (*Das Planetarische*) has inaugurated, some critics aver, a "postglobal age." See, in this regard, Ulrike Bergermann, Isabell Otto, and Gabriele Schabacher, eds., *Das Planetarische: Kultur-Technik-Medien in postglobalen Zeitalter* (Munich: Wilhelm Fink, 2010).

75. Mary Lou Emery, "Caribbean Modernism: Plantation to Planetary," in Wollaeger with Eatough, *Oxford Handbook of Global Modernisms*, 49.

76. Gilroy, *Postcolonial Melancholia*, xv.

77. Song, "Becoming Planetary," 568.

78. Ramazani, "Poetry, Modernity, and Globalization," in Wollaeger with Eatough, *Oxford Handbook of Global Modernisms*, 297.

79. Spivak, *Death of a Discipline*, 72.

80. Spivak, *Death of a Discipline*, 72.

81. Elias, "Dialogical Avant-Garde," 741; Moraru, *Cosmodernism*, 57.

82. Apter, *Against World Literature*, 189.

83. I have attended in more detail to the *monde/mundus* paradigm in *Cosmodernism*, 51–54, 60, 255, 257.

84. Herman Rapaport, *The Literary Theory Toolkit: A Compendium of Concepts and Methods* (Malden, MA: Wiley-Blackwell, 2011), 221.

85. Rapaport, *Literary Theory Toolkit*, 221–222.

86. Emery, "Caribbean Modernism," in Wollaeger with Eatough, *Oxford Handbook of Global Modernisms*, 49.

87. Franco Moretti, *Distant Reading* (New York: Verso, 2013), 44.

88. Emery, "Caribbean Modernism," in Wollaeger with Eatough, *Oxford Handbook of Global Modernisms*, 49.

89. Wallerstein, *World-Systems Analysis*, 16–17.

90. On Heidegger, Merleau-Ponty, and the "world," see, among others, J. E. Malpas, *Place and Experience: A Philosophical Topography* (Cambridge: Cambridge University Press, 1999), 7–9. On Deleuze and Guattari and their "and" and "with" "operators," see, among many other possible sources, Eugene Holland, "Global Cosmopolitanism and Nomad Citizenship," in *After Cosmopolitanism*, ed. Rosi Braidotti, Patrick Hanafin, and Bolette Blaagaard (Abingdon, UK: Routledge, 2013), 153.

91. Wallerstein, *World-Systems Analysis*, 17.

92. Garret Wallace Brown and David Held remind us of this basic tenet of Stoicism with reference to Seneca in the "Editors' Introduction" to *The Cosmopolitanism Reader*, ed. Garrett Wallace Brown and David Held (Cambridge: Polity, 2010), 5, 11. Also see, in the same collection, David Held's essay "Principles or Cosmopolitan Order," 229.

93. On postmodern cartography, see, as part of an ever-larger body of work, Brian Jarvis, *Postmodern Cartographies: The Geographical Imagination in Contemporary American Culture* (New York: St. Martin's Press, 1998), and Peta Mitchell, *Cartographic Strategies of Postmodernity: The Figure of the Map in Contemporary Theory and Fiction* (New York: Routledge, 2008).

94. Pheng Cheah, "What Is a World? On World Literature as World-Making Activity," *Daedalus* 137, no. 3 (Summer 2008): 30. Also see, in the same vein, Cheah's more recent article, "World against Globe: Toward a Normative Conception of World literature," *New Literary History* 45, no. 3 (Summer 2014): 303–329.

95. On "world" as transitive verb in relation to the "worlding" work of comparatists, see Djelal Kadir's articles "To World, to Globalize: Comparative Literature's Crossroads," *Comparative Literature Studies* 41, no. 1 (2004): 1–9, and "To Compare, to World: Two Verbs, One Discipline," *Comparatist* 34 (May 2010): 4–11.

96. On "postcosmopolitanism" and the terminological conflations affecting "planet" and "relation," see Rosi Braidotti, Patrick Hanafin, and Bolette Blaagaard's "Introduction" to their essay collection *After Cosmopolitanism*, 4.

97. In her discussion of "becoming-world," Rosi Braidotti uses "planetary" in a globalist sense and replaces "planet," which she considers a relational *datum,* with "world." See her essay 'Becoming-World' in Braidotti, Hanafin, and Blaagaard, *After Cosmopolitanism*, 8–27.

98. Song, "Becoming Planetary," 572.

99. David Palumbo-Liu, Bruce Robbins, and Nirvana Tanoukhi, "The Most Important Thing Happening," in Palumbo-Liu, Robbins, and Tanoukhi, *Immanuel Wallerstein and the Problem of the World*, 17.

100. Heise, *Sense of Place and Sense of Planet*, 7, 10–15.

101. Wallerstein, *World-Systems Analysis*, 21. On 1989 as a "continuation" of 1968, see, among other places, Almantas Samalavicius's interview with Immanuel Wallerstein, "New World-System? A Conversation with Immanuel Wallerstein," *Eurozine*, February 8, 2013, http://www.eurozine.com/articles/-2013-02-08-wallerstein-en.html.

102. Bruce Robbins, "Blaming the System," in Palumbo-Liu, Robbins, and Tanoukhi, *Immanuel Wallerstein and the Problem of the World*, 55.

103. On the paradox of (geo)culture—always invoked, never attended to—inside the Wallersteinian school, see Richard E. Lee, "The Modern World-System," in Palumbo-Liu, Robbins, and Tanoukhi, *Immanuel Wallerstein and the Problem of the World.*

104. Also see an excellent discussion of Wallerstein's world-systems theory and its bearings on world/comparative literature in Hayot, *On Literary Worlds*, 30–41.

105. Apter, *Against World Literature*, 71–72.

106. Spivak, Susan Stanford Friedman, Dimock, Braidotti, and Emery are only a few of the critics who have insistently linked planetarity and relation. On the "global condition" of "interconnectedness" and its potentially pernicious effects on planetarity itself, see Braidotti's "Becoming-World," in Braidotti, Hanafin, and Blaagaard, *After Cosmopolitanism*, 19.

107. Thomas Pynchon, *Bleeding Edge* (New York: Penguin, 2013), 379.

108. Jacques Derrida, *Specters of Marx: The State of the Debt, the Work of Mourning, and the New International*, trans. Peggy Kamuf, with an introduction by Bernd Magnus and Stephen Cullenberg (New York: Routledge, 1994), esp. 173–176.

109. On Heidegger and eventfulness, see especially Martin Heidegger, *The Event,* trans. Richard Rojcewicz (Bloomington: Indiana University Press, 2013).

110. On September 11, 2011, as "event-world" and the "world-culture" the event attests to, see Jean-François Sirinelli's article "L'événement-monde" in *Vingtième Siècle. Revue d'histoire* 4, no. 74 (2002): 35–38. On the worldwide impact of seem-

ingly local or regional events modeled on Badiou's "universal singular," see Tani E. Barlow, "What Is a Poem? The Event of Women and the Modern Girl as Problems in Global or World History," in Palumbo-Liu, Robbins, and Tanoukhi, *Immanuel Wallerstein and the Problem of the World*, mainly 159–160.

111. It is very tempting, confesses Maurizio Ascari, to settle on September 11, 2001, as the official date of postmodernism's demise. See his book, *Literature of the Global Age: A Critical Study of Transcultural Narratives* (Jefferson, NC: McFarland, 2011), 21. In *Cosmodernism*, I explained why 9/11 should be viewed as an upshot of 1989.

112. This is a reference to Philip Leonard's *Literature after Globalization: Textuality, Technology and the Nation-State* (London: Bloomsbury, 2013). Like mine, the critic's focus is on recent literature's "movement away from narratives of global culture." However, he understands the trend as a testimony to the "reassert[ion] of national sovereignty against technology's transnational effects" (2). In my view, while the ethicization of the netospherical does go against transnational technology's leveling effects, this planetary revaluation of technorelatedness does not necessarily reinforce, nor does it relegitimize, the nation-state.

113. Ascari is one of the critics pointing to a planetary transition out of the postmodern paradigm as a paradoxical effect of the postmodern's "going global." See his *Literature of the Global Age*, 17–40.

114. Simon Gikandi, "Globalization and the Claims of Postcoloniality," *South Atlantic Quarterly* 100, no. 3 (Summer 2001): 631.

115. On networked communication and postcolonial theory, see Mark Poster, "Postcolonial Theory in the Age of Planetary Communications," *Quarterly Review of Film and Video* 24 (2007): 379–393.

116. On "world Englishes literature," see E. Dawson Varughese, *Beyond the Postcolonial: World Englishes Literature* (New York: Palgrave Macmillan, 2012), esp. 1–23, where the book's main concept—the "postcolonial's beyond"—is theorized.

117. John Tomlinson, "Globalization and Cultural Analysis," in *Globalization Theory: Approaches and Controversies*, edited by David Held and Anthony McGrew (Cambridge: Polity Press, 2007), 150.

118. Warnier, *La mondialisation de la culture*, 107.

119. See Jacques Demorgon's books *L'interculturation du monde* (Paris: Anthropos, 2000) and *Critique de l'interculturel: L'horizon de la sociologie* (Paris: Anthropos, 2005).

120. Benjamin Barber, *Jihad vs. McWorld: How Globalism and Tribalism Are Reshaping the World* (New York: Ballantine Books, 1996); John Updike, *Bech at Bay* (New York: Alfred A. Knopf, 1998), 238–239.

121. On "Americanization" theory and the "ready-to-wear" *anti-américanisme* often coloring it, see Jean-François Revel, *L'obsession anti-américaine: Son fonctionement, ses causes, ses inconséquences* (Paris: Plon, 2002), and Pierre Rigoulot, *L'Antiaméricanisme: Critique d'un prêt-à-penser rétrograde* (Paris: Robert Laffont, 2004).

122. Gilroy, *Postcolonial Melancholia*, 69–71.

123. Jameson, *Geopolitical Aesthetic*, 3.

124. Wallerstein, *World-Systems Analysis*, 6.

125. Oana Strugaru, "Globalization and Literature: What Is Left of Literary History?" *Euresis* (2013): 144.

126. On fiction and its "worlding" function, see Medovoi, "'Terminal Crisis?'" 657.

127. Inglis and Robertson, "From Cosmos to Globe," in Rovisco and Nowicka, *Ashgate Research Companion to Cosmopolitanism*, 298.

128. Robbins, "Blaming the System," in Palumbo-Liu, Robbins, and Tanoukhi, *Immanuel Wallerstein and the Problem of the World*, 48.

129. Cheah, "What Is a World?" 26, 34.

130. Nikos Papastergiadis, "Aesthetic Cosmopolitanism," in Delanty, *Routledge Handbook of Cosmopolitanism Studies*, 229. On the thought-event concept, see Foucault, *Language, Counter-Memory, Practice*, 179.

131. Claire Colebrook, "Destroying Cosmopolitanism for the Sake of the Cosmos," in Braidotti, Hanafin, and Blaagaard, *After Cosmopolitanism*, 167.

132. Pratt, "Planetary Longings," in Gallagher, *World Writing: Poetics, Ethics, Globalization*, 219–220.

133. "Connectedness" and "networkedness" are cardinal aspect of literature's "worldedness" according to Hayot. These systemic features of discourse reach beyond intertextuality (*On Literary Worlds*, 73–78).

134. Ascari, *Literature of the Global Age*, 11–17.

135. On the "anthological" and the "ontological," see Doueihi, *Pour un humanisme numérique*, 111.

136. Dimock, "Literature for the Planet," 181.

137. Dimock, "Literature for the Planet," 178.

138. Jérôme David, *Spectres de Goethe: Les métamorphoses de la "littérature mondiale"* (Paris: Les Prairies Ordinaires, 2011).

139. Rebecca L. Walkowitz, "The Location of Literature: The Transnational Book and the Migrant Writer," in Lane, *Global Literary Theory*, 924.

140. Nicolas Bourriaud, ed., *Altermodern: Tate Triennial* (London: Tate Publishing, 2009), 13, 14.

141. See Medovoi, "'Terminal Crisis?'"; Ascari, *Literature of the Global Age*, 11–14, 24; Irr, "Toward the World Novel," and *Toward the Geopolitical Novel: U.S. Fiction in the Twenty-First Century (New York: Columbia University Press, 2013)*; Berthold Schoene, *The Cosmopolitan Novel* (Edinburgh: Edinburgh University Press, 2010; Amitava Kumar, ed., *World Bank Literature*, foreword by John Berger, afterword by Bruce Robbins (Minneapolis: University of Minnesota Press, 2003); Philip E. Wegner, "Soldierboys for Peace: Cognitive Mapping, Space, and Science Fiction as World Bank Literature," in Kumar, *World Bank Literature*, 280–296; Friedman, "Planetarity"; W. Lawrence Hogue, *Postmodern American Literature and Its Other* (Urbana: University of Illinois Press, 2009), 143–188. Franco Moretti, "Conjectures on World Literature," *New Left Review* 1 (January–February 2000), 56–58; *Distant Reading* (New York: Verso, 2013); and *Modern Epic: The World-System from Goethe to García Márquez*, trans. Quintin Hoare (London: Verso, 1996); Spivak, "World Systems and the Creole"; and Wai Chee Dimock, "Genre as World System: Epic and Novel on Four Continents," *Narrative* 14, no. 1 (January 2006): 85–101.

142. Jeffrey T. Nealon's *Post-Postmodernism or, The Cultural Logic of Just-in-Time Capitalism* (Stanford, CA: Stanford University Press, 2012) is only the latest, Jameson-derived, installment in a series of inquiries revolving around the "what comes after postmodernism?" question. On the intensifying disputes around postmodernism's simultaneous obsolescence and endurance, see John Frow's "What

Was Postmodernism?" section of his 1997 *Time and Commodity Culture* (Oxford: Oxford University Press, 1997), 13–63, initially published, in 1990, in Ian Adams and Helen Tiffin, eds., *Past the Last Post: Theorizing Post-Colonialism and Post-Modernism* (Calgary: University of Calgary Press; Hertfordshire: Harvester-Wheatsheaf), 139–152 (Frow's chapter title is, of course, an allusion to Harry Levin's 1960 classical essay, "What Was Modernism?"); Brian McHale's own article with the same title in *Electronic Book Review*, December 20, 2007, http://www.electronicbookreview.com/thread/fictionspresent-/tense?mode-print (accessed March 8, 2013); Andrew Hoberek, John Burt, David Kadlec, Jamie Owen Daniel, Shelly Eversley, Catherine Jurca, Aparajita Sagar, and Michael Berube, "Twentieth-Century-Literature in the New Century: A Symposium," *College English* 64, no. 1 (September 2001): 9–33; Moraru, "Global Turn in Critical Theory" and *Cosmodernism*; Timothy S. Murphy, "To Have Done with Postmodernism: A Plea (or Provocation) for Globalization Studies," *symploke* 12, nos. 1–2 (2004): 20–34; in the same *symploke* issue (53–68), Robert L. McLaughlin's "Post-Postmodern Discontent: Contemporary Fiction and the Social World"; Neil Brooks and Josh Toth, eds., *The Mourning After: Attending the Wake of Postmodernism* (Amsterdam: Rodopi, 2007); Alan Kirby, "The Death of Postmodernism and Beyond," *Philosophy Now* 71 (January–February 2009), http://www.philosophynow.org/issue58/58kirby.htm (accessed February 26, 2009); and other works by Mary Holland, Amy J. Elias, Timotheus Vermeulen and Robin van den Akker (proponents of "metamodernism"), Alison Gibbons, Caren Irr, Leerom Medovoi, Rachel Adams, Min Hyoung Song, Bharati Mukherjee, and the list could go on.

143. Susan Stanford Friedman writes in her 2010 article "Planetarity: Musing Modernist Studies": "As I use the term, . . . planetarity . . . is an epistemology, not an ontology" (494).

144. Wegner, "Soldierboys for Peace," in Kumar, *World Bank Literature*, 218.

145. Amin Maalouf, *In the Name of Identity: Violence and the Need to Belong*, trans. Barbara Bray (New York: Penguin, 2000), 102.

146. On post-biological, "endless kinship," see Dimock, "Genre as World System," 89.

147. Emery, "Caribbean Modernism," in Wollaeger with Eatough, *Oxford Handbook of Global Modernisms*, 49.

148. Paul Giles uses the phrase "writing for the planet" in chap. 8 of Elias and Moraru, *Planetary Turn*, "Writing for the Planet: Contemporary Australian Fiction."

149. Franco Moretti, "World-Systems Analysis, Evolutionary Theory, *Weltliteratur*," in Palumbo-Liu, Robbins, and Tanoukhi, *Immanuel Wallerstein and the Problem of the World*, 68.

150. Pascale Casanova, *The World Republic of Letters*, trans. M. B. DeBevoise (Cambridge, MA: Harvard University Press, 2004), 11–12.

151. Colin MacCabe, "Preface" to Jameson, *Geopolitical Aesthetic*, xi–xii.

PART 2

1. Pratt, "Planetary Longings," in Gallagher, *World Writing: Poetics, Ethics, Globalization*, 211.

2. In Ancient Greek, *drómos* means "race," "running (place)," "track," or "stadium." Recently revivified, primarily by Paul Virilio in his 1977 book *Vitesse et politique: Essai de dromologie* (Paris: Galilée, 1977), "dromology" is the "science of speed" or systematic inquiry into "speed culture." More generally, *drómos* signifies "road" (in Greek and other languages that have borrowed the word) and thus intersects, so to speak, with *hodós*—"way," "street," "road," "path," "journey" (when it is used as a masculine noun), and "threshold" (when one employs its feminine form).

3. Georg Simmel, *Essays on Sociology, Philosophy, and Aesthetics*, ed. Kurt H. Wolff (New York: Harper & Row, 1959), 276–277.

4. Before providing the title of Beigbeder's 2003 novel, Windows on the World was a restaurant on the top floor of the North World Trade Center Tower.

5. Emmanuel Levinas, *Totality and Infinity: An Essay on Interiority*, trans. Alphonso Lingis (Pittsburgh, PA: Duquesne University Press, 1961), 74–75.

6. Friedman, "Planetarity," 494.

7. See Friedman's "Planetarity" (493) for "modernisms" and collage as a "planetary epistemology" within which to read them.

8. In his article "Spatializing Difference beyond Cosmopolitanism: Rethinking Planetary Futures" (*Theory, Culture & Society* 28, no. 5 [2011]), Tariq Jazeel relies on Denis Cosgrove's 2001 book *Apollo's Eye: A Cartographic Genealogy of the Earth in the Western Imagination* to claim that photos of the Earth such as those taken by Apollo 17 in 1972 attest to an "Apollonian gaze" (81), which, Jazeel further contends, betrays an imperial, culturocentric, and totalizing "reverie" redolent of cosmopolitanism's "one-worldist" thrust (87). As it turned out, NASA pictures are no different from those taken since the 1970s by hundreds of other space missions, shuttles, orbiting stations, and satellites belonging to a steadily growing number of countries, Western and non-Western. While the meaning of these images has shifted somewhat in the post–Cold War era, it would be safe to say that even back in the 1970s they meant and suggested much more than what Cosgrove and others think they did. Equally reductive is Jazeel's grasp of cosmopolitanism. Finally, the scalar synergy of the macro and micro categories also plays out in the argument Dimock makes in her essay in *The Planetary Turn*.

9. Bruce Robbins, "Comparative Cosmopolitanisms," in *Cosmopolitics: Thinking and Feeling beyond the Nation*, ed. Pheng Cheah and Bruce Robbins (Minneapolis: University of Minnesota Press, 1998), 253.

10. On the "event" as discontinuous and ambiguously "suspect" occurrence, see, among many others, Jacques Derrida, "Structure, Sign and Play in the Discourse of the Human Sciences," in *Modern Criticism and Theory: A Reader*, ed. David Lodge, 62 (Harlow, UK: Longman, 2000), and Alain Badiou, *Handbook of Inaesthetics*, trans. Alberto Toscano (Stanford, CA: Stanford University Press, 2004), 118, 132.

11. Gilles Deleuze and Félix Guattari, *A Thousand Plateaus: Capitalism and Schizophrenia*, trans. Brian Massumi (Minneapolis: University of Minnesota Press, 1987), 167–191. On "faciality" in Deleuze and Guattari, see, among others, Burcu Canar, "Deleuze and the Face," *Lingua ac Communitas* 21 (2011): 33–52.

12. Where "there is no expression," the face is "asleep," writes Michael Ondaatje in *The English Patient* (New York: Vintage, 1993), 28.

13. Bertrand Westphal, "The White Globe and the Paradoxical Cartography of Berger & Berger: A Meditation on Deceptive Evidence," another essay from Elias and Moraru, *Planetary Turn*.

14. Youri Lotman, *La sémiosphère*, trans. Anka Ledenko (Limoges, France: Presses Universitaires de Limoges, 1999), 9–20.

15. In *On Literary Worlds* (91), Hayot assigns "planet" a cosmographic meaning close to how I understand "earth" here but also to how I define the "spherical" nature of "globe" in part 1, §7.

16. Gilles Deleuze and Claire Parnet, *Dialogues*, trans. Hugh Tomlinson and Barbara Habberjam (New York: Columbia University Press, 1987), 37.

17. Gilles Deleuze and Félix Guattari, *What Is Philosophy?*, trans. Hugh Tomlinson and Graham Burchell (New York: Columbia University Press, 1994), 95.

18. Deleuze and Guattari, *What Is Philosophy?*, 41.

19. Rodolphe Gasché, *Geophilosophy: On Gilles Deleuze and Félix Guattari's* What Is Philosophy? (Evanston, IL: Northwestern University Press, 2014), 21.

20. Gasché, *Geophilosophy*, 35.

21. Deleuze and Guattari, *What Is Philosophy?*, 85.

22. Deleuze and Guattari, *What Is Philosophy?*, 95.

23. Henri Lefebvre, *State, Space, World: Selected Essays*, ed. Neil Brenner and Stuart Elden, trans. Gerald Moore, Neil Brenner, and Stuart Elden (Minneapolis: University of Minnesota Press, 2009), 96.

24. Deleuze and Guattari, *What Is Philosophy?*, 109.

25. Kostas Axelos, *Vers la pensée planétaire: Le devenir-pensée du monde et le devenir-monde de la pensée* (Paris: Minuit, 1984), 29–31.

26. Deleuze and Guattari, *What Is Philosophy?*, 41.

27. In their essay on Deleuze and Guattari's "plan d'immanence" from *Le Vocabulaire de Gilles Deleuze* edited by Robert Sasso and Arnaud Villani (Nice, France: Les Cahiers de *Noesis*, 2003), Maurice Élie and Arnaud Villani observe that "distinct from the *plane of reference*, which characterizes science, consists of 'actuals' [*actuels*], and gives up on the infinite, and also distinct from the *plane of consistence*, which characterizes art, consists of affects and percepts, and brings about the finite so as to regain the infinite, the *plane of immanence* consists of concepts and recovers the infinite [directly]" (272).

28. On "multitude," see Negri, *Art and Multitude*, 7, 75; on "crowd," Badiou's *Handbook of Inaesthetics*, 31–32. Also see Pico Iyer, *The Global Soul: Jet Lag, Shopping Malls, and the Search for Home* (New York: Random House, 2000) and "The Nowhere Man," in *Prospect* 30, no. 3 (February 1997): 30–33; and Alexandar Hemon's novel *Nowhere Man* (New York: Random House, 2002). Also, Masao Miyoshi was among the first to draw attention to, but also to argue for, a turn *to* the planet in a sense that he determined as enabling culturally, politically, and otherwise. On this topic, see his "Turn to the Planet" article discussed in part 1, §10.

29. DeLillo, *White Noise*, 258–259.

30. This is a reference to E. M. Cioran's *Précis de décomposition* (Paris: Gallimard, 1977), originally published in 1949.

31. Bertrand Westphal, *Le monde plausible: Espace, lieu, carte* (Paris: Minuit, 2011), 12–15.

32. On a perceptive discussion of "the spatial turn in contemporary literary historiography," see Andrei Terian, *Critica de export: Teorii, contexte, ideologii* (Bucharest: Editura Muzeului Literaturii Române, 2013), 75–88.

33. For postmodernism's "spatial imagination," also see Julian Murphet, "Post-

modernism and Space," in *The Cambridge Companion to Postmodernism*, ed. Steven Connor (Cambridge: Cambridge University Press, 2004), 116–135.

34. On "lococentrism," see the "Place" chapter in Lawrence Buell's *The Environmental Imagination: Thoreau, Nature Writing, and the Formation of American Culture* (Cambridge, MA: Belknap Press of Harvard University Press, 1995), 252–279. The section has been anthologized in *Modern Criticism and Theory: A Reader*, 3rd ed., edited by David Lodge and Nigel Wood (New York: Longman, 2008), 667–691.

35. "Out is over," variously proclaims, among others, Thomas L. Friedman in *Longitudes and Attitudes: Exploring the World after September 11* (New York: Farrar, Straus and Giroux, 2002), 22, and elsewhere in his books. On the disappearance of the planet's traditional "hiding places," see also Jameson, *Geopolitical Aesthetic*, 66, and David A. Hollinger, *Cosmopolitanism and Solidarity: Studies in Ethnoracial, Religious, and Professional Affiliation in the United States* (Madison: University of Wisconsin Press, 2006), xxii.

36. Moraru, *Cosmodernism*, 2.

37. Moraru, *Cosmodernism*, 307–316.

38. Heidegger, *Being and Time*, 97.

39. For the evolving meaning of "world" as verb (*welten*) in Heidegger, with particular emphasis on the philosopher's early work, see Françoise Dastur, "Heidegger's Freiburg Version of the Origin of the Work of Art," in *Heidegger toward the Turn: Essays on the Work of the 1930s*, ed. James Risser, 129, 140 (Albany: State University of New York Press, 1999).

40. On Heidegger's world concept and its relation to the world of the arts and literature with special application to comparative literature, see Hayot, *On Literary Worlds*, 23–29.

41. Martin Heidegger, *The Question concerning Technology and Other Essays*, trans. and with an introduction by William Lovitt (New York: Garland, 1977), 129. On Schmitt's *nomós*, see Carl Schmitt, *The* Nomos *of the Earth in the International Law of the* Jus Publicum Europaeum, trans. and annotated by G. L. Ulmen (New York: Telos, 2006).

42. Lefebvre, *State, Space, World*, 196.

43. On a possible synthesis of the two reading modes, see N. Katherine Hayles, "Combining Close and Distant Reading: Jonathan Safran Foer's *Tree of Codes* and the Aesthetic of Bookishness," *PMLA* 128, no. 1 (January 2013): 226–231.

44. Heidegger, *Question concerning Technology*, 135.

45. Spivak, *Death of a Discipline*, 72.

46. Spivak, *Death of a Discipline*, 30, 72.

47. Heidegger, *Question concerning Technology*, 135.

48. Spivak, *Death of a Discipline*, 82, 92.

49. See Casanova, *World Republic of Letters*.

50. On "distant reading" and its problematic procedure in Moretti, see his "Conjectures on World Literature," 56–58.

51. See Emery, "Caribbean Modernism" (49), on the cognitive risks of "distance" and spatial-epistemological "detachment." On the latter and its planetary remedies, see Ramazani, "Poetry, Modernity, and Globalization," 301. On this subject, Ramazani leans on Robbins's essay "Introduction[,] Part I: Actually Existing Cosmopolitanism" (in Cheah and Robbins, *Cosmopolitics*, 1–19), which in turn revisits the

community-making dynamic of attachment-detachment discussed by Benedict Anderson in his classic 1983 work *Imagined Communities: Reflections on the Origin and Spread of Nationalism*, rev. ed. (New York: Verso, 1991) and Amanda Anderson in *The Powers of Distance: Cosmopolitanism and the Cultivation of Detachment* (Princeton, NJ: Princeton University Press, 2001).

52. Moretti also makes a rather unpersuasive and, to my mind, unnecessary case against close reading in "Conjectures on World Literature," 57.

53. Neef, *Der babylonische Planet*, 151–152.

54. Simon O'Sullivan, "The Aesthetics of Affect: Thinking Art beyond Representation," *Angelaki* 6, no. 3 (December 2001): 127.

55. On the relationality of place and the need to "work through" the latter, see Jazeel, "Spatializing Difference beyond Cosmopolitanism," 92. For an "inoperative" concept of community, see, of course, Jean-Luc Nancy, *The Inoperative Community*, ed. Peter Conor, trans. Peter Conor, Lisa Garbus, Michael Holland, and Simona Sawhney, foreword by Christopher Fynsk (Minneapolis: University of Minnesota Press, 1991). Critics who move in the same direction overall, also in the context of twenty-first-century geosocial developments, include: Negri, with *Inventer le commun des hommes,* pref. Judith Revel (Paris: Bayard, 2010), Todorov, with *La vie commune: Essai d'anthropologie générale (Paris: Seuil, 1995)*, and Roberto Esposito, with *Communitas: The Origins and Destiny of Community,* trans. Timothy Campbell (Stanford, CA: Stanford University Press, 2010).

56. Negri talks about the community "laboratory" in *Inventer le commun des hommes*.

57. On community as an "illusion" in the global age, see Marc Augé, *La Communauté illusoire* (Paris: Payot, 2010).

58. On distant kinship, see Dimock, *Through Other Continents*, 144–145.

59. Westphal uses the phrase "world reading" (*lecture du monde*) in *Le monde plausible*, 15.

60. Regarding "relational reading," the wider world, and the world library, see Bernadette Brennan's "Worlds Without and Within: Reading Through Patrick White's Library in *The Solid Mandala*," in *Scenes of Reading: Is Australian Literature a World Literature?*, ed. Robert Dixon and Brigid Rooney, 115–126 (Melbourne: Australian Scholarly Publishing, 2014).

61. Dixon and Rooney mention Ken Gelder's "proximate reading" in their introduction to *Scenes of Reading*, xxxi, xxxv.

62. On literary study as a "nation-based discipline" and the field's changes after the "national period," see, among many others, Robert Dixon and Brigid Rooney, "Introduction: Australian Literature, Globalisation and the Literary Province," in Dixon and Rooney, *Scenes of Reading*, x, xi, xv. On this issue, the critics reference in particular Giles's recent books on American Literature.

63. Neil Brenner, "The Space of the World: Beyond State-Centrism?" in Palumbo-Liu, Robbins, and Tanoukhi, *Immanuel Wallerstein and the Problem of the World*, 109.

64. As Fine shows in *Cosmopolitanism* (7), Beck formulated his famous critique of "methodological nationalism" probably for the first time in a 2002 article, then he reformulated it in "Toward a New Critical Theory with a Cosmopolitan Intent," *Constellations* 10, no. 4 (2003), 453–468. After several more elaborations on the

same subject, he takes it up again in "Cosmopolitan Sociology: Outline of a Paradigm Shift," a piece included in Rovisco and Nowicka, *Ashgate Research Companion to Cosmopolitanism*, 17–32. On Giddens, Beck, Martins, "methodological cosmopolitanism," and its "equivocations" (including Beck's "post-universalism"), see Fine's excellent discussion in *Cosmopolitanism*, 1–14.

65. Beck, "Cosmopolitan Sociology, 18.

66. Beck, "Cosmopolitan Sociology, 29.

67. On Beck and the state as a "zombie category," see Fine, *Cosmopolitanism*, 6–7. Paul Giles has commented on territorialism, terrorism, and the "homeland security" approach to literature in his essay "The Deterritorialization of American Literature," in *Shades of the Planet: American Literature as World Literature*, ed. Wai Chee Dimock and Lawrence Buell, 39–61 (Princeton, NJ: Princeton University Press, 2007).

68. Svend Erik Larsen, "Literary History as a Cultural Challenge: Rewriting Local Literary History in the Age of Globalisation," in Dixon and Rooney, *Scenes of Reading*, 62.

69. Mohsin Hamid, *How to Get Filthy Rich in Rising Asia* (New York: Riverhead, 2013), 139.

70. Hamid, *How to Get Filthy Rich in Rising Asia*, 139.

71. Papastergiadis, "Spatial Aesthetics," 373.

72. In the phrase and, presumably, the practice of "world literature," "world" can and does serve as an "alibi for not reading scale politically," claims Peter Hitchcock in his article "The Function of Agon at the Present Time," *Comparatist* 37 (2013): 18.

73. Walkowitz, "Location of Literature," 926, 927. Regarding the distinction between the postcolonial and the global, Rapaport argues that "[w]hereas global studies is quite concerned with transit across the globe—that is to say, with mobility and its expression as power—post-colonial studies has been concerned with intercultural relations and their expression in terms of domination and subjection" (*Literary Theory Kit*, 61).

74. Julia Kristeva, *Nations without Nationalism*, trans. Leon S. Roudiez (New York: Columbia University Press, 1993), 51.

75. Regarding a dynamic of "hearth" and "cosmos" close to the planetary interplay of "here" and "there," see Yi-Fu Tuan, *Cosmos and Hearth*, 187–188. On "egocentric" versus "allocentric space," see Malpas, *Place and Experience*, 44–55.

76. On borders as "quilting points," see Anthony Cooper and Chris Rumford, "Cosmopolitan Borders: Bordering as Connectivity," in Rovisco and Nowicka, *Ashgate Research Companion to Cosmopolitanism*, 273.

77. Dimock, "Literature for the Planet," 178.

78. Daniel Levy and Natan Sznaider, "Cosmopolitan Memory and Human Rights," in Rovisco and Nowicka, *Ashgate Research Companion to Cosmopolitanism*, 197.

79. Dimock, "Scales of Aggregation," 219, 226.

80. Friedrich Nietzsche, *Untimely Meditations*, ed. Daniel Breazeale, trans. R. J. Hollingdale (Cambridge: Cambridge University Press, 2003), 149–150.

81. Julien Benda, *The Treason of the Intellectuals*, with a new introduction by Roger Kinball, trans. Richard Aldington (New Brunswick, NJ: Transaction, 2007).

82. Adrian Florea, "De Facto States in International Politics (1945–2011): A New

Data Set," *International Interactions: Empirical and Theoretical Research in International Relations* (October 2014), http://dx.doi.org/10.1080/03050629.-2014.915543.

83. Dimock, "Literature for the Planet," 175.

84. Among the critics for whom "novel assemblages of territory, authority[,] and rights" would deal successfully with the local (national)-global conundrum, I list here only Saskia Sassen, with her article "Neither Global nor National: Novel Assemblages of Territory, Authority and Rights" (*Ethics & Global Politics* 1, nos. 1–2 [2008]: 61–79), Ramazani, with "Poetry, Modernity, and Globalization" (301), and Beck, with "Cosmopolitan Sociology" (28–29).

85. On methodological "glocalism," see Holton, *Global Networks*, 47.

86. Quoting Robbins in "Poetry, Modernity, and Globalization," Ramazani points to the "multiple attachments" following "detachments" from local bonds. Under planetarity, such detachments are not a prerequisite of with-being. On post-ethnic affiliation, voluntary rather than inherited by background, see David A. Hollinger, *Postethnic America: Beyond Multiculturalism* (New York: Basic Books/HarperCollins, 1995), and *Cosmopolitanism and Solidarity*. Delanty discusses the cosmopolitan local-global and self-other interface in "The Idea of Critical Cosmopolitanism," in Delanty, *Routledge Handbook of Cosmopolitan Studies*, 41.

87. On "nested territorial units," see Thomas Pogge, "Cosmopolitanism and Sovereignty," in Brown and Held, *Cosmopolitanism Reader*, 114.

88. Dumitru Tiutiuca, "Fractology—a Possible Outlook on Literature," *Euresis* 1–4 (2012): 102–108.

89. Dimock, "Genre as World System," 88.

90. Dimock, "Genre as World System," 89.

91. Dimock, "Genre as World System," 90.

92. Emmanuel Levinas, "Peace and Proximity," in Emmanuel Levinas, *Basic Philosophical Writings*, ed. Adriaan T. Peperzak, Simon Critchley, and Robert Bernasconi, 168 (Bloomington: Indiana University Press, 1996).

93. Giorgio Agamben, *The Coming Community*, trans. Michael Hardt (Minneapolis: University of Minnesota Press, 2009), 44.

94. Agamben, *Coming Community*, 43.

95. Agamben, *Coming Community*, 43.

96. Agamben, *Coming Community*, 43–44.

97. Jean Baudrillard, "Global Debt and Parallel Universe," in *Digital Delirium*, ed. and introduction by Arthur and Marilouise Kroker, 38–40 (New York: St. Martin's, 1997).

98. I talk about the "outsourcing of identity" in *Cosmodernism*, 16–17, also in the context of world indebtedness (21, 26). On the latter, see too my recent article "'World,' 'Globe,' 'Planet': Comparative Literature, Planetary Studies, and Cultural Debt after the Global Turn," American Comparative Literature Association, the 2014–2015 Report on the State of the Discipline of Comparative Literature website - Paradigms. http://stateofthediscipline.acla.org.

99. See the previous note. Also see the epilogue of my book *Memorious Discourse*, 224–234.

100. For the "university in ruins" argument, see, of course, Bill Readings's book *The University in Ruins* (Cambridge, MA: Harvard University Press, 1996).

101. Holton, *Global Networks*, 45.

102. Dimock, "Planetary Time and Global Translation."

103. Bruce Robbins, *Perpetual War: Cosmopolitanism from the Viewpoint of Violence* (Durham, NC: Duke University Press, 2012), 4.

104. Jameson, *Geopolitical Aesthetic*, 77.

105. Jameson, *Geopolitical Aesthetic*, 77–78.

106. "New cosmopolitanism," Fine argues in *Cosmopolitanism* (1), is a post-1989 phenomenon.

107. Michael Werner and Bénédicte Zimmermann, "Beyond Comparison: *Histoire croisée* and the Challenge of Reflexivity," *History and Theory* 45 (February 2006): 30, 31, 39, 42, 44.

108. George Konrád, *Antipolitics: An Essay*, trans. from the Hungarian by Richard E. Allen (San Diego: Harcourt Brace Jovanovich, 1984), 179.

109. Mircea Cărtărescu, "Realismul poeziei tinere" (Young Poets' Realism), in *Competiția continuă: Generația 80 in texte teoretice* (The Race Goes On: Theoretical Texts on the 1980s Generation), ed. Gheorghe Crăciun, 183 (Pitești, Romania: Editura Vlasie, 1994).

110. Mircea Cărtărescu, *Totul* (All) (Bucharest, Romania: Cartea Românească, 1985).

111. *Visul* (Bucharest: Cartea Românească, 1989) was republished in complete form in 1993 (Bucharest: Humanitas) and has been translated into a number of languages. For the English version, see *Nostalgia*, trans., with an afterword, from the Romanian by Julian Semilian, introduction by Andrei Codrescu (New York: New Directions, 2005). Later prose works such as novels like *Travesti* (Disguise) (Bucharest: Humanitas, 1994), the *Orbitor* (Blinding) three-volume series (Bucharest: Humanitas, 1996–2007), and the short pieces gathered in the bestseller *De ce iubim femeile* (Why We Love Women) (Bucharest: Humanitas, 2005) detail *Nostalgia*'s description of Bucharest.

112. Dimock, "Literature for the Planet," 185.

113. Jamaica Kincaid, *A Small Place* (New York: Penguin, 1981), 52.

114. *Állos* (masculine plural *álloi*) is "another" in Greek. It may designate either another *like* the self (by and large an other of the same sort) or an other *to* this self, in which case its meaning is closer to *héteros*. "The other of two," the latter marks the other's otherness more emphatically. In Latin, *alius* and *alter* enact roughly the same distinction. While unquestionably significant, the difference between *állos* and *héteros* is not instrumental to my argument.

115. On the spatial ethics of "taking place" and the *ek-static* "outside," see Agamben, *Coming Community*, 13–15, 23–25, and 67–68.

116. Edward W. Soja, *Postmodern Geographies: The Reassertion of Space in Critical Social Theory* (New York: Verso, 1989), 131–137.

117. On the Aleph symbol in writing and inscription systems generally, see Sonja Neef, *Imprint and Trace: Handwriting in the Age of Technology*, trans. Anthony Mathews (London: Reaktion Books, 2011), esp. 7–13.

118. Jorge Luis Borges, "The Aleph," in *Collected Fictions*, trans. Andrew Hurley (New York: Penguin, 1999), 280.

119. On the Zahir as "an unbearable symbol of the infinite, painful circularity, an[d] obsessive counterpart of the elusive Aleph," see Matei Calinescu's *Rereading* (New Haven, CT: Yale University Press, 1993), 12, 11–16.

120. On Borges, the Aleph, the Kabbalah, and Judaic tradition in general, see Jaime Alazraki, *Borges and the Kabbalah and Other Essays on His Fiction and Poetry* (New York: Cambridge University Press, 1988); Edna Aizenberg, *The Aleph Weaver: Biblical, Kabbalistic and Judaic Elements in Borges* (Potomac, MD: Scripta Humanistica, 1984). In Edna Aizenberg, ed., *Borges and His Successors: The Borgesian Impact on Literature and the Arts* (Columbia: University of Missouri Press, 1990), see esp. its fifth section, "Hebraism and Poetic Influence," 249–284, which features two lectures by Borges on the Book of Job and Baruch Spinoza, respectively. Worth mentioning is also Evelyn Fishburn's article "Reflections on the Jewish Imaginary in the Fictions of Borges," in *Variaciones Borges: Journal of the Jorge Luis Borges Center for Studies and Documentation, no.* 5 (1998): 145–156. On Borges's own thoughts on the Kabbalah, see "The Kabbalah," in *Seven Nights*, trans. Eliot Weinberger, introduction by Alasdair Reid (New York: New Directions, 1984), 99.

121. Soja, *Postmodern Geographies*, 223.

122. Edward W. Soja, *Thirdspace: Journeys to Los Angeles and Other Real-and-Imagined Places* (Cambridge, MA: Blackwell, 1996), 54–57.

123. Soja, *Postmodern Geographies*, 222–23.

124. "Shall I project a world?" famously asks Pynchon's Oedipa Maas in *The Crying of Lot 49* (New York: HarperCollins, 1999), 64.

125. Jazeel, "Spatializing Difference beyond Cosmopolitanism," 92.

126. Hollinger, *Cosmopolitanism and Solidarity*, 73, 36.

127. Mircea Cărtărescu, *Blinding*, trans. Sean Cotter (Brooklyn, NY: Archipelago Books, 2013).

128. Cărtărescu, *Blinding*, 75.

129. Cărtărescu, *Blinding*, 48.

130. Mircea Cărtărescu, *Orbitor. Corpul* (Bucharest: Humanitas, 2002), 135, 152.

131. Cărtărescu, *Orbitor. Corpul*, 249.

132. Cărtărescu, *Orbitor. Corpul*, 248–249.

133. Dai Sijie, *Balzac and the Little Chinese Seamstress*, trans. from the French by Ina Rilke (New York: Random House, 2001); *Mr. Muo's Travelling Couch*, trans. from the French by Ina Rilke (New York: Knopf, 2005).

134. Excerpt from a *Boston Herald* review of *Balzac and the Little Chinese Seamstress*, fragment reproduced on the front inside cover of the American translation.

135. Dai, *Balzac and the Little Chinese Seamstress*, 45.

136. Dai, *Balzac and the Little Chinese Seamstress*, 49.

137. Bernadette Delamarre, *Autrui* (Paris: Ellipses, 1996), 4–5.

138. Romain Rolland on himself, quoted in "Romain Rolland," *World Authors, 1900–1950*, ed. Martin Seymour-Smith and Andrew C. Kimmens, vol. 3 (New York: H. W. Wilson, 1996), 2222.

139. Dai, *Balzac and the Little Chinese Seamstress*, 58–59. Critics who have focused on Balzac's presence in Dai's novel include, among others, Dorothée Fritz-Ababneh, in "L'Intertextualité dans Balzac et *La petite tailleuse chinoise* de Dai Sijie," in *French Studies* 77 (Winter 2006): 97–113, and Ian McCall, who zeroes in on the role Balzac plays in the little seamstress's *education sentimentale* in "French Literature and Film in the USSR and Mao's China," in *Romance Studies* 24, no. 2 (July 2006): 159–170. Michelle E. Bloom deals with similar issues apropos of the movie Dai himself made of his novel in 2002. See her article "Contemporary Franco-

Chinese Cinema: Translation, Citation, and Imitation in Dai Sijie's *Balzac and the Little Chinese Seamstress* and Tsai Ming-Liang's *What Time Is It There?*," in *Quarterly Review of Film and Video* 22, no. 4 (October–December 2005): 311–325.

140. Peter Fenves, "Alterity and Identity, Postmodern Theories Of," in *Routledge Encyclopedia of Philosophy*, Edward Craig, general editor (New York: Routledge, 1998), 188.

141. Jacques Derrida, "Geopsychoanalysis: 'and . . . the rest of the world,'" in Christopher Lane, ed., *The Psychoanalysis of Race* (New York: Columbia University Press, 1998), 66, 68.

142. Derrida, "Geopsychoanalysis," 65.

143. Dai Sijie, *Once on a Moonless Night*, trans. Adriana Hunter (New York: Knopf, 2009), 158.

144. Dai Sijie, *Once on a Moonless Night*, 158.

145. Zadie Smith, *On Beauty* (New York: Penguin, 2005), 93.

146. E. M. Forster, *Howards End*. Complete, Authoritative Text with Biographical and Historical Contexts, Critical History, and Essays from Five Contemporary Critical Perspectives, ed. Alistair M. Duckworth (Boston: Bedford/St. Martin's, 1997), 168.

147. Smith, *On Beauty*, "Acknowledgements." On Smith and Forster's "Only connect . . . ," see, among others, Georgia Garett's book note in *Publishers Weekly*, http://www.powells.com/-biblio/1594200637, and Gail Caldwell's review "Come Together" in the *Boston Globe*, September 11, 2005, http://www.boston.com/ae/books/-articles/2005/09/11/-come_together/.

148. Caldwell, "Come Together."

149. Zadie Smith, *NW* (New York: Penguin, 2012), 85.

150. Zadie Smith, *White Teeth* (New York: Random House, 2000), 257.

151. Zadie Smith, *Autograph Man* (New York: Vintage, 2003), 77.

152. Smith, *On Beauty*, "Acknowledgements."

153. For an extensive version of this historical critique of cosmopolitanism, see my book *Cosmodernism*, esp. 67–73.

154. Seth Jacobowitz, "Hellenism, Hebraism, and the Eugenics of Culture in E. M. Forster's *Howards End*," *CLWeb: Comparative Literature and Culture* 6, no. 4 (December 2004), http://clcwebjournal.lib.purdue.edu/clcweb04-4/jacobowitz04.html. In a footnote to his *Howards End* edition, Alistair M. Duckworth also observes that "[t]he Name *Schlegel* recalls the Schlegel brothers" (25).

155. J. Hillis Miller, *Others* (Princeton, NJ: Princeton University Press, 2003), 195. The critic quotes from *The Manuscripts of* Howards End edited by Oliver Stallybrass. He also proposes "there is no way to tell whether Forster had in mind Friedrich Schlegel or August Wilhelm Schlegel as the 'great critic'" (205). My reading suggests that, in all likelihood, Friedrich is the one Forster refers to even though "August Wilhelm may have had greater importance in Forster's day" (205).

156. Casanova, *World Republic of Letters*, 77–81.

157. Miller, *Others*, 8.

158. Miller, *Others*, 195.

159. Miller, *Others*, 199.

160. Miller, *Others*, 200.

161. Smith, *On Beauty*, 94.

162. My translation of the following French original: "Mais 'l'enfer, c'est les autres' a toujours été mal compris. On a cru que je voulais dire par là que nos rapports avec les autres étaient toujours empoisonnés, que c'étaient toujours des rapports infernaux. Or, c'est autre chose que je veux dire. Je veux dire que si les rapports avec autrui sont tordus, viciés, alors l'autre ne peut être que l'enfer. Pourquoi? Parce que les autres sont au fond ce qu'il y a de plus important en nous-même pour notre propre connaissance de nous-même. Quand nous pensons sur nous, quand nous essayons de nous connaître, au fond nous usons ces connaissances que les autres ont déja sur nous. Nous jugeons aves les moyens que les autres ont, nous ont donné de nous juger. Quoique je dise sur moi, toujours le jugement d'autrui entre dedans. Ce qui veut dire que, si mes rapports sont mauvaises, je me mets dans la totale dépendance d'autrui. Et alors en effet je suis en enfer." See Jean-Paul Sartre, No Exit *and Three Other Plays* (New York: Random House, 1973); "*Huis clos* de Jean-Paul Sartre," http://www.alalettre.com/sartre-huisclos.htm.

163. Smith, *On Beauty*, "Author's Note," 445. However, the painter is not Jean Hyppolite (the French philosopher), but Haitian artist Hector Hyppolite.

164. Paul Gilroy, *Against Race: Imagining Political Culture beyond the Color Line* (Cambridge, MA: Belknap Press of Harvard University Press, 2000), 41.

165. Milan Kundera, *Testaments Betrayed: An Essay in Nine Parts*, trans. Linda Asher (New York: HarperCollins, 1995), 50–51.

166. Elaine Scarry, *On Beauty and Being Just* (Princeton, NJ: Princeton University Press, 1999), 47.

167. Scarry, *On Beauty and Being Just*, 95.

168. On Levinas, Derrida, and hospitality, see Derrida's *Adieu to Emmanuel Levinas, Of Hospitality*, and esp. the "Hostipitality" chapter of *Acts of Religion*, ed. and with an introduction by Gil Anidjar (New York: Routledge, 2002), 358–420. Also see J. Hillis Miller's classical essay "The Critic as Host," in *Theory Now and Then* (Durham, NC: Duke University Press, 1991), 143–170.

169. Orhan Pamuk, *Snow*, trans. from the Turkish by Maureen Freely (New York: Vintage, 2005), 306.

170. Pamuk, *Snow*, 306–307.

171. See Ka's cosmic "snowflake" in Pamuk, *Snow*, 283.

172. Sorj Chalandon, "Entretien. Sorj Chalandon dans le vertige de la guerre," *L'Orient Littéraire* 97 (July 2014), http://www.lorientlitteraire.com/article-_details.php?cid=6&nid=4293.

173. Chalandon, "Entretien. Sorj Chalandon dans le vertige de la guerre."

174. Andrés Fabián Henao Castro, "Antigone Claimed: 'I Am a Stranger!' Political Theory and the Figure of the Stranger," *Hypathia* 28, no. 2 (Spring 2013): 317.

175. Sorj Chalandon, "'Je vis avec la mort et la trahison en essayant de me garder de l'une et de l'autre,'" interview by Nicolas Norrito, illustrations by Yann Levy, *CQFD* 115 (October 2013), http://cqfd-journal.org/Je-vis-avec-la-mort-et-la-trahison.

176. Jean Anouilh, *The Collected Plays, Volume 2: Time Remembered, Point of Departure, Antigone, Romeo and Jeanette, Medea* (London: Methuen, 1967), 218.

177. Anouilh, *Collected Plays, Volume* 2, 222.

178. Bertolt Brecht, *Sophocles'* Antigone, adapted by Bertolt Brecht, based on the German translation by Friedrich Hölderlin, trans. Judith Malina (New York: Applause, 1990), 34.

179. Anouilh, *Collected Plays, Volume 2*, 225.

180. Judith Butler, *Antigone's Claim: Kinship between Life and Death* (New York: Columbia University Press, 2000), 6.

181. Butler, *Antigone's Claim*, 6.

182. Sophocles, *The Complete Sophocles, Volume I: The Theban Plays*, ed. Peter Burian and Alan Shapiro (New York: Oxford University Press, 2011), 64.

183. George Steiner, *Antigones* (New York: Oxford University Press, 1984); Slavoj Žižek, *Enjoy Your Symptom: Jacques Lacan in Hollywood and Out* (New York: Routledge, 1992), 46, 77, 91–92.

184. Sorj Chalandon, *Le quatrième mur* (Paris: Grasset, 2013), 241.

185. Chalandon, *Le quatrième mur*, 181.

186. Anouilh, *Collected Plays, Volume 2*, 218–219.

187. Brecht, *Sophocles'* Antigone, 35.

188. Brecht, *Sophocles'* Antigone, 35.

189. Anouilh, *Collected Plays, Volume 2*, 182.

190. Castro, "Antigone Claimed: 'I Am a Stranger!'" 307.

191. Castro, "Antigone Claimed: 'I Am a Stranger!'"

192. Sophocles, *Complete Sophocles, Volume I*, 99.

193. Chalandon, "Je vis avec la mort et la trahison en essayant de me garder de l'une et de l'autre."

194. Chalandon, "Je vis avec la mort et la trahison en essayant de me garder de l'une et de l'autre."

195. Chalandon, "Je vis avec la mort et la trahison en essayant de me garder de l'une et de l'autre."

196. Chalandon, *Le quatrième mur*, 178.

197. Chalandon, *Le quatrième mur*, 127.

198. Chalandon, *Le quatrième mur*, 137.

199. Chalandon, *Le quatrième mur*, 213.

200. Chalandon, *Le quatrième mur*, 313.

201. In *Crimes of the Future: Theory and Its Global Reproduction* (New York: Bloomsbury, 2014), Jean-Michel Rabaté reminds us that "Antigone's very name suggests a movement 'against' generation," that is, against the "procreation . . . perverted after Oedipus's transgression" (227).

202. Chalandon, *Le quatrième mur*, 201.

203. I thank Jeffrey J. Williams and John McGowan for pointing out to me some of the divergent readings to which O'Neill's *Netherland* lends itself. Williams touches on this issue briefly in his article "The Plutocratic Imagination," *Dissent* (Winter 2013), http://www.-dissentmagazine.org/article/the-plutocratic-imagination.

204. Joseph O'Neill, *Netherland* (New York: Vintage, 2009), 161.

205. Ulrich Beck, "Global Inequality and Human Rights: A Cosmopolitan Perspective," in Delanty, *Routledge Handbook of Cosmopolitanism Studies*, 306. On "global cities," see Saskia Sassen, *The Global City: New York, London, Tokyo* (Princeton, NJ: Princeton University Press, 2001).

206. Joseph O'Neill, "Bowling Alone," *Atlantic Monthly*, September 11, 2007, http://www.powells.com/review/2007_09_11. I thank John Protevi for mentioning O'Neill's review to me.

207. C. L. R. James, *Beyond a Boundary*, with an introduction by Robert Lipsyte

and a new foreword by Paget Henry (Durham, NC: Duke University Press, 2013), 195–211.

208. "The Art and Practice Part" is the title of part 6 of James, *Beyond a Boundary* (193).

209. Gilroy, *Postcolonial Melancholia*, 111; James, *Beyond a Boundary*, 67, 65.

210. James, *Beyond a Boundary*, 210.

211. O'Neill, "Bowling Alone."

212. O'Neill, "Bowling Alone."

213. O'Neill, "Bowling Alone."

214. James, *Beyond a Boundary*, 233.

215. O'Neill, "Bowling Alone."

216. O'Neill, *Netherland*, 12.

217. Ian McEwan, *The Children Act* (New York: Random House, 2014), 46.

218. Ian McEwan, *Saturday* (New York: Random House, 2005), 35.

219. O'Neill, *Netherland*, 80.

220. O'Neill, *Netherland*, 211.

221. O'Neill, *Netherland*, 211.

222. James Wood, "Beyond a Boundary," *New Yorker*, May 26, 2008. http://www.newyorker.-com/magazine/2008/05/26/beyond-a-boundary.

223. O'Neill, *Netherland*, 210.

224. O'Neill, *Netherland*, 10–11.

225. O'Neill, *Netherland*, 120-121.

226. Jean-Luc Nancy, *Verité de la démocratie* (Paris: Galilée, 2008), 30–32.

227. O'Neill, *Netherland*, 10. My comments on this place in *Netherland* also allude to Heise's *Sense of Place and Sense of Planet*.

EPILOGUE

1. O'Neill, *Netherland*, 15.

2. Don DeLillo, *The Angel Esmeralda: Nine Stories* (New York: Scribner, 2011) 25, 29.

3. Chang-rae Lee, *The Surrendered* (New York: Riverhead, 2010), 102.

4. Colum McCann, *Let the Great World Spin* (New York: Random House, 2009), 325.

5. O'Neill, *Netherland*, 125.

6. O'Neill, *Netherland*, 161.

7. O'Neill, *Netherland*, 35.

8. Michel Houellebecq, *The Map and the Territory* (New York: Knopf, 2012), 46–47.

9. Rey Chow, *The Age of World Target: Self-Referentiality in War, Theory, and Comparative Work* (Durham, NC: Duke University Press, 2006), 31, 41.

10. Deleuze and Guattari, *What Is Philosophy?*, 189.

11. Friedrich Nietzsche, *Beyond Good and Evil: Prelude to a Philosophy*, trans. R. J. Hollingdale, with an introduction by Michael Tanner (London: Penguin, 1990), 102.

12. O'Neill, *Netherland*, 252.

13. O'Neill, *Netherland*, 252.
14. O'Neill, *Netherland*, 252–253.
15. O'Neill, *Netherland*, 254–256.
16. O'Neill, *Netherland*, 256.
17. Deleuze and Guattari, *What Is Philosophy?*, 197.
18. Deleuze and Guattari, *What Is Philosophy?*, 196.
19. Ramazani, "Poetry, Modernity, and Globalization," 301.
20. Ramazani, "Poetry, Modernity, and Globalization," 301.
21. Heidegger, *Question concerning Technology and Other Essays*, 132.
22. Michael Lang, "Mapping Globalization or Globalizing the Map? Heidegger and Planetary Discourse," *Genre* 36 (Fall–Winter 2003): 239–244.
23. On Heidegger and his "essentialist theory of place," also see Harvey, *Cosmopolitanism and the Geographies of Freedom*, 180.
24. Jacques Derrida, *Adieu to Emmanuel Levinas*, trans. Pascale-Anne Brault and Michael Haas (Stanford, CA: Stanford University Press, 1999), 45.
25. Mimi Scheller, "Cosmopolitanism and Mobilities," in Rovisco and Nowicka, *Ashgate Research Companion to Cosmopolitanism*, 349
26. Emmanuel Levinas, *Difficult Freedom: Essays on Judaism*, trans. Seán Hand (Baltimore: Johns Hopkins University Press, 1990), 233–234.
27. Somewhat similar proposals have advanced: Jameson, who talks about the critic as "curator" of the world museum in "New Literary History after the End of the New," *New Literary History* 39, no. 3 (Summer 2008), 385; Spivak, who refers to the "custodial" energies we must spend on behalf of our planet, in "World Systems and the Creole," 108; and Martha Nussbaum, who, in "Toward a Globally Sensitive Patriotism," from *Daedalus* 137, no. 3 (Summer 2008): 78–93, modifies the position previously formulated in her several interventions from *For Love of Country* (ed. Joshua Cohen [Boston: Beacon Press, 2002]). See also Kennedy Graham, ed., *The Planetary Interest: A New Concept for the Global Age* (New Brunswick, NJ: Rutgers University Press, 1999). Some of these suggestions and recommendations are more or less in line with global studies' "ethical turn," for which see Mervyn Frost, *Global Ethics: Anarchy, Freedom and International Relations* (London: Routledge, 2009), esp. 18–41.
28. Arjun Appadurai, "Grassroots Globalization and the Research Imagination," *Public Culture* 12, no. 1 (2000): 8, 12.
29. Levinas, *Totality and Infinity*, 74–75.

BIBLIOGRAPHY

Adams, Rachel. "The Ends of America, the Ends of Postmodernism." *Twentieth-Century Literature* 53, no. 3 (Fall 2007): 248–272.

Adamson, Joni. "American Literature and Film from a Planetary Perspective: Teaching Space, Time, and Scale." *Transformations* 21, no. 1 (Spring–Summer 2010): 23– 41.

Agamben, Giorgio. *The Coming Community.* Translated by Michael Hardt. Minneapolis: University of Minnesota Press, 2009.

Aizenberg, Edna. *The Aleph Weaver: Biblical, Kabbalistic and Judaic Elements in Borges.* Potomac, MD: Scripta Humanistica, 1984.

Aizenberg, Edna, ed., *Borges and His Successors: The Borgesian Impact on Literature and the Arts.* Columbia: University of Missouri Press, 1990.

Alazraki, Jaime. *Borges and the Kabbalah and Other Essays on His Fiction and Poetry.* New York: Cambridge University Press, 1988.

Anderson, Amanda. *The Powers of Distance: Cosmopolitanism and the Cultivation of Detachment.* Princeton, NJ: Princeton University Press, 2001.

Anderson, Benedict. *Imagined Communities: Reflections on the Origin and Spread of Nationalism.* Rev. ed. New York: Verso, 1991.

Andrade, Jorge Carrera. *Selected Poems of Jorge Carrera Andrade.* Translated and with an introduction by H. R. Hays. Albany: State University of New York Press, 1972.

Anouilh, Jean. *The Collected Plays, Volume 2: Time Remembered, Point of Departure, Antigone, Romeo and Jeanette, Medea.* London: Methuen, 1967.

Appadurai, Arjun. "Grassroots Globalization and the Research Imagination." *Public Culture* 12, no. 1 (2000): 1–19.

Apter, Emily. *Against World Literature: On the Politics of Untranslatability.* London: Verso, 2013.

Arendt, Hannah. *The Origins of Totalitarianism.* New edition with added prefaces. New York: Harcourt, 1985.

Ascari, Maurizio. *Literature of the Global Age: A Critical Study of Transcultural Narratives.* Jefferson, NC: McFarland, 2011.

Augé, Marc. *La Communauté illusoire.* Paris: Payot, 2010.

Axelos, Kostas. *Vers la pensée planétaire: Le devenir-pensée du monde et le devenir-monde de la pensée.* Paris: Minuit, 1984.

Badiou, Alain. *Handbook of Inaesthetics.* Translated by Alberto Toscano. Stanford, CA: Stanford University Press, 2004.

Barlow, E. Tani. "What Is a Poem? The Event of Women and the Modern Girl as Problems in Global or World History." In Palumbo-Liu, Robbins, and Tanoukhi, *Immanuel Wallerstein and the Problem of the World*, 155–183.

Baudrillard, Jean. "Global Debt and Parallel Universe." In *Digital Delirium*, edited and introduced by Arthur and Marilouise Kroker, 38–40. New York: St. Martin's, 1997.

Baudrillard, Jean. Telemorphosis *Preceded by* Dust Breeding. Translated by Drew S. Burk. Minneapolis: Univocal, 2011.

Bauman, Zygmunt. *Globalization: The Human Consequences.* New York: Columbia University Press, 1998.

Beck, Ulrich. "Cosmopolitan Sociology: Outline of a Paradigm Shift." In Rovisco and Nowicka, *Ashgate Research Companion to Cosmopolitanism*, 17–32.

Beck, Ulrich. "Global Inequality and Human Rights: A Cosmopolitan Perspective." In Delanty, *Routledge Handbook of Cosmopolitanism Studies*, 302–315.

Beck, Ulrich. "Toward a New Critical Theory with a Cosmopolitan Intent." *Constellations* 10, no. 4 (2003): 453–468.

Beck, Ulrich. *What Is Globalization?* Translated by Patrick Camiller. Cambridge: Polity Press, 2000.

Beigbeder, Frédéric. *Windows on the World.* Translated from the French by Frank Wayne. New York: Hyperion, 2004.

Beigbeder, Frédéric. *Windows on the World* [2003]. Paris: Gallimard, 2005.

Benda, Julien. *The Treason of the Intellectuals* [1927]. With a new introduction by Roger Kinball. Translated by Richard Aldington. New Brunswick, NJ: Transaction, 2007.

Bergermann, Ulrike, Isabell Otto, and Gabriele Schabacher, eds. *Das Planetarische: Kultur—Technik—Medien in postglobalen Zeitalter.* Munich: Wilhelm Fink, 2010.

Berlant, Lauren. *Cruel Optimism.* Durham, NC: Duke University Press, 2011.

Bloom, Michelle E. "Contemporary Franco-Chinese Cinema: Translation, Citation, and Imitation in Dai Sijie's *Balzac and the Little Chinese Seamstress* and Tsai Ming- Liang's *What Time Is It There?*" *Quarterly Review of Film and Video* 22, no. 4 (October–December 2005): 311–325.

Borges, Jorge Luis. *Collected Fictions.* Translated by Andrew Hurley. New York: Penguin, 1999.

Borges, Jorge Luis. *Seven Nights.* Translated by Eliot Weinberger. Introduction by Alasdair Reid. New York: New Directions, 1984.

Bourriaud, Nicolas, ed. *Altermodern: Tate Triennial.* London: Tate Publishing, 2009.

Bourriaud, Nicolas. *Relational Aesthetics.* Dijon: Les Presses du réel; New York: Idea Books, 2002.

Braidotti, Rosi. 'Becoming-World.' In Braidotti, Hanafin, and Blaagaard, *After Cosmopolitanism*, 8–27.

Braidotti, Rosi, Patrick Hanafin, and Bolette Blaagaard, eds. *After Cosmopolitanism.* Abingdon, UK: Routledge, 2013.

Braidotti, Rosi, Patrick Hanafin, and Bolette Blaagaard. "Introduction." In Braidotti, Hanafin, and Blaagaard, *After Cosmopolitanism*, 1–7.

Brecht, Bertolt. *Sophocles'* Antigone. Adapted by Bertolt Brecht. Based on the German translation by Friedrich Hölderlin and translated into English by Judith Malina. New York: Applause, 1990.

Brennan, Bernadette. "Worlds Without and Within: Reading Through Patrick White's Library in *The Solid Mandala.*" In Dixon and Rooney, *Scenes of Reading*, 115–126.

Brennan, Timothy. "From Development to Globalization: Postcolonial Studies and Globalization Theory." In Lane, *Global Literary Theory*, 877–887.

Brenner, Neil. "The Space of the World: Beyond State-Centrism?" In Palumbo-Liu, Robbins, and Tanoukhi, *Immanuel Wallerstein and the Problem of the World*, 101–137.

Brown, Garrett Wallace, and David Held, eds. *The Cosmopolitanism Reader*. Cambridge: Polity, 2010.

Brown, Garrett Wallace, and David Held. "Editors' Introduction." In Brown and Held, *Cosmopolitanism Reader*, 1–14.

Brown, Marshall. "Globalism or Globalization?" *Modern Language Quarterly* 68, no. 2 (2007): 137–143.

Buell, Frederick. *National Culture and the New Global System*. Baltimore, MD: Johns Hopkins University Press, 1994.

Buell, Lawrence. *The Environmental Imagination: Thoreau, Nature Writing, and the Formation of American Culture*. Cambridge, MA: Belknap Press of Harvard University Press, 1995.

Buell, Lawrence. "Place." In *Modern Criticism and Theory: A Reader*, 3rd ed., edited by David Lodge and Nigel Wood, 667–691. New York: Longman, 2008.

Butler, Judith. *Antigone's Claim: Kinship between Life and Death*. New York: Columbia University Press, 2000.

Caldwell, Gail. "Come Together." *Boston Globe*, September 11, 2005. http://www.boston.com/ae/books/- articles/2005/09/11/-come_together/.

Calinescu, Matei. *Rereading*. New Haven, CT: Yale University Press, 1993.

Calvino, Italo. *Invisible Cities*. Translated from the Italian by William Weaver. New York: Harcourt Brace Jovanovich, 1974.

Burcu, Canar. "Deleuze and *the Face*." *Lingua ac Communitas* 21 (2011): 33–52.

Cărtărescu, Mircea. *Blinding*. Translated from the Romanian by Sean Cotter. Brooklyn, NY: Archipelago Books, 2013.

Cărtărescu, Mircea. *Orbitor. Aripa stîngă*. Bucharest: Humanitas, 1996.

Cărtărescu, Mircea. *Orbitor. Aripa dreaptă*. Bucharest: Humanitas, 2007.

Cărtărescu, Mircea. *Orbitor. Corpul*. Bucharest: Humanitas, 2002.

Cărtărescu, Mircea. *Nostalgia*. Translated, with an afterword, from the Romanian by Julian Semilian. Introduction by Andrei Codrescu. New York: New Directions, 2005.

Cărtărescu, Mircea. *Pururi tînăr, înfăşurat în pixeli*. Bucharest: Humanitas, 2003.

Cărtărescu, Mircea. "Realismul poeziei tinere." In *Competiţia continuă: Generaţia 80 in texte teoretice*, edited by Gheorghe Crăciun. Piteşti, Romania: Editura Vlasie, 1994.

Cărtărescu, Mircea. *Totul*. Bucharest: Cartea Românească, 1985.

Cărtărescu, Mircea. *Visul*. Bucharest: Cartea Românească, 1989.

Casanova, Pascale. *The World Republic of Letters*. Translated by M. B. DeBevoise. Cambridge, MA: Harvard University Press, 2004.

Cassin, Barbara, ed. *Vocabulaire européen des philosophies: Dictionnaire des intraduisibles*. Paris: Seuil, 2004.

Castells, Manuel. *The Information Age: Economy, Society, and Culture*. Vol. 1, *The Rise of the Network Society*. 2nd ed. Oxford: Blackwell, 2000.

Castro, Andrés Fabián Henao. "Antigone Claimed: 'I Am a Stranger!' Political Theory and the Figure of the Stranger." *Hypathia* 28, no. 2 (Spring 2013): 307–322.

Caws, Mary Ann. "The Poetics of the Manifesto: Nowness and Newness." In *Manifesto: A Century of Isms*, edited by Mary Ann Caws, xix–xxxi. Lincoln: University of Nebraska Press, 2000.

Chalandon, Sorj. "Entretien: Sorj Chalandon dans le vertige de la guerre." *L'Orient Littéraire* 97 (July 2014). http://www.lorientlitteraire.com/article_- details.php?cid=6&nid=4293.

Chalandon, Sorj. "Je vis avec la mort et la trahison en essayant de me garder de l'une et de l'autre." Interview by Nicolas Norrito. Illustrations by Yann Levy. *CQFD* 115 (October 2013). http://cqfd-journal.org/Je-vis-avec-la-mort-et-la-trahison.

Chalandon, Sorj. *Le quatrième mur.* Paris: Grasset, 2013.

Chandra, Sarika. *Dislocalism: The Crisis of Globalization and the Remobilizing of Americanism.* Columbus: Ohio State University Press, 2011.

Cheah, Pheng. "What Is a World? On World Literature as World-Making Activity." *Daedalus* 137, no. 3 (Summer 2008): 26–38.

Cheah, Pheng. "World against Globe: Toward a Normative Conception of World Literature." *New Literary History* 45, no. 3 (Summer 2014): 303–329.

Cheah, Pheng, and Bruce Robbins, eds. *Cosmopolitics: Thinking and Feeling beyond the Nation.* Minneapolis: University of Minnesota Press, 1998.

Chow, Rey. *The Age of World Target: Self-Referentiality in War, Theory, and Comparative Work.* Durham, NC: Duke University Press, 2006.

Clarke, Bruce. "Autopoiesis and the Planet." *Impasses of the Post-Global: Theory in the Era of Climate Change.* Vol. 2. Edited by Henry Sussman. Ann Arbor: Open Humanities Press/Michigan Publishing, 2012. http://quod.lib.umich.edu/- o/ohp/10803281.0001.-001/1:4/—impasses-of-the-post-global-theory-in-the-era-of-climate?rgn=div1;view-=fulltext.

Cochrane, Allan, and Kathy Pain. "A Globalizing Society?" In *A Globalizing World? Culture, Economics, Politics*, edited by David Held, 5–46. London: Routledge in association with The Open University, 2000.

Cole, Teju. *Open City.* New York: Random House, 2011.

Colebrook, Claire. "Destroying Cosmopolitanism for the Sake of the Cosmos." In Braidotti, Hanafin, and Blaagaard, *After Cosmopolitanism*, 166–182.

Cooper, Anthony, and Chris Rumford. "Cosmopolitan Borders: Bordering as Connectivity." In Rovisco and Nowicka, *Ashgate Research Companion to Cosmopolitanism*, 262–276.

Dai Sijie. *Balzac and the Little Chinese Seamstress.* Translated from the French by Ina Rilke. New York: Random House, 2001.

Dai Sijie. *Mr. Muo's Travelling Couch.* Translated from the French by Ina Rilke. New York: Knopf, 2005.

Dai Sijie. *Once on a Moonless Night.* Translated from the French by Adriana Hunter. New York: Knopf, 2009.

Damrosch, David. "World Literature as Figure and as Ground." American Comparative Literature Association. The 2014–2015 Report on the State of the Discipline of Comparative Literature website—Paradigms. http://stateofthediscipline.acla.- org/entry/world-literature-figure-and-ground-0.

D'Argoun, Jean. *La mutation planétaire.* Paris: Véga, 2005.

Dastur, Françoise. "Heidegger's Freiburg Version of the Origin of the Work of Art." In *Heidegger toward the Turn: Essays on the Work of the 1930s*, edited by James Risser, 119–142. Albany: State University of New York Press, 1999.

David, Jérôme. *Spectres de Goethe: Les métamorphoses de la "littérature mondiale."* Paris: Les Prairies Ordinaires, 2011.

Delamarre, Bernadette. *Autrui.* Paris: Ellipses, 1996.

Delanty, Gerard. "The Idea of Critical Cosmopolitanism." In Delanty, *Routledge Handbook of Cosmopolitanism Studies*, 38–46.

Delanty, Gerard, ed. *Routledge Handbook of Cosmopolitanism Studies.* Abingdon, UK: Routledge, 2012.

Deleuze, Gilles, and Félix Guattari. *What Is Philosophy?* Translated by Hugh Tomlinson and Graham Burchell. New York: Columbia University Press, 1994.

Deleuze, Gilles, and Félix Guattari. *A Thousand Plateaus: Capitalism and Schizophrenia.* Translated by Brian Massumi. Minneapolis: University of Minnesota Press, 1987.

Deleuze, Gilles, and Claire Parnet. *Dialogues.* Translated by Hugh Tomlinson and Barbara Habberjam. New York: Columbia University Press, 1987.

DeLillo, Don. *The Angel Esmeralda: Nine Stories.* New York: Scribner, 2011.

DeLillo, Don. *Cosmopolis.* New York: Scribner, 2004.

DeLillo, Don. *Underworld.* New York: Scribner, 1997.

DeLillo, Don. *White Noise.* Text and Criticism. Edited by Mark Osteen. New York: Penguin, 1998.

Derrida, Jacques. *Acts of Religion.* Edited and with an introduction by Gil Anidjar. New York: Routledge, 2002.

Derrida, Jacques. *Adieu to Emmanuel Levinas.* Translated by Pascale-Anne Brault and Michael Haas. Stanford, CA: Stanford University Press, 1999.

Derrida, Jacques. "Geopsychoanalysis: 'and . . . the rest of the world.'" In *The Psychoanalysis of Race*, edited by Christopher Lane, 65–90. New York: Columbia University Press, 1998.

Derrida, Jacques. *On Touching—Jean-Luc Nancy.* Translated by Christine Irizarry. Stanford, CA: Stanford University Press, 2005.

Derrida, Jacques. *Specters of Marx: The State of the Debt, the Work of Mourning, and the New International.* Translated by Peggy Kamuf. With an introduction by Bernd Magnus and Stephen Cullenberg. New York: Routledge, 1994.

Derrida, Jacques. "Structure, Sign and Play in the Discourse of the Human Sciences." In *Modern Criticism and Theory: A Reader,* edited by David Lodge. Revised and expanded by Nigel Wood, 62–87. Harlow, UK: Longman, 2000.

Díaz, Junot. *The Brief Wondrous Life of Oscar Wao.* New York: Penguin, 2008.

Dimock, Wai Chee. "Genre as World System: Epic and Novel on Four Continents." *Narrative* 14, no. 1 (January 2006): 85–101.

Dimock, Wai Chee. "Literature for the Planet." *PMLA* 116, no. 1 (January 2001): 173–188.

Dimock, Wai Chee. "Planetary Time and Global Translation: 'Context' in Literary Studies." *Common Knowledge* 9, no. 3 (Fall 2003): 488–507.

Dimock, Wai Chee. "Scales of Aggregation: Prenational, Subnational, Transnational." *American Literary History* 18, no. 2 (Summer 2006): 219–228.

Dimock, Wai Chee. *Through Other Continents: American Literature across Deep Time.* Princeton, NJ: Princeton University Press, 2008.

Dimock, Wai Chee, and Lawrence Buell, eds. *Shades of the Planet: American Literature as World Literature.* Princeton, NJ: Princeton University Press, 2007.

Dixon, Robert, and Brigid Rooney, eds. *Scenes of Reading: Is Australian Literature a World Literature?* Melbourne: Australian Scholarly Publishing, 2014.

Dixon, Robert, and Brigid Rooney. "Introduction: Australian Literature, Globalisation and the Literary Province." In Dixon and Rooney, *Scenes of Reading*, ix–xxxvi.

Doueihi, Milad. *Pour un humanisme numérique*. Paris: Seuil, 2011.

Doyle, Laura, and Laura Winkiel, eds. *Geomodernisms: Race, Modernism, Modernity.* Bloomington: Indiana University Press, 2005.

Edson, Laurie. *Reading Relationally: Postmodern Perspectives on Literature and Art.* Ann Arbor: University of Michigan Press, 2000.

Elias, Amy J. "The Dialogical Avant-Garde: Relational Aesthetics and Time Ecologies in *Only Revolutions* and *TOC*." *Contemporary Literature* 53, no. 4 (Winter 2012): 738–778.

Elias, Amy J. "Interactive Cosmopolitanism and Collaborative Technologies: New Foundations for Global Literary History." *New Literary History* 39, no. 3 (Summer 2008): 705–725.

Elias, Amy J., and Christian Moraru, eds. *The Planetary Turn: Relationality and Geoaesthetics in the Twenty-First Century.* Evanston, IL: Northwestern University Press, 2015.

Élie, Maurice, and Arnaud Villani. "Plan d'immanence." In *Le Vocabulaire de Gilles Deleuze*, edited by Robert Sasso and Arnaud Villani, 272–275. Nice, France: Les Cahiers de *Noesis*, 2003.

Emery, Mary Lou. "Caribbean Modernism: Plantation to Planetary." In Wollaeger with Eatough, *The Oxford Handbook of Global Modernisms*, 48–77.

Fenves, Peter. "Alterity and Identity, Postmodern Theories Of." In *Routledge Encyclopedia of Philosophy*, vol. 1, edited by Edward Craig, 187–192. London: Routledge, 1998.

Ferguson, Frances. "Planetary Literary History: The Place of the Text." *New Literary History* 39, no. 3 (Summer 2008): 657–684.

Fine, Robert. *Cosmopolitanism.* New York: Routledge, 2007.

Fishburn, Evelyn. "Reflections on the Jewish Imaginary in the Fictions of Borges." *Variaciones Borges: Journal of the Jorge Luis Borges Center for Studies and Documentation*, no. 5 (1998): 145–156.

Florea, Adrian. "De Facto States in International Politics (1945–2011): A New Data Set." *International Interactions: Empirical and Theoretical Research in International Relations* (October 2014). http://dx.doi.org/10.1080/03050629.2014.915543.

Forster, E. M. *Howards End.* Complete, Authoritative Text with Biographical and Historical Contexts, Critical History, and Essays from Five Contemporary Critical Perspectives, edited by Alistair M. Duckworth. Boston: Bedford/St. Martin's, 1997.

Foucault, Michel. *Language, Counter-Memory, Practice: Selected Essays and Interviews.* Edited by Donald F. Bouchard. Translated by Donald F. Bouchard and Sherry Simon. Ithaca, NY: Cornell University Press, 1977.

Friedman, Susan Stanford. "Planetarity: Musing Modernist Studies." *Modernism/Modernity* 17, no. 3 (September 2010): 471–499.

Friedman, Thomas L. *Longitudes and Attitudes: Exploring the World after September 11.* New York: Farrar, Straus and Giroux, 2002.

Fritz-Ababneh, Dorothée. "L'Intertextualité dans Balzac et *La petite tailleuse chinoise* de Dai Sijie." *French Studies* 77 (Winter 2006): 97–113.
Frost, Mervyn. *Global Ethics: Anarchy, Freedom and International Relations.* London: Routledge, 2009.
Frow, John. *Time and Commodity Culture.* Oxford: Oxford University Press, 1997.
Garett, Georgia. "Book Note." *Publishers Weekly.* http://www.powells.com/biblio/-1594200637.
Gasché, Rodolphe. *Geophilosophy: On Gilles Deleuze and Félix Guattari's* What Is Philosophy? Evanston, IL: Northwestern University Press, 2014.
Gikandi, Simon. "Globalization and the Claims of Postcoloniality." *South Atlantic Quarterly* 100, no. 3 (Summer 2001): 627–658.
Giles, Paul. "The Deterritorialization of American Literature." In Dimock and Buell, *Shades of the Planet*, 39–61.
Gilroy, Paul. *After Empire: Melancholia or Convivial Culture?* London: Routledge, 2004.
Gilroy, Paul. *Against Race: Imagining Political Culture beyond the Color Line.* Cambridge, MA: Belknap Press of Harvard University Press, 2000.
Gilroy, Paul. "Planetarity and Cosmopolitics." *British Journal of Sociology* 61, no. 3 (September 2010): 620–626.
Gilroy, Paul. *Postcolonial Melancholia.* New York: Columbia University Press, 2005.
Gish Jen. *World and Town.* New York: Knopf, 2010.
Graham, Kennedy, ed. *The Planetary Interest: A New Concept for the Global Age. New Brunswick, NJ:* Rutgers University Press, 1999.
Grausam, Daniel. *On Endings: American Postmodern Fiction and the Cold War.* Charlottesville: University of Virginia Press, 2011.
Greenblatt, Stephen, with Ines G. Županov, Reinhard Meyer-Kalkus, Heike Paul, Pál Nyíri, and Friederike Pannewick. *Cultural Mobility: A Manifesto.* Cambridge: Cambridge University Press, 2010.
Hamid, Mohsin. *How to Get Filthy Rich in Rising Asia.* New York: Riverhead, 2013.
Hamid, Mohsin. *The Reluctant Fundamentalist.* New York: Mariner Books, 2008.
Harvey, David. *The Condition of Postmodernity: An Enquiry into the Origin of Cultural Change.* Cambridge, MA: Blackwell, 1990.
Harvey, David. *Cosmopolitanism and the Geographies of Freedom.* New York: Columbia University Press, 2009.
Hayles, N. Katherine. "Combining Close and Distant Reading: Jonathan Safran Foer's *Tree of Codes* and the Aesthetic of Bookishness." *PMLA* 128, no. 1 (January 2013): 226–231.
Hayot, Eric. *On Literary Worlds.* New York: Oxford University Press, 2012.
Heidegger, Martin. *Being and Time: A Translation of* Sein und Zeit. Translated by Joan Stambaugh. Albany: State University of New York Press, 1996.
Heidegger, Martin. *The Event.* Translated by Richard Rojcewicz. Bloomington: Indiana University Press, 2013.
Heidegger, Martin. *The Question concerning Technology and Other Essays.* Translated and with an introduction by William Lovitt. New York: Garland, 1977.
Heise, Ursula K. *Nach der Natur: Das Artensterben und die Moderne Kultur.* Berlin: Suhrkamp, 2010.
Heise, Ursula K. *Sense of Place and Sense of Planet: The Environmental Imagination of the Global.* New York: Oxford University Press, 2008.

Held, David. "Afterword." In Held, *A Globalizing World?*, 169–177.

Held, David, ed. *A Globalizing World? Culture, Economics, Politics.* London: Routledge in association with The Open University, 2000.

Held, David. *Global Transformations: Politics, Economics, and Culture.* Stanford, CA: Stanford University Press, 1999.

Held, David. "Principles or Cosmopolitan Order." In Brown and Held, *Cosmopolitanism Reader,* 229–247.

Hitchcock, Peter. "The Function of Agon at the Present Time." *Comparatist* 37 (2013): 5–20.

Hogue, W. Lawrence. *Postmodern American Literature and Its Other.* Urbana: University of Illinois Press, 2009.

Holland, Eugene. "Global Cosmopolitanism and Nomad Citizenship." In Braidotti, Hanafin, and Blaagaard, *After Cosmopolitanism*, 149–165.

Hollinger, David A. *Cosmopolitanism and Solidarity: Studies in Ethnoracial, Religious, and Professional Affiliation in the United States.* Madison: University of Wisconsin Press, 2006.

Hollinger, David A. *Postethnic America: Beyond Multiculturalism.* New York: Basic Books/HarperCollins, 1995.

Holton, Robert J. *Global Networks.* New York: Palgrave Macmillan, 2008.

Houellebecq, Michel. *The Map and the Territory.* New York: Knopf, 2012.

Inglis, David, and Roland Robertson. "From Cosmos to Globe: Relating Cosmopolitanism, Globalization and Globality." In Rovisco and Nowicka, *Ashgate Research Companion to Cosmopolitanism*, 295–311.

Irr, Caren. *Toward the Geopolitical Novel: U.S. Fiction in the Twenty-First Century.* New York: Columbia University Press, 2013.

Irr, Caren. "Toward the World Novel: Genre Shifts in Twentieth-First-Century Expatriate Fiction." *American Literary History* 23, no. 3 (2011): 660–679.

Jacobowitz, Seth. "Hellenism, Hebraism, and the Eugenics of Culture in E. M. Forster's *Howards End.*" *CLWeb: Comparative Literature and Culture* 6, no. 4 (December 2004). http://clcwebjournal.lib.purdue.edu/clcweb04-4/jacobowitz04.html.

James, C. L. R. *Beyond a Boundary.* Introduction by Robert Lipsyte and new foreword by Paget Henry. Durham, NC: Duke University Press, 2013.

Jameson, Fredric. *The Geopolitical Aesthetic: Cinema and Space in the World System.* Bloomington: Indiana University Press; London: BFI Publishing, 1995.

Jameson, Fredric. "New Literary History after the End of the New." *New Literary History* 39, no. 3 (Summer 2008): 375–387.

Jameson, Fredric. *A Singular Modernity: Essay on the Ontology of the Present.* London: Verso, 2002.

Jarvis, Brian. *Postmodern Cartographies: The Geographical Imagination in Contemporary American Culture.* New York: St. Martin's Press, 1998.

Jay, Paul. *Global Matters: The Transnational Turn in Literary Studies.* Ithaca, NY: Cornell University Press, 2010.

Jazeel, Tariq. "Spatializing Difference beyond Cosmopolitanism: Rethinking Planetary Futures." *Theory, Culture & Society* 28, no. 5 (2011): 75–97.

Jones, Andrew. *Dictionary of Globalization.* Cambridge: Polity, 2006.

Joronen, Mikko. *The Age of Planetary Space: On Heidegger, Being, and Metaphysics of Gobalization.* Turku, Finland: Painosalama Oy, 2010.

Kadir, Djelal. "To Compare, to World: Two Verbs, One Discipline." *Comparatist* 34 (May 2010): 4–11.

Kadir, Djelal. "To World, to Globalize: Comparative Literature's Crossroads." *Comparative Literature Studies* 41, no. 1 (2004): 1–9.

Kincaid, Jamaica. *A Small Place.* New York: Penguin, 1981.

Kollmeyer, Christopher J. "Globalization, Class Compromise, and American Exceptionalism: Political Change in 16 Advanced Capitalist Countries." *Critical Sociology* 29, no. 3 (October 2003): 369–391.

Konrád, George. *Antipolitics: An Essay.* Translated from the Hungarian by Richard E. Allen. San Diego: Harcourt Brace Jovanovich, 1984.

Kristeva, Julia. *Nations without Nationalism.* Translated by Leon S. Roudiez. New York: Columbia University Press, 1993.

Kumar, Amitava, ed. *World Bank Literature.* Foreword by John Berger. Afterword by Bruce Robbins. Minneapolis: University of Minnesota Press, 2003.

Kundera, Milan. *Testaments Betrayed: An Essay in Nine Parts.* Translated by Linda Asher. New York: HarperCollins, 1995.

Lane, Richard J., ed. *Global Literary Theory: An Anthology.* London: Routledge, 2013.

Lang, Michael. "Mapping Globalization or Globalizing the Map? Heidegger and Planetary Discourse." *Genre* 36 (Fall–Winter 2003): 239–250.

Larsen, Svend Erik. "Literary History as a Cultural Challenge: Rewriting Local Literary History in the Age of Globalisation." In Dixon and Rooney, *Scenes of Reading*, 60–70.

Lee, Chang-rae. *The Surrendered.* New York: Riverhead, 2010.

Lee, Richard E. "The Modern World-System: Its Structures, Its Geoculture, Its Crisis and Transformation." In Palumbo-Liu, Robbins, and Tanoukhi, *Immanuel Wallerstein and the Problem of the World*, 27–40.

Lefebvre, Henri. *State, Space, World: Selected Essays.* Edited by Neil Brenner and Stuart Elden. Translated by Gerald Moore, Neil Brenner, and Stuart Elden. Minneapolis: University of Minnesota Press, 2009.

Leonard, Philip. *Literature after Globalization: Textuality, Technology and the Nation- State.* London: Bloomsbury, 2013.

Levinas, Emmanuel. *Basic Philosophical Writings.* Edited by Adriaan T. Peperzak, Simon Critchley, and Robert Bernasconi. Bloomington: Indiana University Press, 1996.

Levinas, Emmanuel. *Difficult Freedom: Essays on Judaism.* Translated by Seán Hand. Baltimore: Johns Hopkins University Press, 1990.

Levinas, Emmanuel. *Totality and Infinity: An Essay on Interiority.* Translated by Alphonso Lingis. Pittsburgh, PA: Duquesne University Press, 1961.

Levy, Daniel, and Natan Sznaider. "Cosmopolitan Memory and Human Rights." In Rovisco and Nowicka, *Ashgate Research Companion to Cosmopolitanism*, 195–209.

Lodge, David, with Nigel Wood. *Modern Criticism and Theory: A Reader.* Edited by David Lodge. Revised and expanded by Nigel Wood. Harlow, UK: Longman, 2000.

Lotman, Youri. *La sémiosphère.* Translated by Anka Ledenko. Limoges, France: Presses Universitaires de Limoges, 1999.

Maalouf, Amin. *Disordered World: Setting a New Course for the Twenty-First Cen-*

tury. Translated from the French by George Miller. New York: Bloomsbury, 2011.

Maalouf, Amin. *In the Name of Identity: Violence and the Need to Belong*. Translated from the French by Barbara Bray. New York: Penguin, 2000.

Maalouf, Amin. *Le dérèglement du monde*. Paris: Grasset & Fasquelle, 2009.

MacCabe, Colin. "Preface." In Jameson, *Geopolitical Aesthetic*, ix–xvi.

Malpas, J. E. *Place and Experience: A Philosophical Topography*. Cambridge: Cambridge University Press, 1999.

Maus, Derek C. *Unvarnishing Reality: Subversive Russian and American Cold War Satire*. Columbia: University of South Carolina Press, 2011.

McCall, Ian. "French Literature and Film in the USSR and Mao's China." *Romance Studies* 24, no. 2 (July 2006): 159–170.

McCann, Colum. *Let the Great World Spin*. New York: Random House, 2009.

McCann, Colum. *TransAtlantic*. New York: Random House 2013.

McEwan, Ian. *The Children Act*. New York: Doubleday, 2014.

McEwan, Ian. *The Innocent*. New York: Random House, 1998.

McEwan, Ian. *Saturday*. New York: Random House, 2005.

McEwan, Ian. *Sweet Tooth*. New York: Random House, 2012.

McGurl, Mark. "The Posthuman Comedy." *Critical Inquiry* 38, no. 3 (Spring 2012): 533–553.

Medovoi, Leerom. "'Terminal Crisis?' From the Worlding of American Literature to World-System Literature." *American Literary History* 23, no. 3 (2011): 643–659.

Miller, J. Hillis. *Others*. Princeton, NJ: Princeton University Press, 2003.

Miller, J. Hillis. *Theory Now and Then*. Durham, NC: Duke University Press, 1991.

Mitchell, David. *Cloud Atlas*. New York: Random House, 2004.

Mitchell, Peta. *Cartographic Strategies of Postmodernity: The Figure of the Map in Contemporary Theory and Fiction*. New York: Routledge, 2008.

Miyoshi, Masao. "Turn to the Planet: Literature, Diversity, and Totality." *Comparative Literature* 53, no. 4 (Fall 2001): 283–297.

Moïsi, Dominique. *The Geopolitics of Emotion: How Cultures of Fear, Humiliation, and Hope Are Reshaping the World*. New York: Doubleday, 2009.

Moraru, Christian. *Cosmodernism: American Narrative, Late Globalization, and the New Cultural Imaginary*. Ann Arbor: University of Michigan Press, 2011.

Moraru, Christian. "The Global Turn in Critical Theory." *symploke* 9, nos. 1–2 (2001): 74–82.

Moraru, Christian. "Invisible, Ink.: Classics, Programmers, and the Reprogramming of Cultural History in the Aftermath of the 'Book Crisis.'" *Canadian Review of Comparative Literature* 39, no. 4 (December 2012): 415–426.

Moraru, Christian. *Memorious Discourse: Reprise and Representation in Postmodernism*. Madison, NJ: Fairleigh Dickinson University Press, 2005.

Moraru, Christian. "Thirteen Ways of Passing Postmodernism: Introduction to Focus." *American Book Review* 34, no. 4 (May–June 2013): 3–4.

Moraru, Christian. "'World,' 'Globe,' 'Planet': Comparative Literature, Planetary Studies, and Cultural Debt after the Global Turn." American Comparative Literature Association, the 2014–2015 Report on the State of the Discipline of Comparative Literature website - Paradigms. http://stateofthediscipline.acla.org.

Moretti, Franco. "Conjectures on World Literature." *New Left Review* 1 (January–February 2000): 54–68.
Moretti, Franco. *Distant Reading.* New York: Verso, 2013.
Moretti, Franco. *Modern Epic: The World-System from Goethe to García Márquez.* Translated by Quintin Hoare. London: Verso, 1996.
Moretti, Franco. "World-Systems Analysis, Evolutionary Theory, *Weltliteratur.*" In Palumbo-Liu, Robbins, and Tanoukhi, *Immanuel Wallerstein and the Problem of the World,* 67–77.
Mukherjee, Bharati. "Immigrant Writing: Changing the Contours of a National Literature." *American Literary History* 23, no. 3 (2011): 680–696.
Mukherjee, Bharati. *The Tree Bride.* New York: Hyperion, 2004.
Murphet, Julian. "Postmodernism and Space." In *The Cambridge Companion to Postmodernism,* edited by Steven Connor, 116–135. Cambridge: Cambridge University Press, 2004.
Nancy, Jean-Luc. *La création du monde ou la mondialisation.* Paris: Galilée, 2002.
Nancy, Jean-Luc. *The Inoperative Community.* Edited by Peter Conor. Translated by Peter Conor, Lisa Garbus, Michael Holland, and Simona Sawhney. Foreword by Christopher Fynsk. Minneapolis: University of Minnesota Press, 1991.
Nancy, Jean-Luc. *Verité de la démocratie.* Paris: Galilée, 2008.
Neef, Sonja A. J. *Der babylonische Planet: Kultur, Übersetzung, Dekonstruktion under den Bedingungen der Globalisierung.* Heidelberg, Germany: Universitätsverlag Winter, 2013.
Neef, Sonja A. J. *Imprint and Trace: Handwriting in the Age of Technology.* English translation by Anthony Mathews. London: Reaktion Books, 2011.
Negri, Antonio. *Art and Multitude: Nine Letters on Art, Followed by Metamorphoses: Art and Immaterial Labor.* Translated by Ed Emery. London: Polity, 2011.
Negri, Antonio. *Inventer le commun des hommes.* Preface by Judith Revel. Paris: Bayard, 2010.
Nicolescu, Basarab. "The Challenge of Transdisciplinarity: From Postmodernity to Cosmodernity." Paper abstract. Centre of Transdisciplinarity, Cognitive and State-System Sciences—Indexicals. http://indexicals.ac.at/abstractvienna05bnicolescu.html (accessed December 31, 2006).
Nicolescu, Basarab. *From Modernity to Cosmodernity: Science, Culture, and Spirituality.* Albany: State University of New York Press, 2014.
Nicolescu, Basarab. *La transdisciplinarité: Manifeste.* Paris: Éditions du Rocher, 1996.
Nicolescu, Basarab. *Manifesto of Transdiciplinarity.* Translated from the French by Karen-Claire Voss. Albany: State University of New York Press, 2002.
Nicolescu, Basarab. *Théorèmes poétiques.* Preface by Michel Camus. Paris: Rocher, 1994.
Nicolescu, Basarab, et al. "Ce este cosmodernitatea?" Center for Research of the Imaginary, Cluj, Romania. http://phantasma.ro/dezbateri/masa/masa14.html.
Nietzsche, Friedrich. *Beyond Good and Evil: Prelude to a Philosophy.* Translated by R. J. Hollingdale. With an introduction by Michael Tanner. London: Penguin, 1990.
Nietzsche, Friedrich. *Untimely Meditations.* Edited by Daniel Breazeale. Translated by R. J. Hollingdale. Cambridge: Cambridge University Press, 2003.

Nussbaum, Martha. *For Love of Country.* Edited by Joshua Cohen for *Boston Review.* Boston: Beacon Press, 2002.

Nussbaum, Martha. "Toward a Globally Sensitive Patriotism." *Daedalus* 137, no. 3 (Summer 2008): 78–93.

Ondaatje, Michael. *The English Patient.* New York: Random House, 1993.

O'Neill, Joseph. *Netherland.* New York: Vintage, 2009.

O'Neill, Joseph. "Bowling Alone." *Atlantic Monthly,* September 11, 2007. http://www-powells.com/review/2007_09_11.

O'Sullivan, Simon. "The Aesthetics of Affect: Thinking Art beyond Representation." *Angelaki* 6, no. 3 (December 2001): 125–135.

Palumbo-Liu, David, Bruce Robbins, and Nirvana Tanoukhi, eds. *Immanuel Wallerstein and the Problem of the World: System, Scale, Culture.* Durham, NC: Duke University Press, 2011.

Palumbo-Liu, David, Bruce Robbins, and Nirvana Tanoukhi. "The Most Important Thing Happening." In Palumbo-Liu, Robbins, and Tanoukhi, *Immanuel Wallerstein and the Problem of the World,* 1–23.

Pamuk, Orhan. *Snow.* Translated from the Turkish by Maureen Freely. New York: Vintage, 2005.

Papastergiadis, Nikos. "Aesthetic Cosmopolitanism." In Delanty, *Routledge Handbook of Cosmopolitanism Studies,* 220–232.

Papastergiadis, Nikos. "Spatial Aesthetics: Rethinking the Contemporary." In Smith, Enwezor, and Condee, *Antinomies of Art and Culture,* 363–381.

Perloff, Marjorie. *Unoriginal Genius: Poetry by Other Means in the New Century.* Chicago: University of Chicago Press, 2010.

Phillips, Anne. *Multiculturalism without Culture.* Princeton, NJ: Princeton University Press, 2007.

Pogge, Thomas. "Cosmopolitanism and Sovereignty." In Brown and Held, *Cosmopolitanism Reader,* 114–133.

Poster, Mark. "Global Media and Culture." *New Literary History* 39, no. 3 (Summer 2008): 685–703.

Poster, Mark. "Postcolonial Theory in the Age of Planetary Communications." *Quarterly Review of Film and Video* 24 (2007): 379–393.

Pratt, Mary Louise. "Planetary Longings: Sitting in the Light of the Great Solar TV." In *World Writing: Poetics, Ethics, Globalization,* edited by Mary Gallagher, 207–223. Toronto: University of Toronto Press, 2008.

Pynchon, Thomas. *Bleeding Edge.* New York: Penguin, 2013.

Pynchon, Thomas. *The Crying of Lot 49.* New York: HarperCollins, 1999.

Rabaté, Jean-Michel. *Crimes of the Future: Theory and Its Global Reproduction.* New York: Bloomsbury, 2014.

Ramazani, Jahan. "Poetry, Modernity, and Globalization." In Wollaeger with Eatough, *Oxford Handbook of Global Modernisms,* 288–309.

Ramazani, Jahan. *A Transnational Poetics.* Chicago: University of Chicago Press, 2009.

Rancière, Jacques. *Dissensus: On Politics and Aesthetics.* Edited and translated by Steven Corcoran. London: Continuum, 2010.

Ransom, John Crowe. "The Planetary Poet." *Kenyon Review* 26, no. 1 (Winter 1964): 233–264.

Rapaport, Herman. *The Literary Theory Toolkit: A Compendium of Concepts and Methods.* Malden, MA: Wiley-Blackwell, 2011.

Raulet, Gérard. *Critical Cosmology: On Nations and Globalization—A Philosophical Essay.* Lanham, MD: Lexington Books, 2005.

Readings, Bill. *The University in Ruins.* Cambridge, MA: Harvard University Press, 1996.

Robbins, Bruce. "Blaming the System." In Palumbo-Liu, Robbins, and Tanoukhi, *Immanuel Wallerstein and the Problem of the World*, 41–63.

Robbins, Bruce. "Comparative Cosmopolitanisms." In Cheah and Robbins, *Cosmopolitics*, 246–264.

Robbins, Bruce. "Introduction[,] Part I: Actually Existing Cosmopolitanism." In Cheah and Robbins, *Cosmopolitics*, 1–19.

Robbins, Bruce. *Perpetual War: Cosmopolitanism from the Viewpoint of Violence.* Durham, NC: Duke University Press, 2012.

Robertson, Roland. "Social Theory, Cultural Relativity and the Problem of Globality." In *Culture, Globalization and the World-System: Contemporary Conditions for the Representation of Identity*, edited by Anthony D. King, 69–90. Minneapolis: University of Minnesota Press, 1997.

"Romain Rolland." In *World Authors, 1900–1950.* Vol. 3. Edited by Martin Seymour-Smith and Andrew C. Kimmens, 2220–2223. New York: H. W. Wilson, 1996.

Roth, Philip. *Letting Go.* New York: Random House, 1961.

Rovisco, Maria, and Magdalena Nowicka, eds. *The Ashgate Research Companion to Cosmopolitanism.* Farnham, UK: Ashgate, 2011.

Samalavicius, Almantas, and Immanuel Wallerstein. "New World-System? A Conversation with Immanuel Wallerstein. *Eurozine,* February 8, 2013. http://www.eurozine.com/articles/-2013-02-08-wallerstein-en.html.

Sartre, Jean-Paul. "*Huis clos* de Jean-Paul Sartre." http://www.alalettre.com/sartre-huisclos.htm.

Sartre, Jean-Paul. No Exit *and Three Other Plays.* New York: Random House, 1973.

Sassen, Saskia. *The Global City: New York, London, Tokyo.* Princeton, NJ: Princeton University Press, 2001.

Sassen, Saskia. "Neither Global nor National: Novel Assemblages of Territory, Authority and Rights." *Ethics & Global Politics* 1, nos. 1–2 (2008): 61–79.

Scarry, Elaine. *On Beauty and Being Just.* Princeton, NJ: Princeton University Press, 1999.

Scheller, Mimi. "Cosmopolitanism and Mobilities." In Rovisco and Nowicka, *Ashgate Research Companion to Cosmopolitanism*, 349–365.

Schmitt, Carl. *The* Nomos *of the Earth in the International Law of the* Jus Publicum Europaeum. Translated and annotated by G. L. Ulmen. New York: Telos, 2006.

Schoene, Berthold. *The Cosmopolitan Novel.* Edinburgh: Edinburgh University Press, 2010.

Sesé, Bernard. "Pierre Teilhard de Chardin, prophète de la mondialisation?" *Etudes* 3964 (April 2002): 483–494.

Simmel, Georg. *Essays on Sociology, Philosophy, and Aesthetics*. Edited by Kurt H. Wolff. New York: Harper & Row, 1959.

Singer, Peter. *One World: The Ethics of Globalization.* New Haven, CT: Yale University Press, 2002.

Sirinelli, Jean-François. "L'événement-monde." *Vingtième Siècle. Revue d'histoire* 4, no. 74 (2002): 35–38.

Smith, Terry. *What Is Contemporary Art?* Chicago: University of Chicago Press, 2009.

Smith, Terry, Okwui Enwezor, and Nancy Condee, eds. *Antinomies of Art and Culture: Modernity, Postmodernity, Contemporaneity.* Durham, NC: Duke University Press, 2008.

Smith, Zadie. *Autograph Man.* New York: Vintage, 2003.

Smith, Zadie. *NW.* New York: Penguin, 2012.

Smith, Zadie. *On Beauty.* New York: Penguin, 2005.

Smith, Zadie. *White Teeth.* New York: Random House, 2000.

Soja, Edward W. *Postmodern Geographies: The Reassertion of Space in Critical Social Theory.* New York: Verso, 1989.

Soja, Edward W. *Thirdspace: Journeys to Los Angeles and Other Real-and-Imagined Places.* Cambridge, MA: Blackwell, 1996.

Song, Min Hyoung. "Becoming Planetary." *American Literary History* 23, no. 3 (2011): 555–573.

Sophocles. *The Complete Sophocles, Volume I: The Theban Plays.* Edited by Peter Burian and Alan Shapiro. New York: Oxford University Press, 2011.

Spivak, Gayatri Chakravorty. *An Aesthetic Education in the Era of Globalization.* Cambridge, MA: Harvard University Press, 2011.

Spivak, Gayatri Chakravorty. *Death of a Discipline.* New York: Columbia University Press, 2003.

Spivak, Gayatri Chakravorty. "World Systems and the Creole." *Narrative* 14, no. 1 (January 2006): 102–112.

Steiner, George. *Antigones.* New York: Oxford University Press, 1984.

Stevens, Wallace. *The Collected Poems of Wallace Stevens.* New York: Vintage, 1990.

Stråth, Bo. "World History and Cosmopolitanism." In Delanty, *Routledge Handbook of Cosmopolitan Studies,* 72–84.

Strugaru, Oana. "Globalization and Literature: What Is Left of Literary History?" *Euresis* (2013): 140–146.

Surin, Kenneth. "'A Question of an Axiomatic of Desires': The Deleuzian Imagination of Geoliterature." In *Deleuze and Literature,* edited by Ian Buchanan and John Marks, 167–193. Edinburgh: Edinburgh University Press, 2000.

Sussman, Henry. *Around the Book: Systems and Literacy.* New York: Fordham University Press, 2011.

Taylor, Bron. *Dark Green Religion: Nature, Spirituality, and the Planetary Future.* Berkeley: University of California Press, 2010.

Teilhard de Chardin, Pierre. *The Human Phenomenon.* A new edition and translation of *Le phénomène humain* by Sarah Appleton-Weber, With a foreword by Brian Swimme. Brighton, UK: Sussex Academic Press, 1999.

Teilhard de Chardin, Pierre. *Le Phénomène humain.* Paris: Seuil, 1955.

Terian, Andrei. *Critica de export: Teorii, contexte, ideologii.* Bucharest: Editura Muzeului Literaturii Române, 2013.

Tiutiuca, Dumitru. "Fractology—a Possible Outlook on Literature." *Euresis* nos. 1–4 (2012): 102–108.

Tomlinson, John. "Globalization and Cultural Analysis." In *Globalization Theory:*

Approaches and Controversies, edited by David Held and Anthony McGrew, 148–168. Cambridge, UK: Polity Press, 2007.

Turnbull, Neil. "The Ontological Consequences of Copernicus: Global Being in the Planetary World." *Theory, Culture & Society* 23, no. 1 (2006): 125–139.

Ugrešić, Dubravka. *The Ministry of Pain*. Translated from the Croatian by Michael Henry Heim. New York: Harper, 2007.

Updike, John. *Bech at Bay*. New York: Alfred A. Knopf, 1998.

Varughese, E. Dawson. *Beyond the Postcolonial: World Englishes Literature*. New York: Palgrave Macmillan, 2012.

Walkowitz, Rebecca L. "The Location of Literature: The Transnational Book and the Migrant Writer." In Lane, *Global Literary Theory*, 918–929.

Wallerstein, Immanuel. *Geopolitics and Geoculture: Essays on the Changing World-System*. Cambridge: Cambridge University Press; Paris: Maison des Sciences de l'Homme, 1991.

Wallerstein, Immanuel. *The Modern World-System*. Vol. 1. New York: Academic Press, 1974.

Wallerstein, Immanuel. "New Revolts against the System." *New Left Review*, 2nd ser., 18 (November–December 2002): 29–39.

Wallerstein, Immanuel. *Utopistics, or Historical Choices of the Twenty-First Century*. New York: New Press, 1998.

Wallerstein, Immanuel. *World-Systems Analysis: An Introduction*. Durham, NC: Duke University Press, 2004.

Warnier, Jean-Pierre. *La mondialisation de la culture*. 3rd ed. Paris: La Découverte, 2004.

Wegner, Philip E. "Soldierboys for Peace: Cognitive Mapping, Space, and Science Fiction as World Bank Literature." In Kumar, *World Bank Literature*, 280–296.

Werner, Michael, and Bénédicte Zimmermann. "Beyond Comparison: *Histoire croisée* and the Challenge of Reflexivity." *History and Theory* 45 (February 2006): 30–50.

Westphal, Bertrand. *La Géocritique: Réel, fiction, espace*. Paris: Minuit, 2007.

Westphal, Bertrand. *Le monde plausible: Espace, lieu, carte*. Paris: Minuit, 2011.

Williams, Jeffrey J. "The Plutocratic Imagination." *Dissent* (Winter 2013). http://www.- dissentmagazine.org/article/the-plutocratic-imagination.

Wollaeger, Mark, with Matt Eatough. *The Oxford Handbook of Global Modernisms*. New York: Oxford University Press, 2012.

Wood, James. "Beyond a Boundary." *New Yorker*, May 26, 2008. http://www.newyorker.com/magazine/2008/05/26/beyond-a-boundary.

Yi-Fu Tuan. *Cosmos and Hearth: A Cosmopolite's Viewpoint*. Minneapolis: University of Minnesota Press, 1996.

Žižek, Slavoj. *Enjoy Your Symptom: Jacques Lacan in Hollywood and Out*. New York: Routledge, 1992.

INDEX